PENGUIN BOOKS
THE BILL

Steven Waldman is a national correspondent for *Newsweek*, for which he has worked since 1988. He has also written cover stories for *The New Republic* and *The Washington Post Magazine*. He was formerly an editor at *The Washington Monthly*. He lives in Washington, D.C., with his wife, writer Amy Cunningham, and their son, Joseph.

D1622945

THE BILL

How Legislation

Really Becomes Law:

A Case Study of the

National Service Bill

STEVEN WALDMAN

Revised and Updated

PENGUIN BOOKS

To Joseph

PENGUIN BOOKS
Published by the Penguin Group
Penguin Books USA Inc., 375 Hudson Street, New York, New York 10014, U.S.A.
Penguin Books Ltd, 27 Wrights Lane, London W8 5TZ, England
Penguin Books Australia Ltd, Ringwood, Victoria, Australia
Penguin Books Canada Ltd, 10 Alcorn Avenue, Toronto, Ontario, Canada M4V 3B2
Penguin Books (N.Z.) Ltd, 182-190 Wairau Road, Auckland 10, New Zealand

Penguin Books Ltd, Registered Offices: Harmondsworth, Middlesex, England

First published in the United States of America by Viking Penguin,
a division of Penguin Books USA Inc., 1995
Published in Penguin Books 1996

9 10 8

Grateful acknowledgment is made for permission to reprint excerpts from *A City Year*
by Suzanne Goldsmith. © 1993 by Suzanne Goldsmith.
Reprinted with permission of The New Press.

THE LIBRARY OF CONGRESS HAS CATALOGUED THE HARDCOVER AS FOLLOWS:
Waldman, Steven.
The bill: how the adventures of Clinton's national service bill reveal what is corrupt,
comic, cynical—and noble—about Washington/Steven Waldman.
p. cm.
Includes index.
ISBN 0-670-85300-3 (hc.)
ISBN 0 14 02.3304 0 (pbk.)
1. National service—United States.   2. Student loan funds—United States.
3. United States—Politics and government—1989–
I. Title.
HD4870.U6W35   1995
378.3'62—dc20   94–23014

Printed in the United States of America
Set in Postscript Elante
Designed by Kathryn Parise

Acknowledgments

I am deeply indebted to a generous team of readers, including Charles Peters, Howard Fineman, Matthew Cooper, Paul Massimiano, Scott Shuger, Timothy Noah, John Zimmerman, Mickey Kaus, Martin Waldman, Amy Cunningham, Bob Cohn, Steve Tuttle, and, most important, Paul Glastris, who, in the ultimate demonstration of friendship (or masochism), read much of the manuscript twice.

I'm also grateful to my brother Michael Waldman for being completely unhelpful. Mike, who works in the White House, had to recuse himself from any internal discussions about national service. He then maintained a strict fire wall, neither interrogating me about my project nor, alas, telling me anything he was hearing from inside the White House.

Since most of the reporting for this book was done originally for a *Newsweek* article, I also would like to thank my editors Evan Thomas, Dorothy Wickenden, and Maynard Parker. They gave me an unusual amount of time to work on this project in the belief that an in-depth case study would provide *Newsweek* readers with special insight into the Clinton administration and government. It was Evan who introduced me to Rafe Sagalyn, my skillful agent, who, in turn, introduced me to Nan Graham, Courtney Hodell, and the rest of Viking's excellent team.

My research assistant, Alan Greenblatt, saved me countless hours and headaches tracking down stray facts. Lucinda Sikes of the Public

Citizen Litigation Group helped me use the Freedom of Information Act to obtain documents from the Office of National Service and the Department of Education.

My parents, Sandra and Martin Waldman, were, as usual, insightful and supportive. My wife, Amy, was stunning throughout. She skillfully critiqued manuscripts, bolstered my morale, brought me beautiful meals as I typed, and, in the middle of my project, produced a little miracle named Joseph.

Scores of people spent hundreds of hours tutoring me on community service and student-aid reform. Without their generosity, this book would not have been possible.

Finally, I'd like to express my admiration for those who do hands-on service. Occasionally I think working in politics, or even in journalism, is serving the public. But the connection between these professions and actually solving social problems is usually distant and ambiguous. Men and women who put themselves inches away from the problems they are trying to address subject themselves to physical discomfort, low pay, and less glamour—but at least they know, at the end of the day, if they've done any good.

Contents

Cast of Characters

THE CAMPAIGN

Bill Clinton, the candidate

Bruce Reed, issues director and key advisor on national service

Charles Moskos, sociology professor, DLC advisor, and father of the loans-for-service idea

Stanley Greenberg, pollster

WHITE HOUSE OFFICE OF NATIONAL SERVICE

Eli Segal, director, and longtime friend of Clinton

C. Richard Allen, deputy director, and glamorous LA businessman

Jack Lew, general counsel and chief wonk

Robert Gordon, Harvard undergrad on leave to work as policy analyst

Diana Aldridge, director of public affairs

OTHER WHITE HOUSE STAFF

George Stephanopoulos, senior advisor to the president

Gene Sperling, deputy director, National Economic Council; chief White House advocate of pay-as-you-can loans

Bill Galston, deputy director, Domestic Policy Council; White House point man on student-loan reform; head of transition team on national service

Shirley Sagawa, special assistant, Domestic Policy Council; former Kennedy aide; key author of national service legislation

DEPARTMENT OF EDUCATION

Richard Riley, secretary

Madeleine Kunin, deputy secretary

David Longanecker, assistant secretary for post-secondary education

SENATE LABOR COMMITTEE

Sen. Edward M. Kennedy (D-MA), chairman
Nick Littlefield, staff director and chief counsel
Suzanne Ramos, staff on student aid
Tom Sander, staff on national service

Sen. Nancy Landon Kassebaum (R-KS), ranking Republican and lead op-
ponent of national service and student-loan reform
Susan Hattan, minority staff director
Kimberly Barnes O'Connor, staff on national service

Sen. Paul Simon (D-IL), leading advocate of Clinton's loan reform
Bob Shireman, staff on student aid, led efforts to combat industry lobbying
David Carle, press secretary

Sen. Harris Wofford (D-PA), helped floor-manage national service
Martin Rodgers, staff on national service

Sen. Claiborne Pell (D-RI), chairman, education subcommittee, and surprising opponent of Clinton's student-aid reform plan
David Evans, staff director, education subcommittee

Sen. James Jeffords (R-VT), ranking Republican, education subcommittee,
and Pell ally

Sen. David Durenberger (R-MN), chief Republican backer of Clinton's national service and student-loan reform plans

HOUSE EDUCATION AND LABOR COMMITTEE

Rep. Bill Ford (D-MI), chairman, staunch Clinton ally on national service
and student-loan reform plans
Tom Wolanin and Omer Waddles, staff on student aid
Gene Sofer, staff on national service
Pat Rissler, staff director

Rep. Bill Goodling (R-PA), ranking Republican, leading critic of Clinton plan
on service and student loans

Rep. Susan Molinari (R-NY), critic of Clinton service plan

Rep. Rob Andrews (D-NJ), aggressive young Turk and loan reform supporter

OTHER MEMBERS OF CONGRESS

Sen. Robert Dole (R-KS), Senate minority leader
Sen. George Mitchell (D-ME), Senate majority leader
Rep. Sonny Montgomery (D-MS), chairman, Veterans Affairs Committee
Rep. David McCurdy (D-OK), early national service supporter
Rep. Bart Gordon (D-TN), direct lending opponent

Rep. Chris Shays (R-CT), lead Republican supporter of national service

Rep. Bill Clay (D-MO), chairman, Post Office and Civil Service Committee

NATIONAL SERVICE GROUPS

Catherine Milton, executive director, Commission on National and Community Service

Roger Landrum, executive director, Youth Service America

Kathleen Selz, director, National Association of Service and Conservation Corps, and critic of race-mixing programs

Elizabeth Dole, president, American Red Cross

Alan Khazei and Michael Brown, founders, City Year

STUDENT-AID GROUPS

Barmak Nassirian, American Association of State Colleges and Universities (AASCU), opponent of national service and supporter of loan reform

Terry Hartle, director of governmental relations, American Council on Education

Bill Gray, president, United Negro College Fund, key opponent of Clinton's plan

John Dean, partner, Clohan & Dean, representing Consumer Bankers Association in opposition to Clinton's plan

Bud Blakey, partner, Clohan & Dean, representing United Negro College Fund and historically black colleges

Dan Cheever, president, American Student Assistance Corporation (ASA), guaranty agency in Massachusetts, and opponent of Clinton's student-aid plan

Joe Clayton, director of government affairs, ASA

Lawrence Hough, CEO, Sallie Mae

Winfield "Winkie" Crigler, lobbyist, Sallie Mae

Jerry Hultin, consultant, Sallie Mae, and former Clinton campaign official

THE PROMISE
FALL 1991

| WHITE HOUSE OFFICE OF NATIONAL SERVICE Dir: Eli Segal | U.S. DEPARTMENT OF EDUCATION Secy: Richard Riley Deputy Secy: Madeleine Kunin |

| THE NATIONAL SERVICE PLAN SERVICE IN EXCHANGE FOR $5000 Unveiled: April 30, 1993 | PAY-AS-YOU-CAN LOANS LOAN REPAID AS % OF INCOME Unveiled: May 6, 1993 | DIRECT LENDING (PART OF BUDGET BILL) |

| HOUSE EDUCATION AND LABOR COMMITTEE Passed H.R. 2010: June 16, 1993 | SENATE LABOR AND HUMAN RESOURCES COMMITTEE Passed S. 919: June 16, 1993 | HOUSE EDUCATION AND LABOR COMMITTEE Passed: May 12, 1993 | SENATE LABOR AND HUMAN RESOURCES COMMITTEE Passed: June 12, 1993 |

| FULL HOUSE Passed: July 28, 1993 | FULL SENATE Passed: Aug. 3, 1993 | FULL HOUSE Passed: May 29, 1993 | FULL SENATE Passed: June 25, 1993 |

| HOUSE-SENATE CONFERENCE NATIONAL SERVICE Passed: August 3, 1993 | HOUSE-SENATE CONFERENCE STUDENT AID Passed: July 29, 1993 |

| FULL HOUSE Passed: Aug. 5, 1993 | FULL SENATE Passed: Sept. 8, 1993 | FULL HOUSE Passed: Aug. 5, 1993 | FULL SENATE Passed: Aug. 6, 1993 |

| CLINTON SIGNS NATIONAL SERVICE Sept. 21, 1993 | CLINTON SIGNS LOAN REFORM (AS PART OF BUDGET BILL) Aug. 10, 1993 |

Preface

"Everyone! Spit out your gum!" yelled Melinda Hudson, a public-relations consultant working with the White House. Fifty volunteers from community service programs had gathered on the South Lawn for the historic bill-signing ceremony, and Hudson wanted it to be visually perfect. "Don't spit it on the White House lawn!" She collected seven or eight pieces, wrapping them neatly in wads of paper.

Under an enormous wedding-style tent nearby, the grunge band Soul Asylum warmed up the audience with its hit song "Runaway Train." Dignitaries struggled to chat over the ruckus. Some of "the youths," as they were called by the event planners, were wearing the snazzy red-and-black bomber jackets of City Year, a Boston program that brought together Ivy Leaguers and high school dropouts to work in low-income communities. Others wore the Smokey Bear hats and khaki fatigues of the Pennsylvania Service Corps, which refurbished state parks. Four activists showed up in dress shirts and ties instead of T-shirts. "They're wearing ties!" complained a White House staffer, who wanted them to look idealistic, not businesslike. Hudson skipped across the lawn to fetch some white T-shirts to conceal their button-downs.

The conspicuously multicultural group of volunteers, most in their early twenties, had already practiced walking from the White House to the podium—at least five times—and felt they were ready to play their parts in this historic occasion. At last, they saw Secret Service

1

men, and then Bill Clinton, emerge from a limousine just inside the White House gate. They burst into whoops and hollers. The president proceeded according to a predetermined path up the gradual slope of the lawn, then motioned to the group to follow him. Like a shepherd with his flock, Clinton led the youths up the hill. At that moment, the dreadlocked lead singer of Soul Asylum broke into a coarse version of "Don't Stop Thinking About Tomorrow," the cheerful 1992 campaign theme song. The crowd erupted into applause, and Clinton, smiling with his mouth open a half inch, marched triumphantly to the podium surrounded by service volunteers.

"I have harbored this dream for years," Clinton told the gathered politicians, congressional staff, and activists under the tent. He was referring to his promise for a new national service program, which would allow young people to pay back their college loans in small increments over time or, preferably, by doing service in their communities as teachers, social workers, or police officers. Clinton's vow that he would institute such a program had become the most consistently popular applause line in the '92 campaign.

There on the South Lawn that day, September 21, 1993, Clinton recalled some of the service programs he'd visited before his election. "I watched people's dreams come to life, I watched the old and the young relate in ways they hadn't. I watched mean streets turn into safer and better and more humane places." National service, he said slowly, "will help us to strengthen the *cords* that bind us together as a people."

The Generation Xers listened reverentially—not an eye rolled, or a lip curled—as Clinton said, "There are millions of Americans who are not really free today because they cannot reach down inside and bring out what was put there by the Almighty."

Clinton walked over to a small wooden desk. Using the pens with which John F. Kennedy had signed the Peace Corps legislation and Franklin Roosevelt, the Civilian Conservation Corps, Bill Clinton signed into law the National and Community Service Trust Act of 1993.

In the euphoria of that moment, it seemed hard to believe that over the course of the previous year something intended to bring out the best in people had nearly been defeated by a Washington culture that brings out the worst.

1

Anatomy of a
Campaign Promise

In 1980, sociologist Charles Moskos had an idea. The Northwestern University military expert thought he saw a way to bolster the military, keep seniors out of nursing homes, broaden access to college, and revitalize the Democratic Party—all in one visionary step. Moskos, a stocky man who looks like a Greek version of the chief on *Get Smart*, tried selling his plan in various academic settings through the early 1980s but had attracted little attention. In 1986, he had finally drawn some interest from the Democratic Leadership Council, a new group formed by moderate and conservative politicians to push the Democratic Party toward the center.

In March 1988, Moskos traveled to historic Williamsburg, Virginia, to describe his idea to a DLC conference. He made his pitch in a breezy and informal style, but the plan was quite dramatic: Every American who wanted federal financial aid for college would *have* to perform "national service."

He wasn't talking about "softheaded" volunteerism for the idle wealthy, Moskos told the two hundred men and women gathered in the conference hall. National service would mean either military service—which could ease impending manpower shortages—or two years of tough, full-time civilian work helping to alleviate real social problems. For instance, service volunteers could perform household chores for elderly people so they wouldn't have to enter expensive nursing homes. Or volunteers could help staff mental hospitals or give

3

more care to the homeless. It was time, Moskos argued, to balance rights—particularly the "right" to government benefits—with responsibilities. "We now spend nine billion dollars a year in federal aid to college students," he said in a calm, professorial tone. "We have created, really, a GI Bill without the GI.".

"National service moves us beyond the sort of something-for-nothing, every-man-for-himself, me-first philosophy that has been prevalent in the American ruling groups," he concluded. "The time is right to rekindle the idealism called forth by John F. Kennedy in the Peace Corps, Harry Truman in the GI Bill, Franklin Delano Roosevelt in the Civilian Conservation Corps." National service is, he told the audience, "both good politics and good for the country."

After the speech, a handful of people went up to Moskos to talk about his presentation. One man, taller than the others, waited patiently for Moskos's attention. He congratulated Moskos, and said he'd never before really appreciated this idea. "Thank you," Moskos said, embarrassed that he didn't know who this voluble man was. "But you have me at a disadvantage, sir."

"I'm Bill Clinton of Arkansas," the man replied.

Clinton had been one of the founding members of the DLC, which was created in the belief that the Democratic Party had become a morally suspect, politically inept captive of liberal special-interest groups. Labor, blacks, feminists, gay rights activists—they had seduced the party into supporting policies that lost elections and made the public distrust government. By the time of the Williamsburg conference, the DLC had adopted Moskos's service idea as its central, defining proposal. On January 29, 1989, Senator Sam Nunn of Georgia and Representative David McCurdy of Oklahoma, both leading DLC members, unveiled legislation based on the plan. Liberal senator Barbara Mikulski of Maryland, as well as Kathleen Kennedy Townsend, Robert F. Kennedy's daughter, endorsed the bill and toured the country with Nunn and McCurdy to promote the idea. The alliance of the sullen, conservative Nunn with the pugnacious former social worker Mikulski seemed to validate Moskos's prediction that the plan would unite left and right.

Liberals and conservatives did indeed unite—to attack the legislation as a grave threat to the nation. Veterans' groups resented the fact that the plan gave more benefits to some pampered Harvard graduate who picked up leaves than to a soldier who risked his life for his country. Libertarian conservatives like Milton Friedman compared national service to Hitler's youth corps. Labor leaders complained that these service workers would displace unionized employees. Most significantly, college presidents fumed that the poor, who depend on financial aid, would be compelled to serve while rich kids, who don't need aid, would have no obligations. The plan, declared Representative Bill Ford of Michigan, "holds the educational aspirations of the poor hostage to public service, while excusing the affluent." McCurdy would later remember the hostile reaction with a bittersweet nostalgic smile. "It was like climbing up the walls of the Bastille and them pouring hot wax on me," he said.

So much for unifying left and right, rich and poor.

As Bill Clinton began to plot his run for the presidency in the spring of 1991, he thought back to the DLC plan. Advocates of national service had tried to get both Walter Mondale in 1984 and Michael Dukakis in 1988 to embrace service; neither had done so, in part for fear of alienating traditional liberal interest groups. Clinton wanted to position himself as a more conservative "New Democrat." He wanted to show that Democrats could do more than throw money at the poor; that they could once again advocate mainstream middle-class values such as work, sacrifice, and mutual obligation.

Clinton also wanted to win. He knew the history of Nunn-McCurdy, and realized that to alienate labor, blacks, and liberals might not be the swiftest route to the Democratic nomination.

In the summer of 1991, Clinton came up with a shrewd solution. It wasn't exactly Solomonic in its moral force, but politically it was brilliant.

Instead of requiring service in order to receive aid, he would offer *extra* aid to those willing to do service. It was classic Clinton: a voluntary plan that combined the stern rhetoric of conservatism with the generosity of liberalism. Politically, the proposal could draw support from colleges: more aid, more money! And it might appeal to middle-class families as a federal aid program open not only to the poor but to anyone, regardless of income.

Making service purely voluntary solved another political problem for Clinton. Frank Greer, a consultant who had managed Clinton's gubernatorial race and was helping to plan his presidential launch, knew what the American public would soon find out: that Clinton had avoided service in Vietnam. The campaign anticipated what Greer calls "cheap shots that you were going to require people to serve when you hadn't served yourself."

There was still one problem with the proposal. What if people wanted to take socially useful jobs in the mainstream economy—as public defenders or Head Start teachers, for example—without joining some formal government-run program? Clinton believed that many middle-class kids resisted public service because they had incurred too much debt in college. He turned to an idea called "income-contingent loans," which had been suggested by 1988 Democratic nominee Michael Dukakis. Instead of repaying loans in fixed installments, students could pay a percentage of their future income. Someone with $20,000 in loan debt could still take a $20,000 teaching job if the loan payments were only $50 to $100 a month.

Clinton married this ability-to-pay loan plan with the national service proposal, and on September 21 he unveiled the new initiative.

"Opportunity for all," he told the Democratic National Committee, "means giving every young American the chance to borrow the money necessary to go to college and pay it back . . ." Before he could get to the part about service, the audience interrupted him with lusty applause. "Pay it back as a percentage of income over several years, or with years of national service here at home—a domestic GI bill." Again he was interrupted by applause from an audience of Democratic activists. "A domestic GI bill that would ask young Americans to go to the streets of our cities and be teachers, to be policemen where we need community policemen, to be nurses where there's a nursing shortage, to be family service workers where families are breaking down and children are abused and neglected, to rebuild America from the people point of view. We can do that with a national service."

This became the promise.

———

Is it a coincidence that the first president since Franklin Roosevelt not to have served in the military was also the first to make civilian service central to his presidential campaign? Why *was* Clinton so interested in service?

The image of Clinton that emerged during the 1992 campaign—of a campus radical who grew up despising men in uniform—obscured the real psychological drama behind his failure to serve in Vietnam. The small-town Arkansas in which Clinton grew up revered the military and the flag. The principal at Hot Springs High School, a imposing woman named Johnnie Mae Mackey, would annually exhort a Flag Day assembly to appreciate how the sacrifice of veterans had kept the country free. When Clinton shook hands with President Kennedy in 1963, he did so as a delegate to Boys Nation, the civics program sponsored by the American Legion. And poignantly, young Bill Clinton's most precious souvenir of his father was a World War II service citation.

Each stage of Clinton's development seemed to reinforce the importance of service. He came of age in the *early* 1960s—perhaps the peak idealistic moment of the past fifty years—after Kennedy and King had inspired the nation, after the first batch of Peace Corps volunteers had deployed throughout the world, but before Vietnam, before the assassinations of the Kennedys and King, before the urban rioting that burned away so much of the idealism. The civil rights movement was showing that deeply ingrained social attitudes could be changed through citizen action. Clinton grew up during that brief, astonishing moment in history when government was considered an effective—even noble—way to change society. "It seems perhaps ironic to say in this more cynical time," Clinton explained to me in August 1993, "but when I was a boy, going into public life was considered public service. People gave up certain benefits—money, privacy, vacations."

"You didn't even hear the term *politics*," recalls Clinton's high school friend Carolyn Staley. "It was *statesmanship*. It was a high calling, right up there with clergy or teaching."

Clinton attended college at Georgetown University, a Jesuit-run school that stressed service as an expression of Christian behavior. Campaign biographies often mention that after King's assassination, Clinton slapped a Red Cross sign on his car and drove into rioting neighborhoods of Washington to deliver supplies. What is less well known is that, that same year, he joined the Georgetown University Community Action Program and worked one semester tutoring disadvantaged Washington kids. His one brief stint in a service program was not, however, a positive experience. He came away convinced that sporadic volunteerism did more for the volunteer than for the needy. "It made all the participants feel good and we learned a lot but I became convinced you had to have ongoing grassroots efforts," Clinton recalls.

It was only after his exposure to the Jesuits that friends began to believe there was any religious dimension to Clinton's interest in service. After college, Carolyn Staley reports, Clinton read and reread *Mere Christianity* by C. S. Lewis. Written for those whose intellects wrestled incessantly with their faiths, this popular book argued that good Christians applied Christian behavior in the realm where they excelled, even in politics. "Those who happen to have the right talents should be economists and statesmen," Lewis wrote. "Their whole efforts in politics and economics should be directed to putting 'Do as you would be done by' into action." For Clinton, politics could be rationalized as a form of slightly diluted missionary service. His later speeches regularly stressed that government's responsibility was to help individuals fulfill the potential that God gave them. "Each of us reaches our fullness as human beings by being of service to our fellow men and women," he would say.

At Yale Law School, Clinton met Hillary Rodham, whose background looked little like his, except for her belief in the nobility of service. Raised in a middle-class suburb of Chicago, Hillary had, from age fourteen, attended First Methodist Church in Park Ridge, where the youth minister, Donald G. Jones, had suburban teenagers baby-sit for the children of migrant workers. He took Hillary and others in her youth group to hear Martin Luther King, Jr., speak and to meet black and Hispanic gang members on the South Side of Chicago. While Hillary attended Wellesley College, she was gradually transformed from a Goldwater Republican to a liberal social activist. "The aura of the martyred Kennedys was strong on the campuses then, and everyone was full of talk about doing something about the race crisis, about the Peace Corps," Alan Schechter, one of her professors, has said. "The mood was one of youthful idealism, commitment, that clichéd line of Kennedy's—'Ask not what your country can do for you.' " She wrote her senior thesis on community organizer Saul Alinsky. At Yale Law School she began working in legal services for the poor.

Then there was Vietnam. Because Clinton had been taught that service was admirable, his failure to go to Vietnam must have been humiliating and confusing. "To many of us, it is no longer clear what is service and what is disservice," Clinton wrote in his notorious 1969 "political viability" letter, in which he confessed to Colonel Eugene Holmes his desire to avoid the draft.

In that letter, Clinton mentioned that he had written a paper in college on "selective conscientious objection"—the idea that a young man could morally oppose a particular war instead of conflict generally. "I would like to have been able to take a year out perhaps to teach in a small college or work on some community action project," he wrote to Holmes. Housemates of Clinton at Yale remember sitting around the kitchen table on Trumbull Street debating whether young people morally opposed to the Vietnam war could do *civilian* service instead. In an interview with the president in August 1993, I asked whether he would have chosen to do civilian service if it had been available during Vietnam. He said "Probably," before becoming uncomfortable with the subject and launching into his familiar autopilot claim that he had thought he was going to be drafted. Charles Moskos speculates that "national service was a way for Clinton to resolve his own ambivalence about what he did during the Vietnam War." One thing is clear: his "domestic GI bill" could, in effect, elevate civilian service—the type he has performed—closer to a moral par with military service, which he had not.

Clinton's experiences as a young man also shaped his views about the government's role in opening the doors of college. The largest social program in America during his childhood, it is important to remember, was the GI Bill. In 1949, the federal government spent $2.7 billion to help ease veterans into mainstream society. That's roughly $17 billion *per year* in today's dollars, more than that spent in 1993 on the Peace Corps, VISTA, student loans, and federal scholarship aid combined. At one point, the GI Bill subsidized almost half of those in college. So the idea of rewarding service with lavish educational benefits had been well established during Clinton's youth.

In fact, Clinton himself had been able to attend Georgetown University in part because of National Defense Education Act loans, which Congress created in 1958 after the Russians launched Sputnik. The bill was supposed to encourage the training of scientists, but it also provided loan forgiveness for those who went into teaching. Clinton got part of his loan wiped out by teaching law school in Arkansas for a year.

Clinton even had direct experience with income-contingent loans. In 1972, Yale University became so concerned that the cost of school deterred graduates from beginning public-service careers that it instituted a radical idea called the Tuition Postponement Option. Yale would offer loans according to need, to be paid back as a percentage of income. A corporate lawyer would end up subsidizing his classmate the public defender by "repaying" loans in excess of what he actually took out. The Yale program faltered in part because the school couldn't get alumni to send in their tax returns, but it planted an important seed: one of those who got a small loan from this program was Yale Law School student Bill Clinton.

Clinton has become convinced that student-loan debt distorts career choices. "I don't have any research to support this, but it is my belief that if you know that the burden of repaying your loans is not a problem, then you are free to take a job that might pay somewhat less but might be somewhat more rewarding," he has said. "I talked to a young couple a few months ago right before the election that had a combined college loan repayment schedule of a thousand dollars a month. It was *a lot* of money for them. Both of them said they would like to have been doing something a little bit more community oriented than what they were doing. But it's all they could do to scramble and put together one thousand dollars a month."

———

Despite the experiences of his youth, it wasn't until Clinton became a grown-up politician that he saw the *utility* of a government-sponsored service program. As governor of one of the poorest states in the country, Clinton had to confront staggering problems with a weak tax base. Service, he began to see, could provide cheap labor for activist social policy. "I saw all kinds of unmet needs in every community that, hell, we simply couldn't raise the taxes to pay for—whether it was working with children or working in nursing homes," he said. In January 1991 the Arkansas legislature passed a police corps bill, establishing scholarships for people who served as law-enforcement officers. Earlier, Clinton had proposed a literacy corps, in which students could work off college loans by teaching kids to read. He helped create the Delta Service Corps, a successful program in which full-time workers recruit and supervise volunteers to staff food pantries, teach reading, or drive seniors to doctors' appointments. In June 1991, he told the Arkansans who were setting up the corps: "If we are going to solve our problems with limited resources, we are going to have to resort to old-fashioned notions of service."

Clinton believed service is one of the few truly effective types of government action, because it addresses the psychological nature of today's social ills. "The more I got involved in the problems of young people and at-risk children in particular," Clinton told me, "the more I realized there was a corollary breakdown literally in the internal life structure of millions of young Americans. They suffered not just economically, but emotionally from having insufficient order and emotional support and insufficient role models."

For Clinton, service was not just about delivering services. It was, ironically, about building character. It was a way that government—so flawed, so decadent, so discredited—could actually help young people to develop upright values. "A lot of the problems with this country are *intensely* cultural, personal, human. I believe that this national service project has the capacity, anyway, to make us believe we don't have anybody to waste, to make us believe we are all in this together, to give us a chance to reach across racial and income lines to work together."

As Clinton campaigned in New Hampshire in January 1992, crowds would applaud and sometimes jump to their feet when he talked about his domestic GI bill. Stanley Greenberg, Clinton's pollster, was surprised that such a squishily peripheral idea would generate this enthusiasm. He decided to investigate. He included a spate of questions about national service and student loans in his surveys and focus groups.

Despite the positive audience reaction, the national service plan didn't register much support in Greenberg's polling in New Hampshire. Voters were too worried about their own economic suffering to hear lectures about sacrifice. They wanted to hear about rights, not responsibilities. But in February, when Greenberg started testing in Georgia, he noticed stronger responses. Intriguingly, neither service nor loans *alone* stirred much excitement in the focus groups. A service program appealed to a narrow segment of do-gooders; and while voters liked the idea of extra college aid, they feared it would be a "bad value" for taxpayers because it would give people "something for nothing."

Slapped together, however, these two pieces of policy deadwood made a spark. When tied to service, the loans didn't seem like profligate liberalism, because Clinton was asking for something in return. The service provision, in effect, "took away the notion of entitlement," Greenberg said. Conversely, the service program no longer seemed elitist, because it was helping middle-class working families send their kids to college. "It showed Clinton was setting a different kind of standard. He was identifying with values of frustrated middle-class America." It enabled the middle class to get a lush new benefit, and still feel selfless.

The program Clinton outlined was enormous in scope and import; it would be available to virtually everyone who wanted to serve and it would pay for most, if not all, college costs. Clinton and Bruce Reed, the campaign's issues director, knew they might run into criticism because of the cost—but "Clinton didn't have any reservations about making it a big program," Reed said. "He wanted to make this as universal as possible."

"During the campaign I thought this would be the most significant domestic program of my lifetime," said Reed. It was Reed who was asked to come up with an estimate on how much the national service plan would cost. In a November 1991 confidential memo to Clinton, Reed confessed it was a guessing game: "We can't predict the costs of your Domestic GI Bill with any certainty because we don't know how many young people will choose to repay their loans through a small percentage of their income . . . or through national service. Not knowing exactly how much the program will cost means you can leave yourself some wiggle room on how to pay for it."

Nevertheless, Reed did some number crunching, all of which showed that the plan—particularly the loan forgiveness side of it—could be shockingly expensive. He figured an average annual cost of $8 billion, rising to a peak of $14.25 billion by 1998, when the program would be in full force with 500,000 volunteers.

Amazingly, during the campaign hardly anyone questioned or criticized the $14-billion price tag. The only scary moment for Clinton came when Senator Paul Tsongas, Clinton's chief rival, cited it as proof that Clinton was a "pander bear" willing to promise anyone anything. The claim would have particular weight coming from Tsongas, a former Peace Corps volunteer. But the press didn't follow up, and the Clinton campaign knew it had the perfect rejoinder if Tsongas pressed an attack: How could Tsongas criticize Clinton's student-loan plan as irresponsible, when the senator had *defaulted* on his student loan? Tsongas dropped this line of assault.

As the primary campaign progressed, Clinton began embellishing the proposal, partially as a result of Greenberg's research. His focus groups had shown that support for the loan plan grew when participants were assured that it would be combined with "tougher collection." Clinton began emphasizing a provision that had been included in the ability-to-pay loan proposals in Congress: that the IRS would collect on the loans. For the rest of the campaign, Clinton pledged to "scrap" the existing program and bring in the IRS.

Not everyone liked Clinton's service fetish. James Carville would have been perfectly happy if Clinton had never mentioned it. The eccentric Cajun consultant who authored the campaign's call to arms—"The Economy, Stupid"—viewed national service as a distraction, if not an indulgence. "Every candidate has one of these things," he said. "You humor him and you move on." Campaign aides struggled to keep Clinton "on message," and anything that diverted his attention away from the economy—particularly something as trivial as "service"—was deemed unwise. The other political advisors "held it in disdain," Greer recalled. He and Reed felt those aides missed the potential political advantage of the approach. "It had appeal to ordinary people for whom service to country means something," Reed said. "People in Washington underestimated just how much ordinary people longed to give something. It *wasn't* just promising another middle-class benefit."

The political consultants certainly didn't mind Clinton talking about national service in his stump speeches—and couldn't control him that much anyway—but they wouldn't prominently feature it in paid campaign advertising. Polling showed that while the issue was popular, generally reinforcing the notion that Clinton was a "new kind of Democrat," it didn't pack the same emotional punch as welfare reform. Consultant Mandy Grunwald attempted to put together a thirty-second ad on service, but decided she couldn't capture Clinton's enthusiasm in such a short block of time. "It takes too long to explain," she said. "There was no way to compress it and keep the emotion."

By June, Clinton had the nomination wrapped up, but was limping across the finish line. Polls had him running *third* behind Ross Perot and George Bush. As the Democratic convention approached, his rhetoric grew even more grand. "If you do that [service] for two years at a reduced salary," he told a studio audience brought together by CBS *News This Morning,* "then you don't owe any money anymore." Clinton won the nomination with barely any scrutiny of national service. At the triumphant Democratic convention on July 16, Clinton once more declared that his plan would create "an America in which the doors of college are thrown open once again to the sons and daughters of stenographers and steelworkers. We'll say: Everybody can borrow the money to go to college. But you must do your part. You must pay it back, from your paychecks, or better yet by going back home and serving your communities."

On September 11, at Notre Dame, he gave his most expansive talk yet about service. He offered no new details about the plan but, in a speech partially shaped by Senator Harris Wofford of Pennsylvania, Clinton discussed the role of service in the Catholic social tradition. Again he talked about "millions of energetic young men and women serving their country" in exchange for student aid. But he emphasized the spiritual context, and personally added to the speech a quote from JFK: "Here on earth God's work must truly be our own."

So far neither Bush nor the press had attacked Clinton on the service plan. Lucky for Clinton. Behind the scenes, his aides were slowly realizing that, for all its inspiration and political utility, the proposal had some huge practical problems. All year, when citing the cost of the plan, the campaign had been using the memo Bruce Reed had dashed off in November 1991. Reed recognized he needed a better estimate, and asked for help from Jerry Hultin, a financial consultant who was helping to run Clinton's Ohio campaign. Hultin's secret September 16 memo was not good news. For starters, Clinton's promise to open up the college loan program to middle- and upper-income students no longer carried any weight. In August, Congress had passed a new law providing government guaranteed loans to anyone, *regardless of income*. Clinton was making a campaign promise that had already been met—by Bush! "An unconditional call for 'universal access,'" Hultin wrote, "is no longer a viable campaign issue."

Second, Hultin argued, the income-contingent loan program would require massive up-front costs that Reed had not considered. Reed had assumed $6 billion in savings from changing the management of the student-loan program; Hultin said the savings were fictitious.

Third, Reed had estimated stipends and overhead at $9,000 per volunteer; Hultin figured that was $3,000 too low. The bottom line: instead of costing an average of $8 billion annually, a program for 500,000 young people would cost $17 billion. "When one begins to look at the details of national service, loan forgiveness, and student loans," Hultin wrote, "it is clear we face significant programmatic and cost choices in implementing these policies." He suggested funding a mere 25,000 slots instead of 500,000.

To his credit, Reed adjusted the proposal to accommodate the new estimates, although he rejected the idea that only 25,000 servers could be funded. As the campaign headed into its final months, he told the few reporters who bothered to ask that the program would be limited to 250,000 volunteers, and would be pegged to the average debt incurred at a public school, not a private college. Of course, Reed didn't go out of his way to advertise the fuzzy numbers. And despite the changes Reed made in his own computer files, Clinton and the campaign publicly continued to imply a massive, universal program that could wipe out all debt, large or small. He continued to promise he would open up the college loan program to everyone "regardless of financial need"—which made him perhaps the first candidate in recent history to offer a pre-kept campaign promise.

Even Clinton's rhetoric about rights and responsibilities didn't quite make sense anymore. He kept saying that young people would have to give something back to their country in exchange for benefits, a line he'd been using since early 1991, when he was touting the original DLC plan. *That* plan had required young people to give something back. Under Clinton's revised version, one could still get a loan and pay it back without doing a minute of community service.

As the election neared, some policy advisors grew worried that the inconsistencies would harm Clinton. "I assumed they had figured out what they wanted to do before they put out a proposal," recalled Mike Cohen, who had worked for Clinton at the National Governors Association. "I was wrong. It became clear that whatever the hell the program would turn out to be, it could cost gazillions of dollars."

Cohen said he told Reed this. But Reed knew that while the two-sentence applause line seemed unobjectionable, fleshing out the details would stir ancient and ferocious passions in the higher education and service communities. "The last thing he wanted was for this to get out during the campaign," Cohen says. "We reached an understanding that the less said, the better."

More ominously, Reed got a grumpy call during the fall campaign from Congressman Bill Ford, the same man who had attacked the Nunn-McCurdy bill in 1990. Ford had since become the chairman of the House Education and Labor Committee, which would have jurisdiction over the national service legislation. "This national service is awfully expensive," Ford warned Reed.

As Clinton entered the final stretch, he took the rhetoric to new levels of extravagance. Talking to patrons at the Candlewick Diner in New Jersey on October 30, just a week before the election, he said, "I have a proposal that I think is the most innovative proposal that I've made, that could revolutionize education in America, which would permit everybody to get a loan and turn it into a grant. . . . So if you borrow four years' worth of education, you can do two years of work at reduced pay . . . doing community service, and pay off your college loan."

Clinton and his staff knew by this point that it would be a practical impossibility to let "everybody" turn their loans into grants. But as Cohen said later, "A campaign is not the place for a lot of deep thinking."

The mood in Little Rock on election day progressed rapidly from anxiety to numbness to delirium. By noon, exit polls had already come in to Clinton headquarters showing strong leads in tough states like Michigan and Illinois. As voting sites started officially closing, campaign aides like Mandy Grunwald, James Carville, and Gene Sperling gathered in the legendary "War Room," where so much of the campaign had been run. New Hampshire and Georgia were projected for Clinton, leading to one of the first loud cheers of the night. Pennsylvania, Illinois, and Michigan fell to Clinton in rapid succession, prompting a flurry of hollers and high fives. Grunwald, Carville, and George Stephanopoulos hugged. Consultant Paul Begala entered with a Mickey Mouse hat, giving a rebel yell. The War Room was turning into a frat party. New Jersey and Massachusetts came next. ABC projected Missouri and Maryland for Clinton, then Connecticut. A chant broke out, "More! More! More!"

The war-room group rushed out toward the State House, a few blocks away, where Clinton would soon appear. After a half hour of anxious waiting, a few simple piano chords crackled from the speakers. The crowd immediately recognized the notes as the beginning of the campaign theme song, "Don't Stop Thinking About Tomorrow," and burst into a collective scream. Clinton and Gore emerged, hugged their wives, hugged each other, hugged the crowd. The president-elect launched into a breathless speech about what his victory meant. "When we seek to offer young people the opportunity to borrow the money they need to go to college and the challenge to pay it back through national service," he yelled, "all of this is part of a new patriotism to lift our people up and enable all of us to live to the fullest of our potential."

In the sheer ecstasy of the moment, absolutely anything seemed possible, particularly something as noble and idealistic as national ser-' vice. Maybe the president-elect *could* change the way young people viewed their responsibilities; perhaps he *could* lead a new movement to draw out the best impulses of each American. After Clinton left the stage, the crowd scattered to hit the circuit of victory bashes. In the midst of the mob was Bruce Reed with his wife, en route to a party. He looked dazed, as if he were just beginning to absorb what had happened. When asked about national service, Reed became suddenly and surprisingly pragmatic.

"That's going to be the tough one."

2

The Swiss Army Knife

Shortly after the 1992 election, *Newsweek* assigned me to follow one campaign promise as it transformed over many months into a public law. I chose national service because no other idea so typified Clinton's approach and vision. Clinton remembered a time when Democrats had made government work not only to improve conditions, but to tap the patriotism and even enrich the character of citizens. The Democratic Party, after all, gave us Franklin Roosevelt's Civilian Conservation Corps and John F. Kennedy's Peace Corps. National service was Clinton's one chance to create from scratch a program that would help reestablish faith in government. But it also would be a test case of how he rationalized the two strains of his political personality, his expansive idealism and his aggressive pragmatism. Clinton would have to watch and react as his dreamy rhetoric collided with the reality of governing in an era of limits.

The one campaign proposal would eventually split into two pieces of legislation. A service bill would set up the system so that young people could serve their communities in exchange for a college scholarship. A separate student aid reform bill would "scrap the existing student loan program" and allow any graduate to repay loans "as a small percentage of their earnings over time." In each case, the applause line became a bill, which became a law.

Despite their apparent popularity, both initiatives faced great obstacles. Early in 1993, the Republicans would filibuster to death

President Clinton's economic stimulus package, demonstrating a near-veto power over his initiatives. To fulfill this campaign promise, Clinton would have to create two major social programs at the same time he tried to reduce the deficit.

But the budget was only the most obvious problem. In different ways, these proposals would highlight all the most nagging ailments of American politics. The drive to change the college-aid program would showcase many of the most common forms of legal corruption that regularly warp public policy: manufactured grassroots campaigns, phony polls, Democratic influence peddlers working to undermine the agenda of a new Democratic administration. Also on display were some of the more unorthodox lobbying techniques, such as using computer bulletin boards to cyberlobby, slipping dirt to an investigative reporter to humiliate an opponent, or waiting outside a men's room to ambush a senator. National service's journey, on the other hand, would expose all the raw nerves of Democratic Party politics—race, class, and the struggle between the poor and middle class for government resources. Both bills would demonstrate that the interest-group mentality is no longer characteristic only of paid lobbyists. Even groups doing "good works," like local conservation corps, would become infected by reflexive narrowmindedness. Throughout the journey of these bills, conflict would inevitably center on the least important elements, while major policy shifts got smuggled into law under cover of legislative darkness. Little complications would manhandle big ideas, as the system often seemed incapable of working toward a broad national purpose.

———

Clinton clearly had enormous expectations as to what service could accomplish. Was this typical Clintonian excess? No. National service can be a powerful program and idea. Done properly, it could be the public policy equivalent of a Swiss Army knife, performing numerous useful functions in one affordable package. Such a program could simultaneously help address unmet social needs—from carrying meals to the elderly to rebuilding urban playgrounds—and bring people of different backgrounds together in a common mission, as the World War II draft did for millions of Americans. It could build discipline and self-confidence among young people and at the same time create a powerful civic ethic.

Many severe social problems persist because the solutions are labor intensive and expensive. But the nation could reap long-term gain if people were willing to perform these tasks for submarket wages outside the confines of lethargic government bureaucracies. For instance, seniors over eighty-five are the fastest-growing segment of the elderly population. This poses not just a massive humanitarian problem but a financial one as well, as most elderly end up in nursing homes paid for by Medicare and Medicaid. Already, long-term-care costs were $79 billion in 1993, an amount projected to rise to $202 billion in constant dollars by 2020. Tragically, many seniors leave their homes not because of acute medical needs but because they have become unable to manage ordinary daily tasks. Many could be kept in their homes if they had volunteers to clean up, pick up groceries, bring in meals, wash the windows, or transport them to doctors' appointments. As William F. Buckley writes in his book promoting national service, *Gratitude*, "Just to give family members a *temporary* break from caring for an Alzheimer's victim, either through home visits or adult day-care centers, would be a major help." In Germany, where more than 100,000 young people perform civilian work to fulfill a national service requirement, some nonprofit groups have been able to create entirely new services previously considered uneconomical, such as transportation services for seriously disabled persons. A Ford Foundation study that attempted to catalogue useful assignments for national service volunteers in the United States, speculated that 438,000 servers could be effectively used just for home care. While cost-benefit analyses are notoriously creative, it's worth mentioning that studies by local service corps in Pennsylvania, California, Michigan, and Washington State have claimed benefits ranging from $1.70 to $2.88 per dollar spent.

There is an additional advantage that's impossible to quantify: invigorating stultified government bureaucracies. Older career employees sometimes became reenergized working side-by-side with highly motivated young people. Some simply remember why they'd gotten into public service in the first place; others realize their sloth is too obvious in contrast to the newcomer's vigor.

Similarly, national service workers can vastly expand the capacity and effectiveness of existing charities. Groups like the Red Cross or Habitat for Humanity sometimes have to turn away volunteers for lack of full-time employees to train and coordinate them. And some organizations need people they can call on day or night. "Victim assistance" programs, for instance, send volunteers to crime sites to comfort victims, or, later, make sure their interests are represented in the labyrinthine criminal justice system. Unfortunately, crimes don't always occur when unpaid volunteers are available.

Service can be a tool to support broader social goals. As society tries to push mothers off welfare and into the workforce, the need for child-care services will increase dramatically. Yet as of 1993, the waiting lists for publicly assisted day care were 25,000 in Florida, 15,000 in Georgia, and 30,000 in Illinois. The Ford Foundation study estimated that the economy could fruitfully absorb 272,000 to 1,360,000 volunteers in the day-care area alone.

While some social problems seem to defy solution, most environmental woes fit into another category: remedies are conceptually simple but logistically daunting. The best example is lead paint. One in eleven kids has blood-lead levels above the amount at which neurological damage starts occurring. In some inner-city areas, one half of the kids have too much. Lead helps keep kids poor and undereducated by reducing IQ levels and attention spans and increasing their proclivity for violence. It is not hard to teach volunteers how to test and clean up chipped or flaking paint. But three million tons of lead line the walls and fixtures of 57 million American homes, and most health departments have a tiny fraction of the people they need to perform inspections.

Despite these many potential benefits, government has in the past found numerous ways to squander service money. (Nomination for most creative: the War on Poverty grant in the 1960s that funded a LeRoi Jones play in which Rochester, the sidekick on Jack Benny's radio shows, rose up to kill his white oppressors.) Even the Peace Corps, the most successful recent service program, had a mix of high- and low-quality programs. Charles Peters, the director of evaluation for the agency in the 1960s, concluded that while volunteers teaching in Africa dramatically increased the quality of education, those doing "community development" in Latin America had unrealistic goals and accomplished little. "The volunteers could empower the powerless and array the heretofore helpless campesino against the oligarchs who were oppressing him," he writes. "The catch was that actually accomplishing all this required a volunteer who was a combination of Jesus Christ and John Kennedy, with a little bit of Tip O'Neill thrown in."

Truth is, more forces push service programs away from meaningful work than toward it. Social workers may claim that only those with masters' degrees can directly assist public aid recipients (therefore the volunteer should assist by doing paperwork back at the office). Unions might push volunteers toward being teachers' assistants instead of teachers. Ominously, the scores of local youth corps that sprouted up during the 1980s usually emphasized helping the servers themselves more than the communities around them. "Some said theneed is to engage and solve the country's problems like crumbling cities," explained Thomas Ehrlich, chairman of the Commission on National and Community Service and a defender of server-oriented programs. "Others, including myself, say that if that is the goal it is doomed to fail. We focus on the effect on the individual—self-esteem, confidence, character." When the mission is to help the participants, the services rendered become incidental. Several local youth corps have had the "volunteers" perform "fee for service" work, like mowing lawns in affluent suburbs or painting yellow lines down newly paved roads. Not exactly the Lord's work.

Programs succeed when they give volunteers specific, *useful* tasks. Clinton would never face a yea-or-nay vote on "make work" versus "real work." But in deciding who gave out the money, what types of programs qualified, and the role of unions, the White House and Congress would, in essence, determine whether national service emphasized real work. To achieve his desired goals, this New Democrat president would have to battle not only conservative critics but his friends.

Clinton also viewed national service as a remedy—one of the few remaining—for the fragmentation and polarization that threaten the country. "If we can do [service] across lines of race and income and neighborhood and work," Clinton said in June 1991, "we will be able to make a major stride toward reestablishing a sense of community, without which this country cannot begin to solve its long-term problems."

Clinton was right to identify fragmentation as a nation-threatening problem. After all society's efforts to bring races together, housing segregation has persisted, college campuses have balkanized, and political separatism has grown. Even as more blacks prosper economically, the cultural divides continue to grow: In 1992, the top ten TV shows among black viewers had not one program in common with the top ten among whites.

More worrisome, class segregation is growing too. As a result of suburbanization, the proportion of individuals residing in neighborhoods alongside families of similar incomes has increased dramatically in the past two decades. Affluent people, white or black, are now less likely to live near low-income people, black or white. Fragmentation has become part of a vicious circle of social decay: middle-class families move to suburbs, cities collapse; low-income people become isolated, schools worsen, crime increases, neighborhoods deteriorate—and more middle-class families leave the cities.

In the past, social and governmental institutions helped bind together Americans. The military, for instance, not only unified the country symbolically, but forced interaction between men who might otherwise never have met. A twenty-six-year-old John F. Kennedy served on a PT boat in the South Pacific with a refrigeration engineer from Macon, Georgia; the left tackle from the Ohio State football team; a machinist from Chicago; a Polish immigrant factory worker; a Princeton grad; a former commercial fisherman; a career navy man; a jazz pianist; a trailer-truck driver; and a railway mechanic.

But these unifying institutions have disintegrated or dwindled. The military is shrinking. Public schools have become more homogeneous as the communities that run them have become more segregated by income. Public parks and transportation, which once provided venues of mixing, have deteriorated. Even television doesn't unite as it once did. While the average household in 1975 received six TV stations—so the odds were decent that you watched the same show as your boss—today's typical family has more than thirty-nine channels.

Clinton viewed his national service plan as a way of slowly building bridges between classes and races. His model was City Year, the program founded in Boston by two Harvard Law School roommates. In December 1991, while campaigning for the nearby New Hampshire primary, Clinton paid a visit to City Year and was impressed by the mix of young people he met—a prep school student, a former drug dealer, a middle-class girl, all of whom seemed profoundly affected by their service experience. "I like the fact that it involves a diverse socioeconomic group—poor kids and kids who take a year off from Ivy League schools and come from wealthy backgrounds, and middle-class kids in between," Clinton said.

Obviously, City Year is not perfect. Journalist Suzanne Goldsmith spent a year in a City Year corps and wrote objectively about the experience. Her team would hardly qualify to be Up With People singers: one member stole from another and was kicked out, another was murdered back in his own neighborhood, one had an abortion, and a few dropped out for lack of interest or motivation. In between those sad tales, though, were the stories of corps members whose minds and horizons stretched dramatically.

Consider Earl, a nineteen-year-old black high school dropout from Newark. A year after the program, he was unemployed and in trouble, not exactly a model turnaround story. But City Year did make him a more tolerant person, and, in the process, enabled Earl to help *other* people:

What was good about City Year was I got to meet a piece of everybody. We got a chance to eliminate some stereotypes that people had in their puny little minds. Before, I couldn't stand white people. The Blackstone School project made me feel good inside, because I haven't done that kind of work before. I felt like a big brother. I felt like, you know, that sentimental feeling. It gave me that role-model feeling. . . .

I can use a power tool now. And I can work an eight-hour day without dying. I got this feeling of accomplishment, like I done something for the community, even though they never did nothin' for me. Before when there was bum on the street askin' for change I would kick him or play with him and pretend like I was gonna give him a quarter and take it back. Now I'll give him a quarter. I gave one dude ten bills.

Rosa, an eighteen-year-old high school graduate, had moved to Boston from Puerto Rico to live with her brother, in what turned out to be a violent, drug-infested neighborhood:

I thought the team would be prejudiced against me because I was Puerto Rican, but they were friendly. If we had a problem, we talked to each other. They asked me things about PR, the culture, stuff like that. We communicated real good. . . . I liked working in the park, things that I never done before. Things that I never thought that I could learn to do. Man jobs. . . . Tony [the team leader] teaches you a lot. He teaches you that things have to be right. Just when you think, "Oh, it's okay, it's okay to do it that way," no; it has to be *right*. You can do better than "okay."

Will graduated from Skidmore College, an expensive private school in upstate New York. He came from a wealthy family in Connecticut, but was painting houses and waiting tables before he joined the program:

I remember walking in the first day and seeing the corps and my heart dropping, realizing that these people were not my age, very few looked like they'd graduated from college, and that this was a diverse group of people. I got very scared. I remember wanting to hold myself differently, not make jokes, thinking that maybe my words would be too long.

I didn't know anybody that had come from the background I had, and it was the one background we [in the group] never talked about. I sort of felt like everybody agreed that blacks had been oppressed and women are oppressed and blue-collar workers are oppressed and the common ground we would all share is that a rich family is disgusting and they're terrible people.

I remember the day that I felt I didn't hold back as part of the team. We had to do a presentation [about the team's activities]. I came in with a script of how I thought it should go, and so I really put it out there, and when the team started to argue about it, I stepped forward and said, "No! This is how I think it should go." And that felt really good, that I could be myself and my teammates would listen to me like I listened to them. That was important to me—I suddenly felt very comfortable with them. And I stopped holding back, I started talking about my family and everything else.

The service projects—when we were in that shelter and the dust was falling all over the place and we were climbing ladders, that was amazing. To look around and see Alison three floors down working with Chris, and I'm up here with Brendan using a nail gun, that was definitely cool. But what was cool about it was the way we would then be at lunchtime—exhausted but feeling accomplished. And the humor that would go on while you're on the work site. . . .

It has totally changed the way I view relationships with friends. And it's changed my relationships with my family completely. When I was fifteen years old, I was this funny, fat, spoiled little snot. Little Lord Fauntleroy. And now my role is absolutely changed. People have the idea that young people doing service will be good for the ex–gang member, but it's equally important and good for society to get somebody like myself turned around through it. I clearly will be a better person because of my experience here, and I will give back to the world in better ways.

Despite the apparent success of City Year, those writing the service legislation had to face a daunting historical fact: No national domestic service program has ever successfully drawn people of different classes. The Peace Corps is disproportionately well educated and white. VISTA began recruiting the affluent, then changed its mission and by the 1980s attracted primarily the poor. Most discouragingly, the vast majority of modern service corps members are disproportionately low-income and minority. City Year organizers found that to get a good mix they had to explicitly discuss the racial and economic background of each volunteer, and shift people from one team to another as if trading baseball cards. It seems that, as with the question of make-work versus "real" work, Clinton would be fighting great odds if he wanted service programs to be powerful tools of socioeconomic mixing. It would not be easy.

Clinton did not spell out exactly how race- or class-mixing should happen under his plan. Many questions remained. Clinton was leader of the political party that fractured over the issue of busing; would he really risk the bipartisan love of "service" to push a more delicate, and important, vision of class and race integration? Would Clinton be willing to say, "This program has too many poor kids—let's cut some"?

———

Besides bridging racial and economic gulfs and solving scores of massive social problems, what else can this policy Swiss Army knife do? As they say on the infomercials, *wait, there's more.* Service programs may "develop" disadvantaged youths more efficiently than traditional training programs. Studies of the California Conversation Corps, the largest existing service program, showed that low-income men earned $726 more in their first year after graduating than similar young men who don't serve. That's about as good as the most successful antipoverty programs like Job Corps, and along the way the youths perform service to others. The hope: young people try harder because implicit in the request for service is the message that they have something worthwhile to give. Participants who don't show up know they are letting down someone in need, not some patronizing social worker.

Finally, national service could foster a new civic ethic. As Buckley writes in *Gratitude*, society has always understood the beneficial civic effects of military service. With the role of the military declining, he argues, society must find other ways of instilling in young people this sense of mutual obligation: "Far from thinking themselves entirely discharged from showing interest in other people, and in other concerns, they would find their appetite stimulated."

These national service goals are *contingent on each other.* Youths will not develop self-confidence and skills if they merely fill, then empty, ditches for eight hours a day. You can't trick them into having self-esteem. But programs that only provide services—without teaching citizenship or mixing classes—become, well, jobs. And the jobs themselves may be of lower quality if the corps are just for the poor. Programs with a middle-class constituency—from jobs programs to public schools—end up retaining higher quality than those for the poor.

Conversely, programs that aspire only toward socioeconomic integration will likely fail too. The mission of the armed forces, after all, is not to bring black and white together, nor to build esprit de corps, but to defend the country. If the U.S. Army were set up as a class-mixing enterprise—"Be All You Can Be; Meet People with Funny Accents"—it would neither successfully mix classes nor defend the country.

In other words, like a Swiss Army knife, if national service doesn't perform several functions well, it's not worth having.

———

Clinton's campaign decision to emphasize something as pedestrian as student loan reform showed his talent for identifying middle-class anxieties. The cost of a college education increased faster in the 1980s than that of cars, food, or houses—and far faster than family income. Private college tuition outpaced even the price of medical care. College costs now take up more than one in each five dollars a family earns—up from one in seven in 1980. During the same period, America revolutionized the way it finances college: in the 1970s, two thirds of all aid came in the form of grants; today, two thirds come in the form of loans. Few public policy developments have been as sudden, massive, and negligibly acknowledged. (If the significance is not clear, consider the difference between someone giving you a car and lending you the money to buy one.) In 1985, the average loan debt was $6,488; by 1991 that had climbed to $16,417. A typical graduate sent $987 a year to the bank in 1985; by 1991 he or she sent $2,161.

The college cost explosion has begun to undermine some basic American principles. From 1982 to 1989, the percentage of private college and university students who were wealthy jumped from 50 percent to 63 percent. The thirty-year trend of expanded opportunity has begun reversing. A family's financial status has become increasingly important in determining a young person's fate.

The debt-driven access squeeze has happened at a most inopportune moment. The importance of college education for individual and national prosperity has never been greater. Over the past fifteen years, real earnings of college-educated workers have risen 2 percent, while earnings of nongraduates have fallen 30 percent. Combine the access problems with the social segmentation described earlier and the outlines of a self-perpetuating caste system become obvious.

That's why income-contingent loans are important.

The idea of easing loan burden through flexible loan repayment comes originally from conservative economist Milton Friedman. "Expenditure on education is a capital investment in a risky enterprise, as it were, like investment in a newly formed small business," Friedman has written. Why not set up a funding system, he asks, in which investors would " 'buy' a share in an individual's earning prospects, to advance him the funds needed to finance his training on condition that he agree to pay the investor a specific fraction of his future earnings."

It is changing the terms of loan repayment, not the promise of aid for service, that could dramatically improve access to college. Income-contingent loans—or pay-as-you-can loans, as they'll be called in this book—can alter the decision calculus of a low-income high school student. Right now, he may look at loans and decide that college is not a sensible wager. His time horizons are short and he finds it's nearly impossible to envision a future lucrative enough so that he could pay off a loan. He sees around him men and women enslaved by shady high-interest loans and few instances of high-wage, well-educated workers. Others in low-income communities might have developed an entitlement mentality that makes them eschew loans and "wait" for grants. In either case, with a pay-as-you-can loan, the government can say: "You have no excuse not to go to college. If you take out a loan, graduate, and still earn nothing, you will pay nothing. But if education pays you dividends, as it does for most people, you will have plenty of cash with which to gratefully repay society."

The benefits are not limited to the poor. Consider middle-class parents who know that their daughter could get into a top-tier private school but fear they can't afford to pay the tuition. Under pay-as-you-can, their child could take out loans knowing that if she doesn't rake it in, she would still have affordable payments. Children with special needs or interests could also thrive under this system. A middle-income boy with great talent on, say, the saxophone, who wanted to go to a private music academy, would have a hard time justifying a loan under the current aid system. Odds are he *wouldn't* earn enough as a saxophonist to pay back the loan. But do we really want a world where only the rich can go to conservatories?

Yet for all the potentially revolutionary effects on access, what appealed most to Clinton about pay-as-you-can loans was the connection to service. He believed that more college students might have pursued careers in teaching, social work, or law enforcement over the past fifteen years had they not been so loaded down with debt. There is little direct evidence of that, but debt levels have begun to affect a range of other life choices. In 1985, 15 percent of graduates surveyed said debt had influenced when to marry; by 1991, 26 percent said it had. In 1985, 32 percent said it had pushed them to rent, not buy, housing; in 1991, 47 percent said so. In 1985, 25 percent said debt had forced them to work two or more jobs; by 1991 almost 40 percent said it had. Obviously, there are other factors that affect career choice; and pay-as-you-can loans do not take away a person's ambition for wealth and comfort. But they do remove extra weight from the shoulders of someone who is inclined toward a public service career. That is most obvious in the realm of graduate education. The average indebtedness of medical students rose from $14,622 in 1979 to a staggering $45,840 in 1990, increasing pressure on graduates to enter high-paying specialties such as dermatology rather than less profitable fields like pediatrics.

The proposal for pay-as-you-can loans got even less critical attention during the campaign than did its fraternal twin, national service, yet in some ways it was more important. National service would touch tens of thousands of people; pay-as-you-can loans would affect millions. While it seemed noncontroversial, the Clinton loan reform really had an extraordinary premise: government should make it easier for people to earn less. At its core was the almost spiritual notion that, as Clinton said in 1993, "people are not really free" if they cannot take advantage of their God-given potential. Ronald Reagan said that if he could get government off their backs, Americans would show their innate creativity and economic energy. Clinton's college-aid reform suggested that if government could get financial debt off their backs, Americans would be better able to serve others.

3

The Puzzle Magnate

"Eli will make national service happen," President-elect Clinton said in announcing the appointment of his old friend Eli Segal to run the White House Office of National Service.

The day after the election, at a press conference in Little Rock, Clinton had surprised some reporters by listing national service as one of the pillars of his administration, along with health care, economic recovery, and campaign finance reform. He then surprised the congressional leadership by telling them in early strategy meetings that national service would be a top legislative priority. But for those who knew Clinton well, it was his selection of longtime friend and advisor Segal that showed most dramatically his seriousness about national service.

In announcing the appointment, Clinton emphasized Segal's real-world experience as a businessman—magazine publisher, direct-mail marketer—the perfect credential for a New Democrat manager. What he didn't mention was that Segal's history of left-liberal political activism had shaped him as much as his time in the business world.

Segal was the son of a hatmaker in Flatbush, Brooklyn. His earliest political memory was of his father making him stay home from school to watch the Army-McCarthy hearings. He began his political career by winning election as freshman class president of the predominantly Jewish Brandeis University in Boston in 1961. Within his first week of college, Segal had, in eerily Clintonesque fashion, studied the yearbook of incoming freshmen and memorized the names, faces, and hometowns of all 325 students in the book.

In college, he helped start an organization to bring to campus famous speakers—among them Malcolm X, radical lawyer Mark Lane, and Dick Gregory—and helped found a group affiliated with the Student Nonviolent Coordinating Committee. Through SNCC, he worked as a mentor, taking groups of black kids to baseball games and museums; but like Clinton, Segal was not terribly impressed with the efficacy of the volunteerism. "I remember being frustrated . . . that that by itself was not going to be sustaining." Segal went to law school at the University of Michigan, and in 1967 began, with his friend Sam Brown, to move into the leadership of the burgeoning antiwar movement. He joined Eugene McCarthy's 1968 presidential campaign, and eventually ran the candidate's organization in states without primaries, such as Oklahoma, North Dakota, and Iowa. The next year he attended a retreat in Martha's Vineyard for antiwar politicos who wanted to reshape the Democratic Party. There he met Bill Clinton.

During the 1968 campaign, Segal had become convinced that the delegate selection system was rigged against insurgent candidates like McCarthy and in favor of party "regulars." In 1969, at age twenty-six, he became chief counsel to the McGovern Commission—the controversial reform panel that helped open up—and some say destroy—the Democratic Party by creating more primaries and reducing the power of political machines.

Segal then became general counsel to the Vietnam Moratorium—handling less-glamorous protest tasks like negotiating permits for rallies and marches—and soon joined George McGovern's 1972 presidential campaign as assistant campaign manager. Looking for a talented Southerner to run McGovern's improbable Texas campaign, he turned to the young fellow he had met a few years earlier—Bill Clinton.

While the protests of the 1960s and 1970s shaped Segal's political views, he also saw firsthand how radicals tended to destroy their own. The movement had so emphasized inclusion and tolerance that it was unwilling to kick out destructive elements. Writer Taylor Branch, who worked with Segal on the McGovern campaign, has noted that the self-righteous radicals of the period trampled over many well-meaning liberals. "I think Eli was one of the tramplees," Branch said.

It was during the 1972 McGovern campaign that Segal decided to become rich. In his brief career as a political activist he had learned that, as he put it, "Those who had resources could have a far more major impact." Segal was about to take a job at the Washington power law firm of Arnold and Porter when Miles L. Rubin, a McGovern fund-raiser and business tycoon, asked him to join his conglomerate, Pioneer Systems Inc. In 1975, when the president of Vogart Crafts Corporation, one of Pioneer's subsidiaries, resigned, Rubin asked Segal to take over as CEO. Segal was skeptical that he could run a business on his own, particularly one that manufactured needlecraft kits—not exactly his primary field of expertise. Rubin then described the similarities between politics and business. "Remember we talked about getting the right image of George McGovern out onto the streets? They call that marketing," he explained. "Remember when we talked about making sure that every congressional district had the right number of brochures? They call that distribution."

Segal then had a string of business successes. He ran Vogart successfully for six years. He took over American Publishing Corporation, which produced jigsaw puzzles and board games, sold it at a major profit, and then created Bits & Pieces in Watertown, Massachusetts, to market puzzles and games. In 1990 he bought a bankrupt publication called *Games* magazine, and built its circulation to 250,000.

Segal remained active in politics during the 1980s. He served as national finance chairman for Gary Hart in 1987, and established himself as one of the major fund-raisers in the Democratic Party. In the fall of 1991, Clinton chose Segal as his campaign chief of staff; after the election, some Washington oddsmakers assumed Segal would become White House chief of staff. When Clinton chose Mack McLarty instead, Segal made plans to return to Massachusetts.

Clinton allies had discussed a range of people to run the national service operation. Senator Harris Wofford of Pennsylvania suggested Hillary Clinton. Alumni of Franklin Roosevelt's Civilian Conservation Corps pushed FDR's grandson David Roosevelt. Kathleen Kennedy Townsend, head of a Maryland high school service effort, wanted to be in charge. There were calls for former Ohio governor Richard Celeste, who had run the Peace Corps under Jimmy Carter; and Richard Danzig, a Washington lawyer who had written a book about national service. But Clinton wanted someone to whom he could give complete control, someone he could trust unequivocally with not only the policy decisions but the politics. This program had to be up, running, and popular by 1996. Although the president-elect became known early on in his administration for grasping policy detail, on noneconomic issues he often delegated authority to key subordinates. National service would be up to Eli.

Segal clearly had a track record of getting things done, but he had two potential weaknesses. Those who have worked for or with him inevitably describe him in terms more appropriate for an airline flight attendant than for a political manager—as "very good-natured," "the world's nicest guy," and "a rabbi at heart." As he turned fifty, Segal even looked like a softy; his small bald spot, short stature, and ever-so-slightly expanding waistline made him seem more roly-poly than awe-inspiring. He was known as someone who had made difficult decisions in the campaign, but some wondered privately whether he was tough enough to drive through legislation without over-compromising. Like Clinton, he was a born conciliator. Was Segal too "nice" for this job? Put into the world of bare-knuckled congressional and interest-group politics, would Segal become, in Taylor Branch's phrase, a "tramplee"?

Segal's other problem was that he was almost totally ignorant of service programs and their history—of what had worked and what hadn't—and didn't seem to understand some of the basics of Clinton's own proposal. "Why do we have to include this student-aid stuff? Can't we just do community service?" Segal asked at one early briefing. How would Segal know the principles for which to fight?

The atmosphere at the new Office of National Service (ONS) in the Old Executive Office Building did not inspire confidence that the job was in the hands of seasoned pros. Staffed by earnest men and women in their late teens and early twenties, some wearing shorts and T-shirts, others wearing buttondown Oxford shirts with the tails dangling from the back of their corduroy pants, it resembled a college newspaper office. Most of the young people worked in one large space with five desks dubbed the Romper Room. A huge posterboard photo of Clinton jogging in a City Year sweatshirt stood propped against the wall in the back. Near the door sat a large box of T-shirts from service programs that wanted the president to sweat into one of *their* shirts on national TV.

The most influential Romper Room kid was Robert Gordon, a gangly twenty-year-old who had taken a leave from Harvard to work on the campaign in Little Rock. Gordon had been in the thick of the War Room operation—the rapid response team immortalized by an Academy Award–nominated film of the same name. Gordon actually had more experience in service projects than Segal, having volunteered in the Boston public schools, taught tennis in inner-city playgrounds, and raised money for a revolving loan fund for the homeless. His voice is soft, low, creaky, and, often, barely audible. While other twenty-somethings in the White House bristled at not being in major policy roles, Gordon maintained an almost quaint deference to his elders, which earned him their affection and, ironically, helped earn him a major policy role. Behind his back, the adult female ONS staffers would joke about how "adorable" he was, but came to respect his writing ability and his constant reminders of what Clinton had emphasized during the 1992 campaign. He became, in the words of one official, "the campaign conscience" in the office.

Segal's first challenge was getting around one of Clinton's pesky campaign promises. The candidate had promised to cut the White House staff by 25 percent. That would leave the Office of National Service with six people, not quite enough to build a massive movement and transform America. So Segal played a classic bureaucratic parlor game, placing at least ten erstwhile national service staffers at other agencies and then having the agencies "lend" them to ONS. Segal chose as his deputy Richard Allen, a dashing, wealthy commercial real estate developer from California who had helped organize Hollywood celebrities to volunteer in South Central LA. The CEO for a company that owned several trendy boutiques on Rodeo Drive, Allen had only slightly more knowledge of service programs than Segal.

With the two top officials skilled at business but inexperienced in service or government, the heavy policy lifting fell to two former congressional aides: Shirley Sagawa and Jack Lew.

In 1978, Congress had created the Young Adult Conservation Corps, a network of state-operated service programs. To run the California Conservation Corps, Governor Jerry Brown hired B. T. Collins, a former marine, who established a boot-camp atmosphere—his motto was "Hard work, low pay, miserable conditions"—requiring physical exercise, sermons on the work ethic, and first-aid training. The corps members planted trees, fought fires, cleaned up oil spills, and battled the Mediterranean fruit fly.

When Congress and the Reagan administration eliminated the YACC in 1982, several state governments decided to maintain their conservation corps. New urban corps sprouted in San Francisco, the Oakland area, and New York City. The programs formed the National Association of Service and Conservation Corps (NASCC), which helped create new efforts around the country.

At about the same time, an eclectic assortment of entrepreneurs began creating from scratch new service models. Twenty-five-year-old Princeton graduate Wendy Kopp started Teach for America, which recruited successful college graduates to work in poor school districts. Alan Khazei and Michael Brown set up City Year, emphasizing class- and race-mixing. Former antipoverty organizer Dorothy Stoneman created the YouthBuild network, which trained low-income minority participants to help rebuild housing in their own neighborhoods. A twenty-seven-year-old from Kansas City named David Battey formed the Youth Volunteer Corps of America, which put tens of thousands of high school students to work. George Bush's Points of Light Foundation helped publicize some of the activity. Meanwhile, Jimmy Carter's work building homes with Habitat for Humanity highlighted the arduous volunteerism of some of the traditional charities.

Volunteerism began having cachet at colleges. Stanford University president Don Kennedy, Brown University president Howard Swearer, and Georgetown president Father Timothy Healy helped start Campus Compact, which committed two hundred college and university presidents to a drive for campus-based service programs. In 1984, students formed the Campus Outreach Opportunity League (COOL), which enlisted hundreds of thousands of students on more than eight hundred campuses to do service. School-reform advocates began viewing service as a way of making education more exciting and habituating kids into helping others. Scores of school districts adopted "service learning" programs that incorporated volunteer work into curricula (a student in a chemistry course might measure soil samples for pollutants to help the local parks department, for instance).

Although the service pioneers emphasized different approaches, most shared a desire to supplement traditional volunteerism with structured, full-time, often-stipended service. They also shared a desire to get some federal cash for their efforts.

In 1986, Roger Landrum and Frank Slobig, two veteran service advocates, drew together these different "streams of service"—youth corps, service learning, campus volunteerism, and "entrepreneurial" programs—into one grand coalition called Youth Service America. With the creation of NASCC and YSA, the standard political life cycle was completed. Noble impulses had given birth to creative ideas, which led to new programs, which converged into a movement, which begat a healthy brood of interest groups.

By 1990, Congress began considering a slew of service proposals ranging from the Moskos-inspired Nunn-McCurdy plan to a proposal to revive a small version of the New Deal's CCC. Senator Edward M. Kennedy decided to draw together the different plans into one piece of legislation that would set up a steady funding source for the local programs. No one on his staff particularly wanted this low-profile project. As a junior staffer, Shirley Sagawa got the assignment.

The soft-spoken twenty-six-year-old hardly fit the image of legislative powerhouse, given her tendency to giggle and shrug after making important points. But she would prove to be an important founding mother, or at least a nursemaid, of the modern service movement. At first, her main interest was defeating the DLC's Nunn-McCurdy bill, which she viewed as a threat to poor students, but Kennedy urged her to focus on service learning. He had fallen in love with the approach when visiting an elementary school that had gotten fourth graders to visit nursing homes.

As Sagawa looked into it, she too became enchanted with service, not so much to solve social problems but to help teach young people a civic ethic. The daughter of a Japanese immigrant, Sagawa had strong memories of her father's lengthy quest in the 1950s to gain American citizenship. She wrote a comprehensive bill that would expand existing corps, promote service learning, and let the DLC have some pilot programs to test their ideas. With Kennedy's aggressive stewardship, the bill eventually passed the Senate by a 79–19 vote. The House Education and Labor Committee showed little interest, so Kennedy took the unusual step of personally lobbying dozens of congressmen.

The law established the Commission on National and Community Service to distribute money among the various programs. (The political circle of life had expanded: impulse . . . idea . . . program . . . movement . . . interest groups . . . *federal grants*.) Sagawa left Kennedy's office and soon became the commission's vice chair. She hired as executive director Catherine Milton, one of the founders of Campus Compact. The commission created dozens of new programs, such as the Delta Service Corps in Arkansas, and helped existing ones, including City Year, to expand. By 1993, the "service movement" and the commission had created, with little national attention, a web of seventy-five new programs, involving fifteen thousand full-time participants—double the size of the Peace Corps and VISTA combined. In the course of the 1993 legislative process these programs would prove important, first, by showing in practical terms what service could do and, more important, by providing grassroots lobbying in nearly every state.

Sagawa had watched the 1992 presidential campaign with mixed emotions. She was thrilled that Clinton had elevated service to such prominence, but deeply suspicious of his ties to the Democratic Leadership Council. The DLC, after all, had wanted to prevent poor kids from getting college aid unless they did service. In August 1992, she teamed up with Melanne Verveer, a former lobbyist for People for the American Way, to convene a series of secret meetings on service policy. Verveer and Sagawa feared that if they didn't have a plan ready when Clinton came into office, he would turn to the smarmy DLC conservatives to write the legislation.

Some of the tension between the Kennedy crowd and the DLC

was personality-driven. The liberals viewed the members of the DLC as militaristic sexists, while the DLC saw the Kennedy clique as naïve bleeding hearts. Still, there were a few substantive policy differences. While the DLC emphasized patriotism, middle-class participation, and the value of services rendered, the liberals tended to view service as a way of helping at-risk youth. Indeed, many of the conservation corps that sprang up in the 1980s were antipoverty programs with a service gloss. Several were run by veterans of the 1960s War on Poverty, recruited mostly low-income minorities, emphasized job training and work experience, and downplayed the civic ethic. In a survey of youth corps participants, only 14 percent said they had joined "to help other people," while the rest cited opportunities to learn skills or get remedial education.

By the time of Clinton's inauguration, Sagawa and Verveer had completed a draft national service plan that had little of the DLC-oriented rhetoric about class- or race-mixing. Hillary Clinton then chose Verveer as her top policy advisor; Verveer asked Sagawa to be Hillary's representative on the Domestic Policy Council; and Segal assigned Sagawa to write the national service legislation. The DLC crowd privately viewed her selection as supremely worrisome. "From the DLC point of view she represents all the forces of evil," one DLC ally complained.

The other key staffer at the Office of National Service, Jack Lew, had been a top policy aide to former House Speaker Tip O'Neill. Capitol Hill veterans knew Lew as one-half of the Orthodox Jewish team —the other being Ari Weiss—that had handled "substance" for the Irishman's legislative operation. A lanky man with a slightly nasal voice, Lew hadn't, in the words of one friend, "thought five minutes about national service" before taking the job. But Segal wanted him because Lew had earned a reputation as a fine legislative craftsman. He loved the arcana of policy, how tweaking a formula here or adding some legal language there could help thousands of people or shift billions of dollars. One of the few men in political Washington who actually put his religious faith above his work, Lew always left the office by sunset on Friday to observe the Sabbath. Like Sagawa, Lew's connection to service came not from participation in formal service programs but from his own family background. He considered community cohesion to be a central part of religious faith; Lew would regularly take his children to nursing homes to visit seniors who had been congregants in his synagogue. And like Sagawa, Lew's father was an immigrant—in his case, from Poland—who expressed tremendous graditude for being able to live in America. On a practical level, this translated for Lew into a belief in the importance of politics, which meant living in Washington, working in Congress, and, ultimately, haggling with the Education and Labor Committee over whether that subclause should end with a comma or a semicolon.

But the prominent roles of liberals like Lew and Sagawa raise a question: What happened to the DLC activists? Bruce Reed, the campaign issues director who had drafted the initial service plan, became a deputy domestic policy advisor but had no responsibility for national service. The DLC's top two officials, Will Marshall and Al From, did not join the White House staff, nor did Charles Moskos, the originator of the loans-for-service concept.

The only DLCer who got a job associated with national service was Bill Galston, a University of Maryland political philosophy professor who had headed up the transition-team subgroup on national service. At first glance, Galston did not exactly look like a hardheaded, promilitary, Moskos-style service advocate. He bore a striking resemblance to a prematurely grey Harpo Marx, albeit with a larger vocabulary. He *sounded* like a philosophy professor, except that he had the inexplicable habit of muttering "yo" in the middle of sentences as an apparent substitute for "uh." Colleagues are inevitably amazed to learn that Galston is a former marine who counts that experience as his most formative. He was drafted in 1968 when the government eliminated the graduate-school deferment. "I believe that if I could get through boot camp, I could get through anything," he said later. "If *I* could climb a rope without getting vertigo, if *I* can take apart an M-14 rifle longer than I was tall and hit a target five hundred yards away with *my* eyes; if I could run twenty miles with a sixty-pound pack—then not only could anyone, but I could do anything. If you're talking about experiences to breed confidence, competence breeds confidence, to use an aphorism." Indeed, while Sagawa's group had been virtually silent on the issue of class-mixing and integration, Galston in his transition recommendations argued that building bridges should be-a key goal. "As we learned during the public programs of the New Deal, in World War II and in every great national endeavor, the surest basis of community is shared experience. By bringing us together across racial, ethnic and class lines, national service can provide such an experience, making our differences a source of strength rather than division."

But once he assumed his job at the Domestic Policy Council, Galston decided Segal could handle the details of service; he would concentrate on making sure student-aid reform didn't asphyxiate in the loving arms of Education Department careerists.

So, in the end, the DLC men had no direct authority over Bill Clinton's national service plan. The DLC scored points in the early battle of ideas, but the Kennedy wing outorganized them. "There's just more of them," said Ed Kilgore, a former aide to Senator Sam Nunn.

The DLC had one remaining hope. "Conservatives during the Bush administration used to say 'Thank God we have Jack Kemp in there' or 'Thank God we have Sununu in there,'" one DLC ally said. "Some of us are saying, 'Thank God we have Clinton in there.'" But Clinton's political personality seemed to split into two equal halves, one espousing the DLC philosophy, the other holding to a traditional liberalism associated with his wife, Hillary. It remained to be seen which hemisphere of Clinton's political brain would govern his decisions on national service.

On January 23, 1993, Eli Segal—the man who had hired twenty-two-year-old Bill Clinton to run the Texas McGovern campaign—walked into the Oval Office and said for the first time, "Good afternoon, Mr. President." Segal wanted Clinton to make a few quick but important decisions. First, did the president want national service on a fast track or a slow track? Segal felt obliged to point out the downside of speed. If the president pushed national service at the same time as campaign finance reform, economic stimulus, deficit reduction, and more, it could easily get lost in the shuffle. Clinton cut him off.

"This is why I ran for president," he said. Fast track.

Segal then talked about whether to send Congress one grand piece of legislation or split it into two, a service bill and a student-aid reform. "If the service and loan reform are linked, it could drag down the service," he said. "If we separate them, we could have the service up and going right away."

Clinton said they had to remain linked. First of all, he had spoken of them together during the campaign. Second, if budget constraints limited the amount of national service slots, at least pay-as-you-can would be available to everyone. Service could help tens of thousands; flexible repayment could help millions. The student-loan reform enabled Clinton to convince himself, however fraudulently, that he was fulfilling the universal spirit of his campaign promise. Finally, Clinton was determined to press ahead with student-loan reform because he believed it would save money—money he would need to pay for national service as well as deficit reduction.

In the subsequent two weeks, Clinton had to make the hardest decision of all: how much money to spend on national service. His sweeping campaign promise had been based on a fantasy: an impossible budget of $8 billion a year. Clinton had made a lot of promises, including deficit reduction; now he had to resolve the contradictions. He had started this process during the transition by announcing—to skeptical tittering from the press—that he would have to cut back some of his initiatives because new estimates of the budget deficit painted a far bleaker picture than expected.

The scaling back of national service began almost immediately. Bill Galston's transition team recommended a program not for 500,000 volunteers or 250,000 but for 100,000. "I did not spend a lot of time asking, 'Does this comport with a maximalist interpretation of what someone said Clinton said?' " Galston explained. "The question I asked was, 'What is the best we can do?' " He was also influenced by the recommendations of the Commission on National and Community Service, which had suggested 100,000 participants. (Galston apparently didn't realize that the commission had contemplated a much larger program but scaled it back in part to avoid embarrassing Clinton by making his program look too puny.) When Segal joined the White House, he read Galston's transition memo, and adopted his funding recommendations. Segal vaguely remembered that the campaign had proposed more. But he feared that proposing anything larger than a couple of billion would instantly damage his credibility with other White House officials, who had begun realizing how hard it would be to reduce the ever-growing deficit. In other words, after the election, *no one* seriously contemplated spending on national service what Clinton had promised during the campaign.

Segal had the delicate task of shifting from ambitious campaign rhetoric to modest reality. Anything too abrupt would be seen as yet another broken promise. In February, Segal began trying to alter expectations. He emphasized to reporters that, to ensure quality, they would insist on starting small and then "ramping up"—that's entrepreneur lingo—to something bigger.

But the press sensed an opportunity to skewer Clinton. COMMUNITY SERVICE PLAN SCALED BACK—DEFICIT PINCHES CLINTON'S DREAM, read the headline on the front page of the February 4 *Washington Post*. Written by White House reporter Ann Devroy, the article stated, "President Clinton is planning to unveil a small pilot program allowing some college students to repay government loans through community service instead of the huge new 'defining initiative' described during his campaign."

Clinton angrily called Segal. "How come the story was written that it was being scaled back?" Clinton asked.

"Apparently 'ramped up' is not a phrase Ann Devroy is comfortable with," Segal said. He assured his friend the president that he most certainly did not think of the national service program as a small pilot project. Other White House aides gently rebuked Segal for forgetting to emphasize to Devroy the universal nature of pay-as-you-can loans. Yet to some extent he was just taking the hit for the inevitable media realization that Clinton had—surprise—oversold the national service program. The *Post* article was followed by a *New York Times* piece labeling the service program a modest effort "to encourage volunteerism." On March 1 NBC's Andrea Mitchell declared that the national service plan had become a "small pilot project."

Segal had to figure out a way to rebut the broken-promise charge. The day after the *Post* piece, he stopped in on a meeting of Youth Service America. "Bill Clinton is as committed as he always has been," Segal told the group. "Nothing you've heard should make you think he has lost his commitment." First, he claimed, inaccurately, that during the campaign Clinton had never actually promised service slots for everyone who wanted to participate. "Obviously, if you read it carefully," Segal claimed, "at no time did Bill Clinton say there would be enough slots for everyone who wanted to serve." People would either be able to serve off their loans *or* get an income-contingent loan, Segal said, like a lawyer pointing to the fine print of a lengthy legal document.

Then careful listeners heard the unmistakable whistle of expectations diving downward. "We will create *thousands and thousands* of slots," he said. "But we're going to do it slowly because we want to do it right. Reporters may call that cutting back on a campaign promise."

"I was stunned to find out," Segal said, "that when the Peace Corps started, it had only *five hundred* volunteers! I guarantee we will have more than five hundred people." The comment drew chuckles from those in the group, most of whom remembered the 500,000-server campaign promise. Segal's appearance did not succeed in lifting spirits in the service community. Rumors began spreading that the program would be postponed. One Democratic senator suggested scrapping the idea entirely as a way of closing the budget gap. Euphoria had quickly turned to depression.

In early February, Bill Clinton sat in the Roosevelt Room of the White House peering over his bifocals at his economic advisors. They were nearing the end of a grueling process, in which Clinton and Gore went over every single line of the proposed 1994 budget. On the mantel behind the president sat Theodore Roosevelt's Nobel Peace Prize and, near it, a dark oil painting of Franklin Roosevelt, who had managed to get 500,000 men enlisted in his Civilian Conservation Corps within four years. When the group arrived at the section known as the "investment budget," Clinton noticed that his advisors had penciled in his national service plan not for $8 billion, but for $2 billion, by 1997 — enough for 70,000 youths.

"Why is there only two billion?" Clinton asked budget director Leon Panetta.

It came from the transition recommendations, Panetta said.

"Isn't that a lot less than we had talked about during the campaign?" Clinton asked. "I don't want people thinking we're not doing a major proposal."

Neither Panetta nor his deputy Alice Rivlin explicitly argued against an increase, but Panetta did say, "Mr. President, whatever you want to do, we will make work. But whatever you add, we'll have to find somewhere else to cut."

Later in the meeting, one of the advisors mentioned a reform they were considering called "direct lending," in which the government, not banks, would provide student-loan capital. This again prompted a brief lecture from Clinton. It was the flexible repayment system, not direct lending, that would allow young people to take low-paying *service jobs*.

"What is really bothering me is that I'm not hearing anyone talk about this proposal the way I thought of it," he scolded the group. "The direct loan is a good thing but that's not the core of my proposal." Pay-as-you-can loans were as important as national service, in his mind. "Everywhere we went people responded to this."

Clinton became even more intense. "There is no proposal that means more to me than national service," he said, putting his hand over his heart. "But you have to understand that that's never going to reach as many people [as flexible loans] and we really have to have both together."

As if to confirm his memories of the campaign, Clinton turned to economic advisor Gene Sperling and asked, "We never talked about this apart, did we? One without the other?"

Sperling then recited from memory the line that students could get loans and "pay them back as a small percentage of their income over time . . ."

The sound of these familiar words spurred Clinton on, and he gently lowered his fist down on the table.

"Absolutely. This was the one thing that I was saying would directly benefit average middle-class families. This has to be prominent. We have got to do both."

After the meeting, one of the economic advisors called Segal to tell him what happened. Be aggressive, the aide advised Segal. Don't be afraid to push for more money. It looked like the president would be receptive.

For Clinton, there were too many signs of trouble: the failure to understand the importance of pay-as-you-can loans, the low budget number, and the *Post* article. Clinton was in the midst of an anguishing process of reconciling himself to the gap between reality and campaign rhetoric, not just on national service but for his entire program. He was being portrayed as a typical, slithering politician who made promises cynically and broke them effortlessly. In fact, his real curse is his capacity for *self*-deception. He really did believe national service could be enormous, and was surprised and disillusioned when it looked like that wasn't true. Clinton has a tendency to rely on lawyerly rationalizations to explain himself out of his own box of contradictions. (The most famous example was his claim that he "didn't break any laws" to imply he'd never smoked marijuana.) Now that he was president, Clinton knew he would have to make compromises but wanted to at least feel badly about them. It was not helpful for overly pragmatic aides to throw in the towel so quickly.

On February 11, Clinton convened another meeting in the Cabinet room. This time Sperling was joined by several cabinet secretaries, Segal, Rick Allen, Jack Lew, Bill Galston, and George Stephanopoulos. As they reviewed the national service budget numbers, Clinton munched on apples he'd taken from a fruit bowl in front of him on the conference table.

He asked Segal what he thought of the $2-billion figure. "Mr. President, we were willing to go with two billion because we thought, with too many budget constraints, we couldn't ask for more," Segal said. "But we feel that with your leadership we could put far more to good use."

Segal and Lew had spent hours reviewing the numbers with staff at the Office of Management and Budget. They had a "decision-making matrix" to figure how many participants one could employ at various budget levels. The key was the amount of loan forgiveness: the more one spent on each server, the fewer people one could put in the field.

Segal concluded that Clinton's ultimate goal was a minimum of 100,000 participants by 1997, which could be done for about $3 billion per year.

Clinton seemed agitated about the growing public perception of his service plan as a policy trinket. *"The Washington Post* was so unfair," he said.

He asked whether these numbers would make his program bigger than the Peace Corps. Yes, bigger in the first year than the Peace Corps had ever been, Segal said.

Stephanopoulos agreed that $3 billion was clearly manageable, and Sperling added, "Tell people that if this program is a success, you'll go back and ask for more money."

Clinton responded to that immediately. "That is exactly right. Can you imagine if we get this program up and going and we have hundreds of thousands of people doing national service and we have a waiting list? We'll go back to the Hill and we'll have a lot of support. If we get this program up and going and there's more kids, there'll be so much support and I will be willing to go up there and work my heart out to get more funds for more kids."

On February 17, Clinton released the economic plan. National service's piece of the pie was not $2 billion in 1997, as his aides had suggested, but $3.4 billion—a cumulative total of $9.4 billion over five years. Real money. As in the campaign, Clinton had pushed service farther and harder than his advisors recommended.

Clinton was halfway through his economic address to a joint session of Congress that evening when a few stock sentences on national service scrolled up on the TelePrompTer screens. Instead of reading, Clinton looked straight ahead—and began to riff.

"A generation ago, when President Kennedy proposed, and the United States Congress embraced, the Peace Corps, it defined the character of a whole generation of Americans committed to serving people around the world," he ad-libbed. It was time for a new service program, where young people could serve as policemen and teachers and nurses, Clinton said, his cadence accelerating. They could help solve so many of society's problems, and the government would return the favor by wiping out college loan debts; so many more young people—from middle-class families—could then pursue the dream of higher education. But they would have to pay it back "at tax time so they can't beat the bill."

Finally, after tripling the portion of the text dedicated to national service, Clinton shifted from lofty rhetoric to a bald appeal to the lawmakers' vanity. "In the future, historians who got their education through the national service loan will look back on you and thank you for giving America a new lease on life, if you meet this challenge."

The legislators rose to their feet.

4

"Ideological Garbage"

Heather Doe is a fictitious college student. She's a junior at Paiselley College, where she studies feminist architecture and literature of the Amazon. After graduation she hopes to do something socially useful as long as it's not too hard.

Heather's father is a junior executive at a major biotech firm, and her mother manages a local franchise of Mail Boxes Etc. Together the Does earn $80,000, not quite enough to cover Paiselley's $25,000 tuition and expenses. The school gave Heather a $7,000 grant, plus a $1,000 work-study job answering phones in the dean's office. She got a $1,000 scholarship from the local church, and her parents put up $11,000. For the rest, she went to her local bank, Union National Federal, and got a $5,000 Stafford loan. She took out loans of varying sizes all four years of college. The Stafford loan has three advantages for Heather. Because the loan is guaranteed by the federal government, she gets a low interest rate (6.2 percent in 1993); she doesn't have to provide collateral; and she doesn't have to pay the interest that accrues while she's in school. After graduation, she will pay $242 a month for ten years to retire what will be a $17,000 debt. Union National Federal executives like the Stafford loan too. They know that if Heather flees to Nicaragua to work in the coffee fields and defaults, the U.S. Treasury will cover the debt.

Until the 1960s, banks were understandably reluctant to give loans to students: they had no jobs, no credit history, no collateral, no proof of future earnings, and strange haircuts. Congress, however, wanted them to go to college anyway. It passed the Higher Education Act of 1965, which gave special incentives—the interest subsidy and the loan guarantee—to those banks willing to help. Within two decades, student loans became highly profitable, more consistently lucrative than even mortgages or car loans.

To further ensure that banks would lend, Congress created a complex network of backup entities to give banks comfort. A system of state-sanctioned "guaranty agencies" would collect defaulted loans, so banks wouldn't have the hassle. If Heather defaults on her loan, Union National Federal would be reimbursed by a guaranty agency, which— follow the bouncing check—would be largely reimbursed by Uncle Sam. That guaranty agency would send collectors after Heather. If they succeeded in getting her to cough up the $20,000, the agency would pocket $6,000 of it. This is on top of a 1 percent fee they collect for every loan they guarantee. Like the banks, these guaranty agencies, some run by state governments and others operated as nonprofit companies, bore little risk.

In 1972, Congress decided that Union National Federal shouldn't have the bother of holding on to Heather's loan, even if she wasn't a deadbeat. They set up a federally chartered corporation called the Student Loan Marketing Association, a "secondary market" better known as Sallie Mae. As soon as Heather graduated, Union Federal could sell her loan to Sallie Mae and never deal with collections at all. As of 1992, Sallie Mae held $20.8 billion in loans—one third of all those outstanding. By using its special status as a government-sponsored entity, Sallie Mae was able to make a handsome profit in the financial markets.

The system has become a classic example of what columnist Michael Kinsley calls capitalizing profits while socializing risk. The financial players earn the profits while the public takes the risk. And Sallie Mae does seem to be doing awfully well for a quasigovernmental entity. Its luxurious Georgetown offices have the power-quiet of a major law firm; corridors are decorated with immense modern paintings and sculptures bearing names like *The Drama of Space* and *The White Peacock*. The glass doors never seem to have fingerprints. The president of the United States appoints one third of Sallie Mae's board of directors, and yet its stock is traded on the New York Stock Exchange and its CEO, Lawrence Hough, earned $1.3 million in 1992.

By 1993, the system had become so jumbled, Rube Goldberg himself would have needed an efficiency consultant to figure it out. There were roughly 8,000 lenders, fifty secondary markets, and an equal number of guaranty agencies. A diagram of the current student-aid system resembles a pinball machine, with loans getting bounced helter-skelter among students, schools, guaranty agencies, secondary markets, and the Department of Education. At large schools that draw students from all over the country, a financial aid officer had to deal with hundreds of different entities to keep track of the loans.

The problem for policymakers was that this inefficient, laughably complicated system had sort of worked. Most students like Heather have been able to get college loans with little difficulty. Loan volume increased from $1.3 billion in 1970 to $15.9 billion in 1993. College enrollment increased too, in part because of the availability of aid.

But as in the case of a successful protection racket—which, after all, does protect the frightened store owner from trouble—the price was high. The U.S. Treasury paid $6 billion in subsidies in 1992, and generated $15 billion in loans. That's a lot of "overhead."

What does all this have to do with Clinton's primary concern, pay-as-you-can loans? Most analysts who had tried to devise flexible repayment plans concluded that it couldn't be done through the banks. For one, the collections would have to be done by someone with accurate, up-to-date information about how much a graduate was earning. Only one entity fits that description: the IRS. And the idea of turning private tax records over to banks didn't sound politically popular or, for that matter, legal. Second, pay-as-you-can loans would complicate life for the banks. And the banks had made it clear over the years that any new burdens would simply drive them into simpler lines of work.

If the government was going to switch to pay-as-you-can loans, then, it makes sense to adopt simultaneously another radical reform: eliminating the entire student-aid industry and adopting "direct lending." In other words, the government would give money directly to Paiselley College, which would then give it to Heather. She would repay the IRS at tax time. No banks would be necessary to originate the loan, or collect the payments; the secondary markets and guaranty agencies could eventually curl up and die.

John Dean was not happy about Clinton's plan to "scrap" the student-aid system. Dean, who must occasionally introduce himself as "John Dean, not the Watergate felon," is the Washington lobbyist for the Consumer Bankers Association, representing more than five hundred banks with a direct stake in the federal student-loan program. Perpetually officious and serious, Dean talks in a rapid, somewhat nerdy monotone, and looks more like a midlevel banker than a pricey Washington lobbyist.

Unlike the high-profile Washington influence peddlers such as Michael Deaver, Dean is a more nuts-and-bolts—and often more effective—Washington lobbyist: a former Republican congressional staffer with enough expertise not just to visit with the congressman but to write his speeches and draft his legislation. And unlike most hired guns who adopt the position of whatever client has hired him, Dean had genuine convictions developed over years of working on the details of the federal student-loan program. He strongly believed that the bank-based system was the most efficient way to get Heather to college.

During the 1992 campaign, while most of the world was following whether candidate Clinton had time to bed a lounge singer in between jogs, Dean monitored every word he uttered on student loans. At several points during the campaign, Dean sent copies of speeches, debate excerpts, and newspaper articles to banks around the country, to alert them to impending troubles. Once Clinton won, Dean explored every possible avenue to get the ideas of the Consumer Bankers Association to the right people. He distributed bank position papers to administration officials and slipped questions to key Capitol Hill staffers so senators would ask about direct lending at the confirmation hearings of Clinton's appointees.

Clinton's election also awakened the guaranty agencies. Daniel Cheever is president of the American Student Assistance Corporation in Boston, the main guaranty agency for New England. By guaranteeing more than 180,000 loans, ASA was able to earn $22.4 million in

1992. Cheever had just joined ASA after having been president of Wheelock College in Boston, and thought the current student-loan system was a mess. But he also realized that Clinton's national service plan involved direct lending—which meant ASA's extinction. A few weeks into November, Cheever told ASA's senior staff: It may not seem like it now, but our very futures are at stake; we need to get actively involved in politics. ASA hired the Widmeyer Group, a Washington-based public-relations firm. In January 1993, ASA formed a coalition with two other major guaranty agencies to block Clinton's student-loan reform—which, in the grand tradition of lobbying doublespeak, they named the Coalition for Student Loan Reform. The two other agencies, based in Ohio and Indiana, would handle the heavy-duty Washington lobbying; ASA's Cheever would be in charge of "message."

Cheever had several advantages that suited him well for that role. As a former college president, he had credibility, although that was undercut a bit by his physical resemblance to TV's Joe Isuzu, a fellow known for his dishonesty. Still, he at least didn't have Dean's accountant-on-an-audit demeanor. More important, Cheever had ties to Senator Kennedy. This would be quite handy, because the committee Kennedy chaired—Labor and Human Resources—had jurisdiction over national service and student-aid reform. ASA handled most loans for students in Massachusetts. Cheever had gone to high school and college with Nick Littlefield, chief of staff for the Labor Committee. Finally, one of the people put on the ASA account at the Widmeyer Group was Lori McHugh-Wytkind, a former aide to Kennedy.

Cheever emphasizes that he isn't opposed to direct lending per se, but wants to try it out as a pilot program first. (Congress had, in fact, set up a pilot program in 1992 involving five hundred schools, or 4 percent of the loan volume.) As a spokesman for the guaranty agencies, Cheever tried to sound moderate but could also scare the bejesus out of schools over what he considered a plausible horror scenario. "Jesse Helms finds out that University of California has in its biology classes films of a sexually explicit nature—which I'm sure it does—and filibusters the student-aid money," Cheever said. "Colleges don't get the money and students aren't able to register. You could have no one registering for classes, no revenue coming, no payroll. The funding of truth can only occur if the search is unfettered!"

———————

By mid-January, rumors started circulating that the administration was going to go with full-scale direct lending. This sent the banks into a minor panic. "I can't talk long," said John Dean when I called on January 29. "There is a crisis atmosphere here. We are attempting to mobilize schools to weigh in with Secretary Riley and with the president."

Sallie Mae's stock began diving. Rumors that Clinton was considering direct lending sent the stock price from almost 75 to below 65. On February 12, Smith Barney began advising its customers not to buy Sallie Mae, sending the price down to $58.625. On February 17, Clinton released his first budget, which included a switch to direct lending. The next day, panicked traders on Wall Street dumped so much Sallie Mae stock that the New York Stock Exchange had to halt trading. By the end of the day, Sallie Mae's stock price was $47.25. The company, one of the one hundred largest in the nation, had just a few months earlier been one of the surest bets on Wall Street. After one month of Bill Clinton's presidency, its stock was in a free-fall.

Lobbyists struggled to get any bit of intelligence about what was going on inside the tightly wound executive branch. After twelve years of ready access to White House information, the student-loan industry found that many of its sources had dried up. Frantic, executives hired more and more Washington lobbyists—particularly those with Democratic Party connections.

The student-loan lobbying roster read like a seating chart at a Democratic Party fundraiser:

At roughly $20,000 a month, USA Group of Indianapolis, the largest guaranty agency in the country, hired Akin, Gump—the lobbying firm of "Mr. Democrat" Robert Strauss, the former chairman of the Democratic Party, and Vernon Jordan, head of Clinton's transition operation. The firm assigned the account to Kirk O'Donnell, a former top aide to Tip O'Neill. USA Group also hired Walker/Free Associates, run by James C. Free, a former Carter White House official and Clinton golf partner; and Sagamore Associates, the lobbying arm of the law firm Baker and Daniels.

The New England Student Loan Marketing Association, the secondary market that buys up many student loans from New England banks, hired Patton Boggs & Blow, former law firm of Ron Brown, the ex–Democratic Party chief who had become Clinton's secretary of commerce.

The Student Loan Funding Corporation of Ohio, a major secondary market, hired the firm of Powell Tate, founded by former Carter press secretary Jody Powell, as well as Winston Strawn, a Chicago-based firm that housed former Vice President Walter Mondale. Winston Strawn assigned the account to Dennis Eckart, who had until a few months earlier been a Democratic congressman from Ohio.

But no one had more lobbying clout than Sallie Mae, which pulled together an all-star team of great Washington influence-peddlers. Following Sallie Mae's stock crash, CEO Hough decided they would have to be extremely aggressive. "When you lose $3 billion in wealth you can't just say to shareholders, 'Hey don't worry,'" Hough said. "You have to *do* something." Hough was not the type to shy away from battle. A former world champion in rowing, he had won a silver medal in the 1968 Olympics before turning to a career in business. He had worked his way up through Sallie Mae over twenty years and didn't want to preside over its demise. The company moved into action. It retained Harry McPherson, special counsel to President Lyndon Johnson and a top Washington rainmaker, and he got Hough an appointment with Al From, the DLC founder, who was heading up Clinton's domestic policy transition team. To lobby the White House, it hired former Carter administration official Anne Wexler and her colleague at the Wexler Group, Dale Snape. On one occasion Wexler enlisted the help of another of the firm's executives, Betsey Wright, a close Clinton aide in Arkansas for years and arguably the most plugged-in lobbyist in Washington. The company hired lobbyist Kent Cushenberry to work specifically with black representatives. The firm that put in the most hours for Sallie Mae was Williams and Jensen, one of the most powerful lobbying houses in the city. Lobbyist Winfield "Winkie" Crigler was close to the wife of Bill Ford, the House Education and

Labor Committee chairman; lobbyist David Starr was a former aide to liberal Senator Howard Metzenbaum.

Perhaps Sallie Mae's most important asset was none other than Jerry Hultin, the man who had run Clinton's Ohio state campaign and helped Bruce Reed prepare cost estimates on national service. A friend of Clinton's from law school—they had worked together on the *Yale Review of Law and Social Action*—Hultin had been a Sallie Mae consultant even before Clinton's campaign began. Reed knew about the Sallie Mae ties, but not that Hultin's campaign analysis—which happened to criticize direct lending—had been partly *paid for* by Sallie Mae. A soft-spoken man, with a thin, graying beard, Hultin says that what he did for Sallie Mae was technical analysis, and not, heaven forfend, lobbying. But after the election, Sallie Mae executives were not shy about exploiting Hultin's connections. In December, Hultin accompanied Hough to meet with transition aide Galston. In February, he and Hough lobbied Deputy Education Secretary Kunin and Sperling. Hultin helped draft a speech by Hough arguing that Sallie Mae could administer Clinton's national service plan, and personally gave copies to the president and senior advisor Bruce Lindsey.

John Dean appreciated the ability of the prominent Democrats to get in doors he couldn't. But he also feared that the stable of big-name influence peddlers would alienate young Clintonites who had probably joined the administration in part to beat up on bad-guy lobbyists. "The Clinton people may feel compelled to take a meeting with [the big-name lobbyists] but they don't feel they have to work with them," Dean said. The industry had to convince the administration they genuinely wanted to be helpful. "We can't just go in there saying, 'Banks are great' or say, 'This is nationalizing lending and that's communism—communism bad, capitalism good.' One of our primary arguments is we think we can help Clinton meet his campaign promises. Here's a way to do it: our gift to you. That's our strategy. I don't know if it will work."

Bill Clinton gave the assignment of revamping the existing student-loan system to two savvy, professional politicians. He named as his secretary of education Richard Riley, who had overcome a devastating physical disability to become one of South Carolina's most popular governors. While serving on a Navy ship one day in 1955, Riley had sneezed, fallen to the floor, and become paralyzed with agonizing back spasms. Soon after, he had learned he had spondylitis, a degenerative disease in which the vertebrae fuse together. Riley would regularly tie himself to a board and wince through the pain for an hour to straighten his spine. Clinton had come to admire Riley when they were both governors; Riley was one of the few in the Cabinet who called the president "Bill."

Clinton appointed as deputy secretary of education another veteran politician: Madeleine Kunin. The three-term governor of Vermont was born in Zurich, Switzerland, in 1933. In 1940, as the Nazis conquered Europe, her family, which was Jewish, fled to New York. She later moved to Vermont, became involved in the environmental and women's movements, and was elected governor in 1978. While Riley oozed Southern charm, Kunin's patrician gray hair and creaky voice made her resemble the aging Katharine Hepburn.

One of the first things Kunin did when she arrived in Washington was read the General Accounting Office report on the Department of Education, which stated that the student-loan program was at "high risk" of catastrophe because of colossal management problems. "So *this* is what we've gotten ourselves into," Kunin said to Riley the next time they met. They soon found out that some Department of Education staff—i.e., the bureaucrats—had no desire to throw out the student-loan program with which they had become comfortable, and had serious doubts about whether pay-as-you-can loans and IRS collection could work. "Like any bureaucracy, they had built relationships with existing players," Kunin said later. The permanent staff at the Office of Management and Budget believed it would be nearly impossible to administer a massive income-contingent loan program. And the IRS careerists feared that handling student loans would drain resources from their mission of collecting taxes.

At least, Riley and Kunin thought, they could count on support from the colleges. But that, too, turned out to be a false assumption.

Higher education is represented in Washington by about forty trade associations, each with a specific constituency—big state schools, private colleges, community colleges, trade schools, financial aid officers, Jesuit schools, medical schools. Each had a slightly different reason for disliking the Clinton plan.

The group representing financial aid officers at schools—the National Association of Student Financial Aid Administrators (NASFAA)—feared direct lending because its members would have the headache of administering the program. The United States Student Association (USSA) hated the idea of the IRS collecting student loans.

The private schools, as represented by the National Association of Independent Colleges and Universities (NAICU), loved pay-as-you-can loans because the loans would help students afford their higher tuition. But they seriously doubted the Education Department could manage a "direct lending" program. Under direct lending, the Department of Education would put up the cash for Heather Doe's loan and Paiselley College would be responsible for disbursing it. College officials were nervous about taking on that role, particularly in partnership with the notoriously incompetent Education Department, which, among other things, had never quite figured out how to keep track of millions of outstanding loans.

The American Association of State Colleges and Universities (AASCU), which represents large public schools like the California state system and the State University of New York, had concerns that ran opposite to those of the private colleges. AASCU officials liked direct lending, but distrusted pay-as-you-can loans and national service loan forgiveness.

Why would schools dislike easier repayment terms? Look at Heather Doe's loan payments. Say Heather left college with $17,000 in debt and then decided to take a low-paying job as a $15,000-a-year Head Start teacher—just as President Clinton hoped. Under the pay-as-you-can system, Heather's loan payments would be quite small, maybe $100 a month. Sounds good so far. The problem is that $100 a month barely pays for the interest on her loans; she'd end up paying for the next forty years. With interest compounding, as it's wont to do, Heather would end up paying nominally three times as much as someone who repaid in ten years. The large public schools viewed not loans but Pell grants—the no-strings-attached scholarships for the poor—as the key to maintaining broad access to school. After fifteen years of deficit-driven politics, they looked at student-aid budgets as a zero-sum game: loans go up, grants go down. And under Bill Clinton, loan volume could explode.

AASCU's director of federal relations, a meticulously dressed Iranian immigrant named Barmak Nassirian, added another potent argument when he spoke to a group of students at a USSA conference in February. A slight, thirty-year-old former philosophy graduate student with short black hair and an olive complexion, Nassirian generally likes to infuse his arguments with quotations from Machiavelli or Kant, but this time he laid out a practical, numerical argument against Clinton's program. National service cost $20,000 per participant and would provide loan forgiveness to only 2 percent of the students, Nassirian said. At the same time, "We live in a society in which the poorest of the poor—families who earn less than $15,000, maybe, *maybe* will get a $2,300 Pell grant. There's something strange about the federal government handing out $20,000 to upper- and middle-income people. You're taking $3.5 billion that could go for increasing the Pell grant from $2,300 to $3,600." In other words, the money the federal government would spend to allow Heather to serve could provide Pell grants to *eight* low income kids. Heather gets a rewarding experience, those eight kids get a life of filling Slurpees at convenience stores.

"National service may lead to a renaissance of citizenship—it may have numerous benefits—but college affordability isn't one of them," Nassirian said bluntly. The students at the conference applauded enthusiastically—and Nassirian was restraining himself that afternoon. Every Tuesday evening after work, a half dozen or so higher education lobbyists would eat, drink, and argue at the Front Page, a bar near their offices at DuPont Circle. One night when I stopped by their darkly lit booth, Nassirian had loosened his bow tie, pulled out a pack of cigarettes, sipped some red wine, and let loose. "This whole national service thing is a bunch of ideological garbage," he ranted between bites of quesadilla. "Combine it with income-contingent loans and it's a real piece of shit."

And these were supposed to be the Clinton administration's *friends*.

In reality, Clinton's most important ally was thirty-one years old, wore sandals to the office whenever possible, kneaded Silly Putty to release tension, and worked for a man with very long earlobes. Bob Shireman was the education aide to Senator Paul Simon of Illinois, who would lead the Senate fight for pay-as-you-can loans and direct lending.

Raised by Republican parents, Shireman had attended Berkeley and worked for several years for public-interest groups, which had taught him how to run grassroots, media-oriented campaigns. After a brief stint teaching in the Boston and Washington public schools, in the fall of 1989, he joined the Employment and Productivity sub-committee that Simon chairs and immediately started searching for an issue with which he could make his mark. He settled on pay-as-you-can loans and direct lending. This change, he insisted, could save billions of dollars and help poor and middle-class families. "It would be impossible for my wife to be a consumer lobbyist if it were not for Harvard Law School's loan forgiveness program," he wrote, "one of the few such programs that exist." He and his wife had ac-cumulated $80,000 in student-loan debt from their years in graduate school.

This idea, Shireman wrote to Simon, also had one major tactical ad-vantage: an easy-to-demonize foe—the banks. Sure there'd be a fight, but "without a fight," he wrote, "there is not media attention."

Simon didn't warm to the idea at the time, for fear that it had too many technical problems. But a year later, he was breezing through the *Congressional Record*—he is one of the few senators, in fact, one of the few human beings, who reads it cover to cover—and came across a statement from Republican Senator David Durenberger of Minnesota, advocating direct lending and income-contingent loans. Simon tore it out, and scrawled on it, "Talk to me, Bob." Simon de-cided he wanted to team up with Durenberger.

In January 1993, Clinton was on the verge of deciding whether to embrace Simon's direct-lending approach—and Shireman was busy turning up the heat. He and his colleagues had already succeeded in putting the industry on the defensive. Simon's press secretary, David Carle, convinced Michael Binstein, who co-authors Jack Anderson's syndicated column, to rail against the "middleman racket" run by Sallie Mae. Sallie Mae officials, wrote Anderson and Binstein, "recently traveled to the home of one transition official to make the case for the status quo." The column implied that the lobbyists had showed up at the doorstep in the middle of the night. (Actually, Bill Galston had invited them to his Washington home.)

Then Shireman got a delicious opportunity. He learned that John Dean's Consumer Bankers Association and another group representing guaranty agencies planned to hold a "Lobby Day" on March 2. Local bankers were to come to town, learn about direct lending, and then visit their congressmen. Shireman and Carle organized a campaign to highlight the lobbying "onslaught." Shireman drafted a hard-hitting letter to senators warning that the greedy bankers would be in their midst soon. Carle contacted reporters with the urgent tone of a botanist alerting colleagues that the thirty-seven-year cicadas were emerging from their pods. "A rare opportunity comes March 2nd to catch a glimpse of members of a powerful special interest as they pad the halls of Congress trying to kill a key provision in the Economic Package that has pocketbook importance to EVERY family needing help in sending a kid to college. . . . Bankers have targeted March 2nd as their lobbying day to try to smother in the cradle the proposed direct student loan plan. During the transition, opponents like Sallie Mae went to great lengths to keep direct loans out of the package (including a nighttime visit to a key transition official at his home.)"

By the day of the event, a flustered John Dean had stopped calling it "Lobby Day" and began insisting it was a "legislative workshop." Although Simon's crew had conjured images of high-powered influence peddlers descending like vultures, most were the midlevel bank executives who deal with the student-loan program. Imagine their confusion when they discovered three camera crews, with brilliant lights, taping their arrival at the Holiday Inn Crowne Plaza in downtown Washington as if they were mobsters testifying before a grand jury. As the workshop proceeded inside, CNN's investigative reporter Brooks

Jackson and *MacNeil/Lehrer NewsHour*'s Judy Woodruff camped outside. Dean stood stiffly in a dark blue suit and (yes) tasseled loafers and assured the public that the bankers were not trying to smother national service. "In 1992 we can make more service opportunities available" if we do it with the current bank-based program, he explained, nervously fiddling with the bottom of his suit jacket. "Anyone who suggests that the lenders are opposed to national service is simply mistaken."

Inside, the bankers listened to a talk from Clohan & Dean attorney William "Buddy" Blakey, a former aide to Paul Simon. Blakey sketched the basic techniques of his trade using catchy aphorisms like "You can't teach what you don't know" (Learn the material before you lobby); "Can't lead where you won't go" (Be willing to put something constructive on the table); and "The long way around is sometimes the short way home" (If you have no credibility, get someone who does to represent you).

The consumer bankers distributed a thirteen-point tip sheet on lobbying, which mostly suggested common courtesies—"Always say thank you"—but did recommend campaign contributions and other signs of thoughtfulness. "If your legislator has won a victory for your industry, it is not uncommon to send key staffers flowers or tickets to the theater with a polite note of thanks. . . ."

Meanwhile, direct-lending advocates gathered in the Senate Radio and TV Gallery to denounce the sinister lobbyists before a packed press conference. The tactic worked magnificently. "More than 100 bankers flocked to Capitol Hill last week in an effort to combat President Clinton's plan to overhaul the government's student loan program," began *The Wall Street Journal* story about direct lending. *MacNeil/Lehrer* ran a piece on direct lending a few days later that was so anti-industry it used illustrations of little green money bags to illustrate the bloated salaries of Sallie Mae executives.

The counteroffensive did nothing if not get under the skin of the industry leaders. "It really irritates the hell out of me," said Hough of the constant harping on his salary. "It's a big company. Compensation is set by directors, directors are hired by the stockholders. They ought to be able to set the compensation levels!" After reading the negative press accounts, Dean fumed, "You have people who are trying to keep a dignified discussion. But the media isn't interested in such nuances as whether the policy is right. It's simply a circus."

By February, Clinton was wavering about direct lending. He'd made a preliminary decision to adopt the program because it seemed to save several billion dollars, but privately he was still skittish. "The president is betwixt and between on direct lending," Galston told Shireman. "I don't know where he'll come out. He's not fully committed on the issue." Keep up the heat, said Galston, who by that time had joined the Domestic Policy Council staff as the White House point man on student-aid reform and become a direct-lending advocate. "Simon is doing a tremendous service. We can't assume the president will come out full square for direct lending. This may sound odd. But it's not a done deal. The president is receiving a range of advice, some from the financial industry. That's all I can say."

That last line was a reference to a conversation between Clinton and Sallie Mae's Jerry Hultin. When Clinton visited Chillicothe, Ohio, for a town meeting on February 19, 1993, he spoke with Hultin, who mentioned that the direct-lending chatter had sent Sallie Mae's stock price plumetting to $47. To fix the problem in Clinton's mind, Hultin offered a vivid analogy. "You know, Mr. President, in Ohio when we build a new barn and decide to burn down the old one, we usually let the horses out first." Clinton said he was aware of the problem. "Yes, I know. I'm very concerned," he said.

On March 5, Clinton gathered his advisors in the Cabinet Room to make his final decision on direct lending and student-aid reform. Scheduled to begin at five o'clock, the meeting didn't begin until six —"Clinton time," in White House argot. The assembly included Riley, Segal, Panetta, Rivlin, and the IRS commissioner-designee Margaret Richardson.

Clinton told the group that when he gave speeches someone already repaying a loan inevitably asked if he'd be able to benefit from the new program. Riley responded that they could set up a system to convert existing loans to the new plan. "That's very interesting. Get back to me with some numbers," Clinton said. From campaign Q-and-A session to policy proposal—just like that.

Riley then recounted for Clinton an internal debate that aides had been having about pay-as-you-can loans. Several Education Department officials were insisting that they be available only for people who were in danger of default. These officials agreed with Barmak Nassirian's argument that widespread use of pay-as-you-can loans would hurt, not help, the poor. Galston and economic advisor Gene Sperling argued that the low payments would help poor students gain access to college and enable middle-income people take public-service jobs. Clinton agreed with Galston and Sperling that pay-as-you-can loans should be open to everyone, but, he added, not required for everyone. That decision would prove helpful in mollifying the public-school lobbyists.

As for the IRS role, Clinton couldn't have been happier. Despite the grumbling in the bowels of the IRS, Richardson said the IRS was "willing and interested" in having students repay loans through the tax system, because it would inculcate a payment mentality.

Aware of the IRS's historic resistance to the approach, Clinton said, "It was worth being elected president just to hear the IRS say that."

When the discussion moved to direct lending, Riley offered three options: pure direct loans, direct lending partially run by private contractors, and the current system with some improvements. Clinton understood the enormity of the shift. He wanted to know how the industry would be affected by the middle approach.

"How would all this be received by Sallie Mae?" Clinton asked.

"Wouldn't be pretty," one advisor said.

"See if there's some role for Sallie Mae," Clinton responded. He mentioned to the group that he had heard from Hultin about the devastating effects of reform on Sallie Mae.

It was Riley who, in his succinct, folksy way, laid out the key reason for going forward with direct lending. "This could save a lot of money," he said in his slow Southern drawl. "And I mean a *lot* of money." Riley recommended the second option: direct government lending plus some private participation. By using private organizations to help run the program, the administration might be able to give the system more stability and preserve a role for segments of the industry.

The option Riley recommended, everyone in the room knew, would embark the administration on a radical overhaul of the way college is financed—a change that could benefit millions of students, or harm just as many. It went farther than advisors had suggested during the transition. The approach would cut off billions in subsidies to thousands of banks and guaranty agencies, and eliminate the mission of the multibillion-dollar corporation Sallie Mae. It would, in fact, scrap the existing student-aid program.

This course of action would also inextricably link pay-as-you-can loans to the proposal for direct lending. Politically, it meant that the fight over loan reform would not be a war of ideas about the best way to improve access to college or encourage public service. It would be a full-throttle, multifront, high-stakes interest-group war over direct lending. The players would not be tweed-jacketed analysts with an intellectual interest in loan debt; they would be major financial institutions with a direct financial interest in preserving the status quo. Indeed, the option Riley recommended to Clinton would take the young administration into a political battle that, if it were lost, could defeat not only the proposals for pay-as-you-can loans and IRS collection, but the national service plan as well.

Finally, Clinton responded simply, "I agree with that recommendation."

5

The Cynical Media

I checked in at Andrews Air Force Base in suburban Maryland at 7:30 a.m. along with about fifty other reporters, photographers, producers, and broadcast technicians for Clinton's March 1 trip to Rutgers University in New Jersey. It was to be his first major national service address as president.

Moving the White House press corps around the country is not a simple matter. Although forty different news organizations want their man or woman traveling with the president, they cannot all fit on Air Force One with POTUS (as insiders call the "president of the United States"). Instead, the press forms a small "pool" that includes reporters representing each form of media. The pool travels with the president and reports back to their colleagues. Of course, "being with" POTUS doesn't always mean you can talk to him or even breathe the same air. On this day, Number One Pool traveled in a plane several thousand feet away from POTUS. What mattered, apparently, was not proximity but sequence. The pool plane arrived before Air Force One so the TV crews could run out to the tarmac and set up their cameras to photograph Clinton getting off the plane.

The rest of the press corps arrived in a third plane and was shuttled to Rutgers Athletic Center, where the White House advance team had constructed an impressive makeshift newsroom behind the bleachers: about twenty rows of tables, forty phones, dozens of electrical outlets, and most important, box lunches. At around 10:45, Clinton engaged in some semispontaneous interactions with Inspirational Individuals who had learned to read as adults. Most reporters in the pressroom were oblivious, since POTUS was at Brunswick Adult Learning Center, several miles away. A few reporters gathered near two small speakers, straining to hear the disembodied voices of the president and the students crackle unintelligibly through a live "audio feed." "Just think, you spend your whole life working as a reporter to get to *here*," said one cynical reporter.

Several hours before Clinton's one p.m. speech, reporters sat down with their laptops and started writing that day's story. Based on handouts the White House had given them, they were able to write at least the background paragraphs. Later they'd get a copy of the "report" from Pool Number One, describing Clinton's arrival ("He picked up one toddler and embraced him; no words"), the high school visit, and the flight back to Washington ("A jaunty wave and a turn and the president bumped his head on the door frame of the little plane").

Pool Number One arrived shortly before the president, and proceeded quickly down a cordoned aisle in the packed Rutgers gymnasium. The reporters looked blasé; they refused to acknowledge what a heady feeling it is to have three thousand college students gawking at you like you're Michael Jackson. About half of the reporters sat in bleachers at the opposite end of the gymnasium from the speaker's platform. The more seasoned ones remained in the filing center behind the bleachers and watched the speech on TV.

The event was designed to highlight the president's national service plan, but reporters were annoyed that there weren't enough new details. A speaker thanked the students for being there for the "major address," which prompted my bitter newspaper friend to exclaim, "Major address! What planet is he on? This is a campaign speech!"

When Clinton appeared, the crowd erupted. Rather than indiscriminately greeting the entire gymnasium, he waved to each section separately. Each time he gazed at a particular set of bleachers, those students waved back and cheered. In the speech itself, Clinton used the vocabulary of military combat to talk about service, again attempting to place civilian service closer to a par with military. "Brave men and women in my own generation waged and won peaceful revolutions here at home for civil rights and human rights," he said.

There was "news" in the speech, but only for those who had been following the policy debates closely. The Office of National Service announced that the program would be open to high-school-age youths, not just the college graduates Clinton had talked about during the campaign. Clinton also unveiled plans for a Summer of Service, a program for one thousand participants, intended to dramatize the potential of service as Congress considered the legislation.

For me, however, the event was more significant in that it illustrated why the White House press corps would never give national service real attention. There was the reporter for a major newspaper who ranted before the speech, "I was afraid I'd have a hard time covering these people because of my liberal bias. It took me about a week before I started hating these guys. I *hate* them."

Then there was the conversation on the plane back home.

"Ten thousand dollars?" one reporter said snidely about the annual scholarship. "What's that gonna buy you?"

His buddy agreed. "Yeah, I mean it costs four thousand to send your kid to nursery school."

That a reporter would think most people send their kids to $4,000 nursery school says a great deal about why the Washington press corps consistently underestimates public outrage over things like congressional pay raises.

Over the course of the year, Clinton was asked 126 questions at press conferences. None dealt with national service, none with pay-as-you-can loans. He had dozens more shouted at him at photo opportunities. Only one dealt with national service—on February 4, someone asked why national service had been "cut back to a pilot program"—and no questions dealt with pay-as-you-can loans. In the course of the year, the three Sunday morning public affairs shows had 205 guests; neither Eli Segal nor Richard Riley was among them. Throughout 1993, NBC evening news did three correspondent-reported stories on national service legislation, ABC two, and CBS one. None of them did stories on pay-as-you-can loans. U.S. News ran three news articles on national service, Newsweek two, and Time—the largest newsweekly in America—none. Of those stories that did appear, almost all were produced by reporters who spent no more than one day doing research.

Besides the petty reasons offered by those grumpy reporters at the Rutgers event, why wasn't national service taken seriously by the media? Several specific tendencies of the Washington press corps influenced the way this policy issue was covered.

On the rare occasions when Washington reporters cover policy instead of politics, they try to apply an easy-to-quantify standard. Among the most obvious of these is: Did the president break his promise? Instead of considering the policy itself, they prefer to compare the reality against the promise, the way police match two sets of fingerprints. In the case of national service, this wasn't hard to do: the reality did not come close to the campaign promise. "Five million students now have college loans and could have assumed they'd be eligible," NBC's Andrea Mitchell reported in early February, "but Clinton's plan would cover only a fraction of them." She nonetheless added the damned-if-you-do, damned-if-you-don't observation: "Some critics worry that Clinton's proposal, small as it is, could be a boondoggle." After a clip of one of those scholars, Mitchell concluded, "Once again, Clinton has proved that there is a big difference between what he promised as a candidate and what he can deliver as president."

What the press failed to explain was that the program could be significant even if it didn't measure up to the campaign rhetoric. World War I had been billed as "the war to end all wars." The fact that it wasn't doesn't mean it was an insignificant skirmish. Where the press failed was in refusing to take national service to the next step.

The reason they didn't bother is that most Washington reporters thought national service was at best innocuous, and more likely a bunch of bull. Cynicism, after all, not liberalism, is the dominant ideology of the Washington press corps. Reporters have always treasured their image as hard-boiled skeptics spitting tobacco juice on the powers that be. They truly believe that the politicians will trumpet the good news, so it is up to the journalists to find the bad. By that logic, anything the president pushes, the press should duly ignore. Clinton wanted us to know about national service—ergo, no story. Reporters have became acutely sensitive to being "stage-managed." As Susan Milligan, a White House correspondent for the New York *Daily News*, puts it, "Everything was so hokey that we got cynical. There's a certain kind of resentment about being manipulated, so you don't look at the substance." (Had the modern press corps covered the parting of the Red Sea, TV reports undoubtedly would have begun, "In a carefully crafted photo opportunity, Moses today . . .") Journalists today live in desperate fear of being labeled "in the tank"—blindly pro-Clinton. Tankophobia runs particularly high in Democratic administrations, because so many reporters are Democrats. Many feared that writing seriously about something as nakedly idealistic as national service would make them seem naïve.

Print reporters get ahead through scoops; TV careers advance through confrontation. Aggressive attitude in the TV age has replaced the aggressive reporting of old. Service is a soft story, and the interesting parts are complicated. Imagine Sam Donaldson shouting across the White House lawn as the president boards a helicopter: "Mr. President, are you going to apply a means test to the post-service benefit?"

Washington reporters try to cast policy debates in terms of conflict, preferably using sports metaphors. At debate time, we learn that one candidate needs to land a "knockout blow"; the president's speech must be a "home run." If it can't be described in athletic terms, there isn't any conflict involved and, ipso facto, the story cannot be made interesting. With national service, the conflicts were ideological and philosophical, dealing with issues like race, class, and the distribution of resources between the middle class and the poor. Should the program require race-mixing? Should volunteers be paid to serve? "Barbs" were not "tossed" by famous politicians, so reporters saw none of the normal signs of conflict—it appeared to them that nothing was happening at all. Explaining why ABC did so little on national service, producer Mark Halperin said, "There was no conflict in the legislative process so no one covered it. All the White House press corps knew —all anyone knew—was that Clinton promised everyone could be in it, and it was much smaller than that."

One of the most fundamental reasons for the shallow press coverage may be the most mundane: that the White House press corps is busy. The networks and newspapers considered national service important enough to be covered by their White House correspondents, but not quite important enough to devote much time to. At most newspapers, there was no national service beat reporter. This new, hybrid program would potentially affect everything from urban affairs to the environment to crime. But the impact was not obvious enough to make national service a top priority for the urban policy or environmental reporter. The program fell through the cracks of the normal beat system. The publications and stations that did the best job covering national service—the *Los Angeles Times*, MTV, the *Chronicle of Philanthropy*—assigned reporters outside the White House press corps to cover it regularly.

Clinton's own advisors reinforced the notion that national service wasn't important. Speaking privately to reporters, spinmasters such as Carville, Paul Begala, and David Dreyer rarely mentioned national service as a top priority. Reporters discount the official positive spin from the White House, but treat private negative spin as the gospel truth. "Our spinners were not saying it was important, so the McLaughlin Group didn't say it was important," explained one administration official.

This lack of faith from Clinton's own political advisors raises a question unrelated to the merits of the press corps: If those within the White House didn't take national service seriously, how could they possibly sell it to the American people?

6

"Ouch!"

She is considered by some to be the most powerful individual in education policy. Her decisions affect billions of dollars of business activity and can send Sallie Mae stock plummeting or soaring on Wall Street. Her views affect millions of students and how much they pay each month on their student loans.

Her name is Deborah Kalcevic. She's not a congresswoman or senator, or a high-level White House official. She is a budget analyst, and she never gives interviews. "Deb," as student-aid insiders know her, is a nineteen-year veteran of the Congressional Budget Office (CBO). When our leaders plan to change policy, someone has to tell them what the cost will be. That job falls to the CBO. Deb, as one administration official puts it, is "the czarina of loan estimating."

Because of the modern budget process, Deb's influence extends far beyond the fluorescent-lit cubicles of the bureaucracy. The federal budget is not a list of what the government has spent, but a prediction of what it will spend the following year. When congressional leaders declare that they have passed a deficit-cutting budget, they are really saying they've made some changes that CBO thinks will save money. It's often hard to predict how much a program will cost: If the economy gets worse, will more kids take out student loans, or fewer?

CBO estimates can do more than measure costs; they can determine policy. In February 1993, the White House budget office estimated direct lending would save $3.7 billion. The student-loan industry considered this bad news. The higher the savings estimate, the more direct lending would appeal to Congress. To stop direct lending, lobbyists could not simply ask legislators to "vote it down"; they had to offer an alternative plan that would also save $3.7 billion—probably by slashing all those sacred subsidies the industry got from the government.

Since CBO analysts work like nuns in a convent, protected from outside pressures or distractions, John Dean and Dan Cheever of ASA, the guaranty agency, really didn't know what Kalcevic thought. Maybe she'd inadvertently help them out by decreeing that direct lending wouldn't save any money. Maybe, just maybe.

In March, Kalcevic's savings estimate became public: $6.52 billion.

In Boston, Cheever looked like he was going to cry when Joe Clayton, his director of government affairs, told him the news. In Washington, Dean railed against the chicanery that had "somehow made the numbers double overnight." Winkie Crigler, one of Sallie Mae's lobbyists, called Tom Wolanin, top education aide to the House Education and Labor Committee, to ask for help in cracking the CBO code. "No," Wolanin grumbled. "Why should I help you to fuck up the president's program?"

Dean did raise a good question: How on earth could the government give out billions of dollars in new loans and *save* taxpayers $6 billion? It depends how one keeps score. It used to be that if the government gave out $10 billion in student loans one year, it immediately increased the deficit by $10 billion. In 1990, Congress passed a law that no one but accountants noticed—but which ended up affecting the fates of millions of students. Under the Credit Reform Act, Congress was allowed to take into account the fact—or at least the hope—that loans eventually would be repaid. So, Congress could lend $10 billion and its effect on the deficit would be minimal in any given year. Suddenly, this innocuous accounting change made direct government lending possible. And because the government was to provide the loans, it would no longer have to pay billions in "incentives" to goose the banks into lending. Kalcevic estimated that, over five years, the government would save $6 billion by eliminating these middleman subsidies.

On March 11, the Senate Budget Committee passed a budget resolution that assumed $6 billion in savings from direct lending. Bob Shireman in Senator Simon's office was quite aware that if the budget resolution passed the full Senate, direct lending supporters like him would be halfway to victory. As the Senate considered the budget, he hoped he could sneak this provision through without a fight. But on Thursday, March 18, he got a call from a staffer on the Labor and Human Resources Committee.

"Have you seen the Kassebaum amendment 'Dear Colleague' letter?" he asked.

"What Kassebaum amendment?" Shireman replied, with a gulp. After trying unsuccessfully for weeks, direct lending opponents had finally snuck up on him.

Leading the frontal attack would be Senator Nancy Landon Kassebaum. The daughter of Alf Landon—the man who lost to Franklin Roosevelt in 1936—the sixty-year-old Kassebaum is not a showy, camera-hogging senator. Her shy, almost apologetic speaking style makes her seem more like a museum docent than a senator. A few months earlier, she'd taken over as the senior, or "ranking," Republican on the Labor and Human Resources Committee, and had begun to assert herself. She strongly doubted the government could run a massive loan program, and believed that, despite the bookkeeping gimmicks, the program would increase the national debt.

She decided to attack when the budget resolution hit the floor of the Senate. "It seems to me that we are taking an enormous risk in dismantling the current student loan program, financing a new program solely with new federal debt, and putting its administration in the hands of federal agencies which may have difficulties in assuming new management responsibilities—with no real debate or deliberation of what we are doing," she wrote to fellow senators on March 18. "Yet, without the opportunity to explore any of these issues, the Senate is being asked to endorse *today* a full fledged direct lending program."

The first battle had begun. Shireman fired off a fax alert to the higher-education groups: "WE NEED LETTERS FROM EDUCATION GROUPS TO ALL SENATORS SUPPORTING DIRECT LENDING. Phone calls from the local level are crucial also." That Friday, congressional aide Suzanne Ramos told her boss, Ted Kennedy, about the Kassebaum amendment. Kennedy was furious about being blindsided. He was going to Massachusetts that weekend and feared he wouldn't have time to prepare. The conventional wisdom about Ted Kennedy in Washington is that, for all his personal troubles, he's been a very effective senator over the years thanks largely to his excellent staff. Tom Butts, a leading direct lending supporter from the University of Michigan, accepted this notion—until that Sunday afternoon, when he answered the phone in his Washington apartment and heard a familiar voice with a Boston accent.

"Hi, this is Ted Kennedy," the caller said. The senator then proceeded to quiz Butts on the intricacies of direct lending.

In a suburb of Boston, Dan Cheever got a similar call. Kennedy asked him about the administrative burden on schools and whether guaranty agencies like Cheever's could help with that, to which Cheever eagerly responded yes. Kennedy fired more questions: Do you think income-contingent loans and IRS collection are good ideas? How do you think students would react? What about the budget savings from direct lending? That gave Cheever a chance to say that not everyone agreed with the administration's view that direct lending would save money. A new Congressional Research Service study, for instance, had concluded the savings would be tiny.

Kennedy was torn. He was thrilled that the new president had come out fighting for national service. And he understood the theory behind direct lending. In fact, in 1978, Kennedy himself had proposed an income-contingent loan and direct-lending program. But by 1992, he'd soured on the idea a bit; he believed that, since the stakes were so high, the idea should be tested through a pilot program first.

When the Simon and Kennedy aides heard the details of the Kassebaum amendment, they discovered she had made one major tactical blunder. The amendment scaled down the direct lending program and dictated that Congress make up the lost money by cutting other "domestic discretionary programs." In order to take out direct lending—which saves money—Congress would probably have to cut other education programs. That gave Simon and Kennedy an opening. They could argue against the Kassebaum amendment without even debating the merits of direct lending.

The colleges, meanwhile, had to decide their position on this crucial Kassebaum amendment. Some education lobbyists disliked national service; others feared pay-as-you-can loans; still others opposed IRS collection. Yet this first political test of Clinton's plan, it turned out, did not hinge on those fractious issues but on whether to kick the banks out of the system. Luckily for the administration, while most college lobbyists disliked Clinton's service plan, they hated the banks.

There was another reason the higher-education lobby decided to help Clinton out on direct lending: It was afraid to challenge a new Democratic president. "This administration decides early on who are its friends and who are its enemies," said Jim Appleberry, the president of the public college group, AASCU. "If we take a hard line on this now, we will not be at the table."

The schools moved into action *supporting* the president. The United States Student Association, an opponent of IRS collection, nonetheless faxed out a release to its state chapters with a banner across the top: "URGENT! URGENT! URGENT! URGENT! URGENT! URGENT! URGENT! URGENT! *Oppose* Senator Nancy Kassebaum's (R-KS) anti-education amendment to the Senate budget resolution!!" AASCU faxed out an "Urgent Request for Immediate Action" to its four hundred members to support direct lending.

The schools also used what has become an increasingly important tool of grassroots lobbying: a computer bulletin board. All across the country, college officials logged on to a special Internet data base to find out the latest wrinkle in federal financial aid policy. AASCU sent Internet messages warning members that the issue was not direct lending, but the fate of education generally. "It is imperative that phone calls and faxes go to all Senate offices IN OPPOSITION TO THE KASSEBAUM AMENDMENT as early as possible on Monday morning."

Attempting to rebut the most common criticisms, AASCU's Barmak Nassirian uploaded a series of questions and answers about direct lending. Cyberspace then buzzed with a debate between dozens of financial aid administrators. One from South Dakota logged on to report that the Nebraska student-loan program (contacted by Kassebaum's office) had urged support for the Kassebaum amendment. An official at the guaranty agency in New York State, Kirsten DeSalvatore, tapped in a message arguing that Nassirian was exaggerating the

Kassebaum amendment's harm to education. That infuriated Nassirian, and he fired off a pointed reply:

> The Kassebaum amendment basically puts it all on the table, and no amount of rhetorical flourishes can change its fundamental effect: the middlemen's profits come before educational spending. . . .
> Folks, this just don't look right.
> Nassirianb@AASCU.NCHE.EDU

In turn, Kassebaum's office requested college administrators in certain states to call their senators. Metro Community College in Omaha, Nebraska, dutifully contacted home-state senators Bob Kerrey and James Exon. Citibank leaned hard on New York Senator Daniel Patrick Moynihan. Bud Blakey, John Dean's law partner, got black colleges in the South to call the offices of Alabama senators Richard Shelby and Howell Heflin as well as Georgia's Sam Nunn.

The amendment came up for a vote after midnight on Wednesday, March 24. At that hour, there were no lobbyists around. Shireman sat with other Democratic staffers on a bench along the wall of the Senate chamber. Kassebaum aide Lisa Ross stood in the lobby with a thick white looseleaf book of briefing papers watching the debate at the guard desk on a tiny black and white portable TV.

Finally, the roll was called. Simon stood near the clerk's desk in his trademark red bow tie, gesticulating to Senator Patty Murray of Washington. Kassebaum spoke with a few members on her side.

The vote was on a "motion to table" the amendment. A nay vote meant the senator supported the Kassebaum amendment; a yea vote supported the Clinton administration. At first, the vote proceeded along party lines, except that Republican Senator David Durenberger, an early proponent of direct lending, voted with the White House as expected.

Then conservative Democrat James Exon of Nebraska voted nay, surprising Shireman, who hadn't heard of a single Democrat considering defection. A few senators later, Heflin of Alabama voted nay as well. The banks' efforts to target conservative Southern Democrats had netted at least one vote.

Shireman began nervously fiddling with his pen. He comforted himself by remembering that Exon and Heflin had often voted with the Republicans. If the defections came from the usual suspects, they were safe.

Then Shireman heard the clerk call, "Senator Kerrey of Nebraska?"

"Nay," Kerrey said.

"Senator Kerrey of Nebraska—nay."

Shireman began frantically checking his own list against that of another staffer. If Kassebaum's amendment passed, the president's plan could unravel—student loans, national service, everything.

Shireman's concern grew to near panic when the clerk said, "Senator Nunn," and the Georgian's voice came back, "Nay!" Shireman's side had expected no defections; it already had four.

"Senator Shelby?"

"Senator Shelby—nay!" Another Southern Democrat defection.

Three more and it would all be over. The president's proposal would be mortally wounded before it was even written. Shireman couldn't help thinking that *he* would get blamed.

"Senator Glenn?" the clerk called. "Senator Glenn—nay."

At first, Shireman wasn't sure if they'd won or lost. Simon leaned over a wooden banister that separated staff from senators, and, in his baritone voice, told Shireman, "We're one vote short of fifty." But as the clerk ran through the list of yea votes one more time, it included Democratic senators Breaux of Louisiana, Sasser of Tennessee, and Boren of Oklahoma. A few of the Southern Democrats had stuck with the president.

The presiding senator announced the final tally: 51–47 against the Kassebaum amendment. Simon punched his right hand into his left triumphantly. He went over to Shireman again: "We lost some votes we shouldn't have. I want to send thank you notes to everyone who voted with us—and send them tomorrow. And I want to sign them."

Shireman nodded and left the floor dazed. He now realized just how hard this was going to be. He returned to his office, sat down in his chair, drained, and looked at his computer. On the terminal was a yellow Post-It note from his boss, Brian Kennedy. In large letters, it read, "Ouch!"

The lobbyists for the higher-education community gathered every Monday morning at the offices of the American Council on Education (ACE) to plot strategy, compare notes, and exchange witticisms. (These are, after all, *higher*-education lobbyists.) At the March 15 meeting, the group had expressed deep worries about Clinton's national service plan. Nassirian—looking particularly natty that morning, in a bow tie and gray sweater vest—launched into an aggressive attack on Clinton's idea of paying people to do service.

"At the risk of sounding philosophical, Kant said it best: 'You can't legislate goodwill,'" Nassirian said. "If you pay them, it's a job, not service. When you think about national service, the standard should be: Is this something important enough that we would force people to do it, like defending the country?" The other college lobbyists viewed Nassirian, fond of quoting the classics during strategy meetings, as a bit of an eccentric. But on student-aid matters, few were more respected, and he continued to press the argument that a major national service program was a lethal threat to financial aid for the poor.

The federal budget deficit had changed the dynamic of interest-group politics on the left. In times of plenty, liberal groups could support each other's pet programs, but in times of scarcity, more money for one worthy cause might mean less for another; the conservation corps' gain was the community college's loss.

As I sat in the ACE meeting each Monday morning, I was struck by this jarring irony: the same process of alchemy that worked in the campaign—two leaden proposals cooked together to form gold—seemed to be reversing in the legislative process. By continuing to emphasize national service as a way of paying for college, the administration had pitted service *against* student aid.

The reasons went beyond Nassirian's point about the limited pot of resources. Implicitly, Clinton's policies represented three shifts that the higher-education community hated.

First, the possibility that in scarce budgetary times national service would grow and Pell grants would shrink represented a shift from "need-based" to "merit-based" aid—in this case, based not on academic but on social merit. The schools believed all aid should be based on financial circumstance.

Second, by emphasizing loans, the administration had virtually ensured that the shift from grants to loans would continue or accelerate. Debt levels in the long run would be higher, not lower, under Clinton's plan. Clinton's proposal, if it could talk, would respond: "Loans are here to stay. The trend will continue no matter what we do. Pay-as-you-can loans help make borrowing far less burdensome."

Third, despite Clinton's rhetoric of expanded aid, the policy actually makes federal aid *less* of an entitlement. The fundamental assumption behind a grant is that society as a whole benefits if everyone is well educated. The assumption behind a loan—and the reason that Milton Friedman suggested income-contingent loans—is that college education provides an enormous *personal* benefit. Clinton took away some of the punitiveness in the original DLC plan, but implicitly his plan carries a similar message: If you don't do service you get a loan; if you do, you get a grant. Clinton's plan, in effect, decrees: We will only treat this as a *social* benefit if society gets something back in the form of service.

One man in the higher-education community thought his colleagues had made an enormous error in supporting the White House and working against the Kassebaum amendment. The day after the Kassebaum amendment vote, the leaders of higher education gathered in the main conference room at the American Council on Education at the request of Bill Gray, former Democratic congressman, former chairman of the House Budget Committee, and now president of the United Negro College Fund. Gray, who continued to preach as a minister in the Bright Hope Baptist Church in Philadelphia, began by speaking in calm, cerebral tones. "Let me just say candidly, our [college] presidents are *for* national service." (Anytime a politician says something "candidly," one can assume he is about to offer a carefully prepared public position, soon to be followed by his true feelings.) "We have no problem," Gray said, "except for some concerns which I will share with you."

Share he did. First, he suggested that small colleges, like those represented by the United Negro College Fund, would be overwhelmed by the extra cost and workload of having to administer Clinton's new direct loan program. The schools, not the banks, would suddenly have to give out the money, process the paperwork, and take responsibility for collecting the loan, he said. These struggling schools, with one or two people in their financial aid offices, could not afford to take on such a huge responsibility.

In a highly deferential voice, Dick Rosser from the private colleges (NAICU) said he shared the concerns about the administrative burden of direct lending, but added, "I think what we're seeing is these concerns being *addressed.*" What's more, Rosser said, the pay-as-you-can loan reform "is going to be a great boon to many students."

Apparently sensing that he was not changing any minds by focusing on the technicalities of direct lending, Gray moved to the more fundamental issue of priorities. Advocates for the poor had been struggling for years to fend off cuts in the Pell grant program, he reminded the group. Here, the Clinton administration comes along and proposes spending $3.4 billion on just 150,000 students, when there are 5 million students whose grants could be increased.

Gray's tone began to change. "It's American pie, you know—national service, doing something for the country, shades of JFK, the whole bit," he said dismissively. "Wonderful images of Americana, et cetera." But he *knew* the legislators who wrote the original national service plans that had inspired Clinton—and *their* goal was to wipe out Pell grants for the poor and replace them with loans. Now Gray's tempo quickened. His words drove across the conference table with the steady beat of a metronome.

"Go . . . back . . . and . . . read . . . the . . . record!" he said, banging the table. Gray was preaching, and several of the white lobbyists at the table began to nod and quietly murmur, "Hmmm hmmmm, hmmmm hmmmm," as if at a Baptist, or at least a Presbyterian, revival.

"And you have a member of Congress who says, 'Gee, I'd like to help all these education programs, but I've got only fifteen billion dollars. So I end up picking the ones that sound best.' And I can tell you right away which they're going to pick. They're going to pick the one for people who vote! *Middle-class* Americans. Middle-class vote! Poor folks don't!"

Around the table, the education lobbyists began to express some agreement. "My personal opinion is, fundamentally, if you've got nine billion dollars—it's misplaced in national service. It should go into Pell grants," said Larry Zaglaniczny of the National Association of Student Financial Aid Administrators.

The representative of the school business officers, Mary Jane Calais, suggested that they push the Education Department to "make every effort" not to burden small, poor schools with extra cost. That prompted a short, black man sitting quietly behind Gray to get to his feet, placing his dashing fedora on his chair. It was Bud Blakey, the law partner of John Dean, who had helped prepare the bankers to argue against direct lending on "Lobby Day." Blakey, it turns out, not only helped the Consumer Bankers Association (which opposed direct lending) and represented the Points of Light Foundation (which supported national service)—but *also* served as the Washington counsel to the United Negro College Fund (which criticized national service and direct lending). Blakey had grown up in a poor neighborhood in Louisville, Kentucky. But his mother (a domestic) and father (a janitor) saved enough that Blakey could, with the help of loans from the Presbyterian Church, attend Knoxville College. After law school he began a career in government, first with a Maryland congressman, then with the Department of Education under Jimmy Carter, and finally with Paul Simon. As a black, liberal former staff director of the House Postsecondary Education subcommittee, Blakey was a prize catch for Clohan & Dean.

"Mary Jane, I'm not going for 'good-faith effort' and 'every effort' and none of that crap. That's why we're in this hole now. If we end up sacrificing low-income students' higher-education aspirations on the altar of national service, then I'm out of here—and our presidents are out of here."

The meeting broke with Gray and ACE officials agreeing to try to work out a compromise that would avoid a bloody rift within the college community.

What was this all about? Some college lobbyists speculated that the

UNCF was opposing direct lending because Citibank was on its board. Others questioned Blakey's role, suggesting that he was pushing the UNCF toward that position because his firm, Clohan & Dean, represented the banks. Blakey said the UNCF had opposed direct lending since 1991 and insisted he just wanted to protect the UNCF schools from undue burden. He scoffed at the idea that he or the distinguished officials of the UNCF could so easily be influenced by a bunch of white bankers. There was, Blakey claimed, a strict Chinese wall between himself and John Dean (although that apparently didn't prevent him from being a key speaker at the Consumer Bankers' Association "Lobby Day").

In a private memo to Gray on February 5, 1993, Blakey rehearsed the argument that direct lending would burden small, poor schools like those in the UNCF, and asked, "Since lenders are paid a 'special allowance' to administer the [current] loan program—why should colleges and universities administer the [direct] loans for free?" In other words, if the UNCF opposed direct lending, it might be able to at least squeeze out some more "administrative" subsidies for UNCF schools.

In classic Washington style, the United Negro College Fund officially supported the "concept of a national service program" but just happened to oppose most of the particulars of Clinton's approach. They suspected that the program was not about uniting classes but pitting the middle and upper classes against the poor. "A Hobson's Choice lurks in the national service option," Blakey wrote to Gray. The "almost exclusive focus on middle and upper income students" would end up "diluting the emphasis on lower income students." By resisting Clinton's program, the UNCF could force increases in aid for the poor, perhaps even getting the long-cherished "Pell Grant entitlement" that would have guaranteed grants to anyone who needed them. Key legislative allies, Blakey wrote, could be counted on "to trade a Pell Grant entitlement for Clinton 'reforms' in the loan programs." He believed the UNCF was bargaining from strength with this Democratic president, and ought to at least try to get something for any acquiescence to national service. "While any opposition must be carefully articulated—the political reality is that the Clinton Administration can ill-afford to be perceived as financing 'access' or 'choice' for upper income white students on the backs of poor blacks."

The UNCF position raised a broader question for Clinton: if Bill Clinton was a "New Democrat," what was his constituency? Was this a sign that traditional members of the old Democratic coalition didn't feel bonded to this New Democratic president?

The next day Blakey met with Terry Hartle, the new chief lobbyist for ACE. Hartle, a few weeks earlier, had been the top education aide to Ted Kennedy—one of the countless examples of Washington's revolving door. Hartle had arrived so recently from his Capitol Hill job that unopened boxes lined his new office at the Dupont Circle building. He was joined by Becky Timmons, another ACE lobbyist, and David Merkowitz, the ACE public affairs director (and, for those keeping track, a former aide to Bill Gray).

Although skeptical of direct lending and national service, Hartle argued that both were now a fait accompli—in part because of the vote two days earlier against the Kassebaum amendment. But (former Simon aide) Blakey continued to argue with (former Kennedy aide) Hartle.

"It's stupid! Our presidents are not willing to buy a bill of goods. To take all the money savings from direct lending and spend it on this is ludicrous! If we're going to do a half-ass job on national service, screw it! Let's go and finish this war [to get more money for] Pell grants. We're half-assing it."

"I just don't think it's a good idea for the higher-education community to say 'Scrap this half-assed idea,' " Hartle responded calmly.

"I don't agree!" Blakey shouted back, shaking his head. "Maybe for you, it's okay. But if we end up trading the interests of upper-income whites for low-income blacks and Latinos . . ." He didn't finish that sentence; instead he skipped to one breathtakingly blunt. "If the race card has to get played to stop this bullshit from happening, then the race card is going to be played here!"

Hartle was sympathetic but felt that Blakey was not facing up to political realities. "Let's be candid," Hartle said. "I don't think Riley and Kunin want to do it. They've been told to, so they're marching into machine-gun fire. We are in a box. Decisions have been made at higher pay grades than mine that this is going to happen. The thing that terrifies me most is if the [education] department has a glitch, the whole thing goes down the drain."

Nevertheless, Hartle continued, "This is a train that's coming down the track and we've got to swallow it."

"I don't accept the train theory," Blakey spat back. "I think this train is going to crash for sure and that's why I don't want to get on it."

"I don't know how to get the education community to pay attention," Hartle said dejectedly. "I don't know what else to do."

This seemed to capture the confusion in the higher-education world. One day, the associations had applied Kantian rigor to critiquing the president's plan. Four days later they had protected the plan from Kassebaum's attack. And the day after that, they had gathered, at Bill Gray's request, and complained that it was now a fait accompli.

Why the schizophrenia? Clearly, the colleges found themselves in a dilemma. They had a genuinely pro-education Democratic president for the first time in twelve years—and they hated most of what he was doing.

7

Race, Class, and Veterans

Bill Clinton was an integrationist in a separatist era. He believed in service as a leveler—a way of bringing races and classes together. Clinton's vision of service was shaped by the three programs he knew best: City Year, Teach for America, and the Delta Service Corps. City Year consciously emphasized race- and income-mixing. Top officials would sit around and swap corps members to get the proper program makeup. Teach for America recruited intensively at top schools to maintain quality, and in the process produced a diverse group of teachers. And the Delta Service Corps has successfully recruited a sixty-forty mix of blacks and whites. But these programs were the exceptions. Most local service corps were racially *homogeneous* and targeted at low-income young people. In total, whites made up about 20 percent of the participants in the existing service corps.

So as the different players in the service world began to meet after Clinton's election, three questions arose: How much did Clinton care about race- and income-mixing? How hard was he willing to push for it? And did he know what he was getting into?

The Commission on National and Community Service, the independent agency created by the 1990 service act, wrestled with these questions at a staff meeting in January. Executive director Catherine Milton argued that, when giving out grants to "demonstration projects," the commission should give preference to those that embraced a mix of races and income groups.

But twenty-four-year-old Michael Camunez, who was in charge of overseeing these programs, suggested that Clinton's commitment to integration would wither if diversity meant devaluing all-minority programs. What would happen, Camunez asked, if Clinton saw a group of "poor minorities doing much-needed community service" in South Central LA? "Do you think Bill Clinton would really stand up in South Central Los Angeles and say that's not service?" And what about the Delta Service Corps, which Clinton himself helped to start? Many corps members worked in their own homogeneous communities. "I don't think we can say the Delta Corps is not national service because it's all white people helping a poor community."

Chris Murphy, a twenty-four-year-old program officer, mentioned YouthBuild, which runs corps that enlist disadvantaged young men and women to rebuild their own neighborhoods. The corps often end up being all black or all white, but are considered quite successful. "Are you willing to say YouthBuild is not national service?"

"Yes," Milton responded bluntly. She believed YouthBuild was worthwhile and should certainly be supported, perhaps by the Department of Housing and Urban Development, as it was in 1992. But, she argued, one of the characteristics that distinguished national service from antipoverty programs was the race- and class-mixing.

Just two weeks earlier, YouthBuild's founder, Dorothy Stoneman, had been in Washington to make the opposite case at a meeting of service groups in the offices of Youth Service America. "It could be counterproductive to say all must be integrated," she said. "In some ways, it shows disrespect for the programs in these segregated communities. I don't want blind allegiance to the word *diversity*."

Sam Halperin, a veteran of the service movement, objected that she "seems to say a segregated program is okay."

Nothing wrong with that implication, Stoneman countered. "Everyone says if it doesn't include middle-class people, it won't get funded," she said, leaning into the table toward Halperin and raising her voice. "That's dangerous thinking."

"People ask the volunteers, 'Wouldn't you be better off working alongside white middle-class kids?' " Stoneman continued. "And they say 'Why?' " She scrunched her face to convey disbelief. " 'I'm work-

ing for my community.' " She concluded simply, "The people who ask
that question really don't understand community development."

Stoneman was not alone in her views. Seated nearby was Kathleen
Selz, the director of the National Association of Service and Conservation Corps (NASCC), which represents the mostly minority local
programs. A chirpy button-nosed woman with short, blond hair, Selz
looks like an elementary school teacher but is actually known as one
of the toughest advocates in the service world. She sat quietly through
the YSA meeting, but later, in a private interview, lashed out. "These
girls from [upper-middle-class] Bethesda at the D.C. Service Corps are
always saying things like, 'Oh, it opened our horizons!' " she said, mim-
icking the syrupy voice of a white suburbanite. "Well you notice the
welfare mother [in such a program] doesn't say much like that." Selz
believed that the integrationist fad could rob money from programs
with proven records of helping the poor. "There is this romantic notion that service is somehow better if there's economic diversity. I
don't begrudge people the opportunity to do that, but it *is* untested.
I disagree very much that we should spend limited resources on an
untested idea."

The issues of race and class didn't come up during the campaign
because Clinton had talked as if the program would be only for college
graduates. But both liberals and conservatives eventually urged him to
open the program to non-college-bound students. During a jog with
Clinton, Representative Dave McCurdy argued that allowing kids to
serve pre-college would be more cost effective since they could live at
home while they served. Liberals argued that it was unfair to shut out
less advantaged kids. Clinton decided in March to open up the program to young people pre- and post-college. The decision had hidden
implications for the integration issue. Since national service would recruit young people with less education, there was a real possibility it
would end up resembling the low-income youth corps touted by Selz.

Clinton fashioned himself a "New Democrat," and the 1970s Democrats nearly self-destructed over integrationist efforts like busing. But
Clinton believed in service as a force for successfully bringing together
people of different backgrounds. The defining issue for Eli Segal and his
White House team, it seemed, would be whether the administration
would explicitly encourage, or even require, programs to be mixed.

Shirley Sagawa, who had largely written the 1990 National and Community Service Act, was in charge of negotiations with Capitol Hill on this issue. She knew quite a bit about City Year—in fact, she had gone to law school with founders Michael Brown and Alan Khazei. But she had also been persuaded by Dorothy Stoneman's argument. Unlike Milton, she was not willing to exclude YouthBuild from national service.

More important, Sagawa was not merely writing an "administration" proposal. Segal had made a strategic decision early on: the White House would not write the legislation and then "send it up" to Capitol Hill, according to standard procedure. Rather, the staff would craft it *with* the key players on Capitol Hill. Throughout February, March, and April, Sagawa and Jack Lew met with Nick Littlefield and Tom Sander of Ted Kennedy's office and Gene Sofer of the House Education and Labor Committee. It was Segal's hope that such collaboration would ease the bill's journey through Congress. Consequently, in dealing with diversity, Sagawa and Lew had to attend not just to national politics, but to committee politics. Bill Clinton may have been elected as a moderate Democrat; the House Education and Labor Committee, in the words of a Senate Democratic staffer, would "approve the Communist manifesto, if it had jurisdiction."

The White House's guide through the House Education and Labor Committee was Sofer, a staff counsel to Chairman Bill Ford. Some DLC allies nearly fainted when they learned the key role Sofer would play, because they believed he had helped orchestrate the tar-and-feathering of Representative Dave McCurdy before the committee back in 1989. Sofer had worked at the time for Gus Hawkins, chairman of the Education and Labor Committee and senior member of the Congressional Black Caucus. Sofer had no background in service; he had come to the Hill as an expert on Latin American policy, and then developed an expertise in the congressional budget process. But Sofer had a soft spot for service. He had quietly helped ease the 1990 service act through the House despite an almost total lack of interest from the members.

Just as dog owners seem to take on the attributes of their pets, congressional staffers often seem temperamentally similar to their bosses. Sofer, like his boss Bill Ford, avoids media coverage and prefers backroom politics. He is intriguingly nondescript, wearing tortoise-shell glasses and standard-issue dark Capitol Hill suits with suspenders. He talks with a New York accent, and often uses blunt or sarcastic language, yet speaks softly and slowly, seeming to measure each phrase. He rarely musters more than a sly grin, but somehow manages to project a sweetness unusual for Capitol Hill. And like his boss, his tart, tough-guy phraseology belies a passionate, traditional liberalism.

Sagawa fully understood that during these early stages Sofer represented not just Ford, but the entire House Education and Labor Committee. It was Sofer's job to analyze the politics of each sentence in the legislation—to predict who would support it, who would oppose, who wouldn't care. Sofer concluded that any language favoring "diverse" programs could be interpreted as a threat to the programs that were not mixed, many of which were in the districts of committee members.

Sofer also had to consider interest-group politics. Youth Service America might like the diversity approach, but Sofer doubted their capacity to produce political backup. On the other hand, the National Association of Service and Conservation Corps and its leader, Kathleen Selz, who disliked the race-mixing push, had always been able to mobilize their members effectively and quickly. "NASCC is the best organized of any of them," said one administration official. "The political decision was that we don't want to offend them. If you didn't have the nondiverse corps fighting for this, we could have trouble getting [national service]."

Even if he had wanted to shoot for race- and class-mixing, Sofer doubted there was a simple, noncontroversial way of encouraging it in law. If the plan specified that a certain percentage of federal money go to diverse corps, that would be, well, a quota. And how does one define *diverse*? Is fifty-fifty black-Hispanic "diverse," or does the term require whites? Is a corps that mixes rich and poor whites considered diverse? What if it is class-homogeneous and race-heterogeneous? Congress could merely require that a program represent the makeup of "the community," but someone would still have to define *community*. Is it Harlem (47-percent black)? New York City (28-percent black)? Or New York State (16-percent black)?

Sofer therefore resisted explicit "diversity" language, and Sagawa and Lew backed down from it—quickly. "Every time diversity would come up [in legislative negotiations, Ford's staff] would say, 'Well, the House is going to have some problems with that,' " one White House official said, "and we'd say, 'Okay, okay, we'll take it out.' " In fact, the key White House staffers barely even discussed it. "It came up in a nondiscussion kind of way," Sagawa says.

Not only did the White House back off from pushing for integrationist language, it took other steps to ensure that a hefty part of the money would go exclusively to low-income communities. As the legislation was being drafted, Representative Xavier Becerra of Los Angeles complained that minorities might lose out and proposed requiring that 50 percent of the money funneled through the states go to programs that served *and placed a priority on recruiting from* "distressed" communities. Becerra got lobbying support from a key NASCC member, the Los Angeles Conservation Corps, which targets low-income minorities. With little discussion, the White House agreed to the seemingly radical Becerra amendment to the House legislation, and later included similar language in the Senate bill. With that concession, the White House seemed to shrink the pool of money that it could, *even in theory*, give to mixed programs.

Why did the White House exert so little effort fighting for diversity when the concept seemed central to Bill Clinton's vision of service? In part, Segal and his team were surrendering to the physics of interest-group politics. If force is being exerted on an object and there is no countervailing pressure, the initial force will control the object's direction. If a squirrel pushes an acorn and no other woodland creatures push back, the squirrel will carry his booty straight home. No squirrels pushed the integrationist agenda in the legislative process.

There was, of course, one person who could have pushed hard for diversity language: Bill Clinton. It is the job of the president, in this increasingly atomized political system, to be the chief advocate for Big Ideas. If Clinton had told Segal he wanted to emphasize class- and race-mixing in the legislation, Segal would have instructed Sagawa and Lew to push harder. Clinton never did. He had chosen his old friend Segal to run the national service effort in part because he didn't want to have to think about it. Clinton had seen the Republicans kill his economic stimulus package on April 21, and faced steep opposition to his budget plan. The principle Clinton cared about most was passing the legislation.

Segal never posed diversity as a dilemma for Clinton. Segal viewed himself as the political operative, the man to drive through the president's program. He did not enter with strong ideas about service, and trusted Lew and Sagawa with figuring out the details of the legislation. As for Lew and Sagawa, they feared that a fight over race- and class-mixing would be a no-win proposition for Clinton and the White House. They were behind-the-scenes staffers who preferred to fight such battles with hidden legislative booby traps and land mines, not with public declarations of war. They could always require mixing *after* the legislation passed—when they were issuing regulations. No need to create a firestorm that could incinerate the entire program before it started. Sagawa had learned this lesson while working on Capitol Hill. She had helped Kennedy fight the Bush administration's efforts to set up a voucher system for day-care centers. Sagawa's side won the legislative battle only to watch the Bush administration put its voucher idea into the regulations implementing the program.

Sagawa viewed the Becerra 50-percent set-aside as a deliciously ideal provision: politically helpful but substantively meaningless. To understand, one has to venture briefly into the actual legislative language, where hidden treasures lurk between every line. Half the money, the Becerra amendment said, must go to programs that recruit from communities "in areas of economic distress described in subsection (c)(6)." Hmmm. Flip to subsection (c)(6) and you begin to see why Sagawa wasn't too worried. The set-aside money was to go to:

(A) "Communities designated as enterprise zones or redevelopment areas, targeted for special economic incentives. . . ." Areas "targeted for special economic incentives" could include any city that got a small business loan for a new strip mall.

(B) "Areas that are environmentally distressed." Beverly Hills has air pollution.

(C) "Areas adversely affected by Federal actions related to the management of Federal lands that result in significant regional job losses and economic dislocation." This cryptic language referred to Pacific Northwest timber areas.

(D) "Areas adversely affected by reductions in defense spending or the closure or realignment of military installations." That brings in California, not to mention every state south of the Mason-Dixon.

(E) "Rural areas adversely affected by unfair trading practices of international competitors." Are there any rural areas that *aren't* affected by unfair trading practice? Rice growers in Louisiana suffer from Japanese import quotas, Nebraskan wheat farmers curse those Belgian grain subsidies.

(F) "Areas that have an unemployment rate greater than the national average unemployment for the most recent 12 months." It is in the nature of "averages" that a large portion of a population often will be above the norm.

So, when you add together all these possible definitions of "distressed communities" it becomes clear that the program managers, if they chose to be coy, could give money out however they wanted. Segal's team allowed the interest groups to pile on so many exemptions that, together, they became meaningless.

There was one final reason the White House didn't fret about diversity language. Staffers thought the key to shaping participant makeup was not legislative language but something else: the amount of the college scholarship.

In writing their initial proposal for the DLC, Will Marshall and Charles Moskos had suggested a $10,000 scholarship for each year of service. Clinton's staff had used the $10,000 figure during the campaign, in part because Bruce Reed thought anything less would be viewed as insufficient to help people pay for college. After the election, Galston had revisited the issue and, in his confidential transition recommendations, agreed with Reed. "A $10,000/year figure would enable national service sponsors to tell pre-college youth: 'Serve your country for two years and you'll be able to go to the public college or university of your choice and graduate debt-free.'"

On this question, Clinton became intimately involved. He preferred $10,000 but faced a dilemma: Which was more important, having a large scholarship or having more kids in the program? Cut the scholarship in half and you can roughly double the size of the program. The Office of National Service was divided. Lew and Sagawa thought a smaller amount would be sufficient to draw plenty of young people. The 1990 law that Sagawa had written offered a $5,000 scholarship. Lew feared that a $10,000 scholarship might cause political problems if it were deemed profligate by Republicans and conservative Democrats.

Gene Sperling and George Stephanopoulos, on the other hand, supported a $10,000 benefit as essential to attracting middle-class kids. Rick Allen, the deputy director of the Office of National Service, argued that, to draw middle-class kids, the amount would have to be fairly close to the average annual cost of attending a four-year college, which was $5,400 for public schools and $13,000 for private. He also argued that students would compare the benefit package against the salary he or she might earn in their first year out of school. If the postservice benefit dropped too low, the kid might head straight to the private sector.

But the most passionate advocate for the large scholarship was Rob Gordon, the twenty-year-old Harvard student who had worked on the campaign and, later, on Galston's transition team. Gordon had gradually become an indispensable part of the operation, writing, among other things, the first draft of a *New York Times* op-ed article that appeared under the byline "Bill Clinton." Gordon fervently argued that the scholarship should be $10,000, first, because that was the campaign promise (as a certified member of the campaign War Room, Gordon was forever reminding the rest of the staff of the principles set out in 1992). Second, he argued, a smaller scholarship wouldn't attract young men and women from elite schools—people like him. Students at expensive institutions, like Harvard, where the cost of a four-year degree now ran over $80,000, would view a $5,000 benefit as pub money.

On February 24, Clinton gathered his national service advisors and a few political aides in the Roosevelt Room to discuss the scholarship level. He had come to the conclusion that $10,000 was preferable for a twenty-one-year-old finishing college, but that it was simply too much to give a teenager.

Deep in Clinton's gut, he really did believe that the graduate would be making more of a sacrifice by taking two years to teach when he could be out making a lot more money. "That's a real gift to society," Clinton told the group. Seventeen-year-olds, on the other hand, had fewer skills and expenses, since many lived at home. They would be sacrificing less financially.

Clinton decided on a compromise: a $10,000 benefit for college graduates, but a $5,000 benefit for those serving before college or those not intending to go to college. It was pointed out that having two different benefit levels might send an inappropriate message that Clinton cared more about the college-bound. But Clinton said he didn't mind the differential treatment: society *should* signal that it values higher education. It was a telling discussion, revealing the extent to which Clinton viewed college education as the ticket to success—as it had been for him. In fact, at the same meeting he rejected a suggestion that volunteers be able to use their postservice benefit for a down payment on a house or to start a new business.

The discussion also revealed Clinton's obsessive political sensitivity to the middle class. At one point in the discussion, Clinton made reference to the liberal criticism that the Nunn-McCurdy plan had discriminated against the poor, and that the poor were the only ones who need student aid. In fact, Clinton pointed out, the middle-class need loans to go to college, and the *rich* don't. The rich would therefore get the least financial benefit from the program.

Sagawa and Susan Stroud, another Office of National Service staffer, were given the task of launching this trial balloon. On March 12, they attended a meeting of the National and Community Service Coalition, an ad hoc lobbying group formed by service groups and charities ranging from the Girl Scouts to the YMCA. The room was packed. Sagawa didn't relish having to defend the split-benefit slant toward college education. "I hope we won't spend hours and hours on this, because that's what he campaigned on and it's what he sees as the mandate—that it focus on access to college," she said. "Of all the things he's most aware of and committed to, that's it."

One activist suggested making the postservice benefit available to young people who want to start up businesses. "There are a lot of youth who want to do service but don't want to go to college," he said.

Stroud's response was blunt. "The president has made the decision that the benefits should be just training and education."

Again, Sagawa brought it back to the campaign. "The focus in the campaign was so much on access to education that he didn't feel he should be adding other benefits."

Finally, Sam Halperin stood up in the back of the room. Halperin spoke with a certain moral authority on this subject. He was the author of the highly acclaimed *The Forgotten Half*, a 1990 report by the W. T. Grant Foundation about society's failure to deal well with the non-college-bound.

"Sometimes it's a difficult position being between friends and a boss," he said in a loud, paternal voice. "But I think he needs to understand that there is *nothing* that would split this movement more quickly than this proposal. The whole message is, 'We value people who go to college more.' "

"Let me ask you this," Sagawa responded. "Would you rather have this split or have it both be ten thousand dollars?" She knew that the service community didn't much like the $10,000 number, that they viewed it as a drain of money that could be used to create more service slots and programs.

"I'd go to the other direction—five thousand is enough," Halperin said.

"That's not one of the options," Sagawa snapped back.

"Well, you can't make me accept that," he responded.

"How would you respond to the argument that the president's campaign promise was to help pay for college and, with five thousand dollars, you can't do that?"

"I'd say 'This is a *start*,' " he said. "This is a time of scarcity. This is a good start."

Sagawa tilted her head, as if to say, "There's just really nothing more I can say." It was an awkward moment. People in the movement were realizing that while they fancied themselves the experts on service, the president simply had his own views.

On April 12, Clinton and his national service team met again in the Roosevelt Room, and the staff conveyed the strength of the opposition to the differential benefit. Segal had also heard, in no uncertain terms, the same message from Senator Barbara Mikulski, the chair of the Appropriations subcommittee that would fund national service. Segal told Clinton about attending a conference on campus volunteerism and asking the crowd of college students whether they would prefer a higher benefit or more participants; the audience favored a broader program.

Clinton was grumpy about the opposition to the split benefit. He again argued that those doing teaching and police work merited a higher reward. "Why can't professionals get more?" he asked. They again reminded him of the political opposition, with Segal inserting a strong note of pragmatism.

"This isn't one to lose the program over," he said.

Finally, Clinton relented and they began discussing what the unified benefit should be. They couldn't peg it to the average cost of a four-year college education, which was more than $20,000. They couldn't tie it to the average indebtedness because that was around $10,000. Someone pointed out that the average indebtedness at a four-year public college was around $6,500. Perfect. Public school debt was a sensible standard to cite, and it happened to be a number that would be politically palatable too.

The benefit level remained at $6,500 throughout April, as the staff worked out other details of the program. All were pushing to get a specific plan before Congress by Friday, April 30, the hundredth day of the Clinton presidency. The staff had already printed and distributed to some reporters a fact sheet listing the $6,500 figure. Who else could possibly object? On April 28, the White House found out.

Veterans.

Veterans! In other words, the last group in America the draft-dodging, gay-soldier-supporting, women-in-combat-loving president could afford to pick a fight with right then. The White House had been warned of this attack. Seven weeks earlier, Herschel Gober, the deputy secretary of veterans' affairs, had sent Segal a handwritten note warning that national service would "meet a lot of resistance from veterans organizations" if the benefit for civilian service was higher than that for soldiers. He wrote to Segal again the next week to report, "I have heard numerous comments from leaders of the veteran community and the Hill that they will oppose if veterans don't get at least equal treatment." Segal had asked his staff to prepare a comparison of benefits under national service and those received by soldiers under the Montgomery GI Bill. The analysis showed that, by their reckoning, the typical military pay and benefits package was more generous than what they were suggesting for national service. At the April 12 meeting, Segal had assured Clinton that lowering the benefit to $6,500 would certainly take care of any veterans' problems. What Segal forgot to do was run this by Representative Sonny Montgomery, the chairman of the Veterans Affairs Committee, or the veterans' groups. Suffice it to say, the veterans read the numbers differently, arguing that the value of their educational scholarship was less than $6,500. On April 28, Montgomery demanded to see Bruce Lindsey, Clinton's closest personal advisor. Lindsey was paged on his beeper, spoke with Montgomery, and heard the troubling news: the veterans were poised to launch a full-scale assault against national service.

When the veterans' issue blew up, the White House called Senator Sam Nunn for help—the same man who had been publicly humiliating Clinton over gays in the military. Nunn, of course, was a big national service fan—as evidenced by the Nunn-McCurdy bill. Nunn pledged to the veterans' groups and Montgomery that he—the veterans' best friend in the Senate—would never support something that hurt them. He promised to hold hearings later if they would just please let go of the president's national service plan.

The White House, to show its extreme level of attentiveness, sent Lindsey to hear the complaints at a meeting with the American Legion, the Veterans of Foreign Wars, and other veterans' groups. Both Segal and George Stephanopoulos also called Montgomery. The veterans were not impressed. They knew they had the administration over a barrel. One of their lobbyists proposed that the benefit for national service be slashed to $3,000. Simultaneously, the Washington office of the American Legion began mobilizing its local chapters. "We were having a national meeting so we had people right there who could make phone calls," said Steve Robertson of the American Legion. Inside the VA, staff had done another analysis that supported the position of veterans' groups: the proposed national service benefit would be more generous than the veterans' benefit.

Morale in the Office of National Service had never been lower. Several of the staffers had felt like they had compromised already in lowering the benefit from $10,000, and here, the veterans had swooped in out of the blue. Gordon remembers thinking it was his first *real* day of work.

As if the veterans problem wasn't enough, Segal was simultaneously hearing that several House Republicans the White House wanted as cosponsors of the bill thought the $6,500 benefit was too costly.

Segal and other advisors were meeting Thursday night in the White House to discuss whether to cut the size of the scholarship. On the one hand, they had a pretty good argument that the veterans' benefits were, in fact, higher. On the other hand, was it a good idea to get into a public argument with the veterans over this? Lowering the scholarship, Segal figured, would appease the interest groups and, if they were lucky, help pick up some Republican support.

Less than twenty-four hours before Clinton was scheduled to unveil his national service plan, the president tracked down Montgomery at the Carlyle Grand Cafe in Virginia, got him on the phone, and agreed to lower the benefit to $5,000. As Will Marshall of the DLC put it later: "Clinton's capitulation to the veterans was the price he had to pay for gays in the military."

So, in the end, what happened to the idea of developing a demographically mixed service corps? Segal and his team didn't explicitly encourage diversity language in part because they figured the scholarship would be large enough to attract a broad cross-section of young people anyway. But that key tool was then cut in compromises: first with the community service groups, then with the veterans' groups. The net result was that little in the legislation seemed to promote the race- and class-mixing that Clinton deemed so important.

What did Clinton get for his concessions? Something not insignificant: the strong support of blacks, House liberals, Bill Ford, and Sonny Montgomery.

8

Real Work

In April Eli Segal stood engrossed behind a one-way mirror. He was watching a politically mixed group of eleven voters from suburban Maryland talk about national service, and it was proving a less than delightful experience. Few of the people in this focus group knew anything about the president's grand plan. Worse, when moderator Peter Hart described it, they seemed profoundly unimpressed. Several of the voters knew deadbeats who hadn't repaid their student loans, and as for national service, they figured the government would devise some creative way of screwing up even something so promising. Hart asked if they could name *any* government programs that worked well. They sat silently for about thirty seconds. Finally, someone mentioned the Peace Corps, and a few of the others nodded. Any others? Another twenty seconds of disconcerting calm. Someone suggested the space program. Then more silence. That was it.

Bill Clinton had decreed that the national service program would be the model of his efforts to "reinvent government." By April, Segal knew just how hard it would be to create something that would win over such a skeptical public. In some ways, he seemed ideally suited for the task of setting up a social program from scratch. His significant business experience combined with his insignificant background in government made him unusually open-minded. Rubbing his hands together as if perpetually washing them in invisible water, Segal would stare directly into the eyes of staffers and fire off question after question challenging their assumptions about whatever they were discussing. He wasn't afraid to ask stupid questions, so he got smart fast.

Most important, Segal was political. He viewed getting Bill Clinton reelected as a major mission of the national service program. To help Clinton, Segal knew, national service would have to produce a product in which "the public would delight." Segal knew from his experiences in the 1960s and 1970s that creating another antipoverty program would guarantee failure. This program had to do real, useful work. "I don't want kids raking leaves or picking up gum wrappers," he told his staff on numerous occasions.

Segal had the right impulses. But he had early on also exhibited disturbing sentimentality about the service programs themselves. Because he had few strong ideas about how good programs worked, he seemed highly reliant on those in the "service community," which included saints and, in the words of Charles Peters, the former Peace Corps chief of evaluation, "some of the biggest con men I've ever met." For instance, Segal talked about weeding out bad programs by requiring them to demonstrate "quantifiable outcomes" from service. But in the hands of a clever grant writer, a program placing teachers' aides to sit blindfolded in the classroom closet can be transformed into a paragon of hard-nosed cost effectiveness. And, as Segal pointed out, picking up 932 gum wrappers would be a quantifiable outcome not worth the money.

In his first week on the job, Segal had gotten a hefty dose of the service world's capacity to put on a good but ultimately meaningless show. Some local Washington, D.C., service corps had arranged for an "urban barn raising" to demonstrate the energy of service during the week of the presidential inauguration. Several hundred young people gathered at the Atlas Theater, in a low-income neighborhood of Washington, to transform the abandoned building into a community center. Some students put down cement, while others painted one-by-one-foot squares on the wall, filling each with an original pattern in Day-Glo blue or orange. Segal came, painted, was wowed by the enthusiasm of the young people, and left the event inspired—a great sign of his naïveté.

The day was a successful photo opportunity—the volunteers finished painting much of the building—but the project as a whole flopped. The group organizing the event, Public Allies, couldn't get appropriate permits and approvals from local community leaders and abandoned the effort to convert the theater to a youth center several weeks later. As Peter Hart's focus group met in Maryland in April 1993, the Atlas Theater sat empty and decaying.

Was Segal too much of a limousine liberal to separate the wheat from the spin? Could someone so ignorant of how service programs worked—including the scams—know *how* to guarantee real work?

On the morning of March 15, 1933, just eleven days into the administration of Franklin Roosevelt, a group of reporters gathered in the White House to question officials about the details of the new president's Civilian Conservation Corps.

The man briefing the reporters began, "This is entirely off the record." Many in Congress, he noted, wanted this to be a broad public-works program with a limitless variety of tasks. The new president disagreed. He wanted it focused on improving natural resources. The skeptical reporters inquired just what kind of work would be done; they fired off detailed questions, such as whether servers would be cutting down trees or planting them.

The briefer took them up on the challenge, and began a lengthy disquisition on forestry. "We have to have another class here on it," he said. "Nearly all of the so-called forest land owned by the government is second-, third-, or fourth-growth land—what we call scrub growth which has grown up on it." The reporters scribbled. "What does that consist of? Probably an average of four or five thousand trees to the acre; little bits of trees, saplings and so forth. . . . Now, take this second-, third-, fourth-growth land. Put men in there. . . . They go in there and take out the crooked trees, the dead trees, the bushes and stuff like that has no value as lumber, and leave approximately one thousand trees to the acre." And so on.

Two things were remarkable about this briefing. First was how focused the administration was on tangible goals so early in its tenure. The official was making it clear that despite the urgent need to put unemployed men to work, the CCC was as concerned with improving the environment as it was with helping the volunteers.

The second was that the man conducting the briefing was Franklin Roosevelt himself. Years earlier, Roosevelt had developed a strong interest and expertise in environmental concerns, and he demanded that the CCC share that focus.

Three decades later, the mission of the Peace Corps was more vague, but it did emphasize an external goal more than a benefit to the servers. The particular mission: to vanquish communism. "On the other side of the globe, teachers, doctors, technicians, and experts desperately needed in a dozen fields by underdeveloped nations are pouring forth from Moscow to advance the cause of world communism," John F. Kennedy declared in his only 1960 campaign speech on the Peace Corps. "I am convinced that our young men and women, dedicated to freedom, are fully capable of overcoming the efforts of Mr. Khruschev's missionaries who are dedicated to undermining that freedom."

What was the goal of Clinton's national service plan? In the campaign, Clinton always emphasized service for service' sake—"giving something back." The second most important goal was the college scholarship, something very much for the server. Only as a fleeting afterthought did he mention particular tasks, which changed throughout the campaign but usually included police work and teaching.

Segal had to decide: Would Clinton's national service program have a single, clearly defined social mission? The White House political honchos had no preference. They cared most about student aid for the middle class; for them, the service performed was incidental. Ironically, this tendency was reinforced by the service movement itself, which concentrated on providing service opportunities for young people, not on solving particular social problems. Most local service corps were set up not by environmentalists or police chiefs or teachers, but by youth activists who wanted to give young people a character-building experience.

Segal did not agree with those service advocates. He really did want the program to accomplish something, and understood, at least in the abstract, the desirability of focus. The question was, focus on what?

The most obvious choice was health care. The administration desperately needed ways to stretch their health-care reform dollars and to capture the public imagination. They could have adopted the German model, which deploys tens of thousands of servers to help seniors with home care; servers could also do immunizations to reduce the incidence of childhood disease, or help low-income pregnant women get good prenatal care. Segal did brief health-care guru Ira Magaziner on such possible uses of the service corps, but his suggestions did not exactly change the course of health-care reform. In the end, when Clinton gave his major health-care speech before Congress, he didn't even mention the connection to his national service program.

Robert Gordon advocated focusing the program on one or two areas, as a way of energizing Americans and increasing impact. But when anyone inside or outside of the administration would suggest an imaginative, dramatic focus for the service plan, interest-group politics intervened. "The education reform folks said we ought to spend it all on education reform," recalls Peter Edelman, counsel to the secretary of health and human services. "I said, 'Gee whiz, the environmental folks won't like that.'"

Shirley Sagawa, ever the pragmatist, inverted the argument. She feared that support for national service was "a mile wide and an inch deep," and that to focus the issue would "cut off three-quarters of the mile." More grants dealing with more issues meant more interest groups supporting national service. "In a political context, it's helpful for the president to go to a community hard hit by a defense base closing and say, 'We're going to put National Conservation Corps people here,' or go to a crime-ridden area and say, 'We're going to put volunteers here to help make your streets safer.'"

The broad-beam approach won. The legislation required that service be focused on the "priority areas" of public safety, *and* health, *and* the environment, *and* education.

Segal did not believe this lack of focus necessarily doomed his vision of volunteers accomplishing real work. There could be many different service corps, each doing different but nonetheless substantial work. Ultimately, the programs would have to be designed well on the grassroots level if they were to avoid the pitfalls of make-work. Within the Peace Corps, volunteers served as teachers in some countries, as nurses in others. If the particular programs were run well, there needn't be one national focus.

Who exactly would run these programs? Would the federal government, as it had run the Peace Corps or the CCC? The answer came from Clinton himself: no. As a former governor, he liked the idea of the states playing a large role; he distrusted the abilities of the federal government—even his federal government—and did not want to leave himself open to attack for being a typical big-bureaucracy Washington liberal. Segal therefore instructed his staff to limit the Washington staff of the new agency to 100. (By comparison, the EPA's Washington staff is 5,000.) This decision from Clinton, and Segal's agreement with it, triggered a series of challenges, the foremost being to figure out how to run a high-quality national program with a small federal bureaucracy.

Nick Littlefield, of Ted Kennedy's office, had one idea for making each dollar go far: to give one-third of the pot to Kennedy's favorite type of project—service learning. Because sixth-graders don't get a salary or a scholarship, the only cost would be for a school administrator. You could produce millions of servers without a large Washington staff. But there were a few problems. Many service-learning programs do stimulate kids, but how much does the *community* benefit from Jessica and Justin collecting pond samples from the nearby creek? And there was the small matter that this did not even faintly resemble Clinton's campaign promise. Lew and Sagawa gently told Littlefield that, while service learning was certainly worthwhile—and they appreciated Senator Kennedy's fine work in this field—one-third of the money was a bit much. They gave him 15 percent.

Another possibility was to model the program on the original GI Bill. Senator Dale Bumpers of Arkansas had proposed that the government provide money just for loan forgiveness and simply specify what type of existing jobs would qualify (i.e., Counseling Addicts: yes. Selling Fruit Dehydrators: no). The GI Bill, after all, did not set up an education program; it merely gave people a check to pay for school if they had served. The colleges took care of the rest.

But Lew, Sagawa, and Segal quickly ruled out this approach. For one thing, determining what counts as college education or military service is relatively easy. But what counts as civilian service? If nursing is a public-service job, then is being a doctor? If a family practitioner should have her loans wiped out, should a cosmetic surgeon? What if he treats low-income burn victims? Would all public employees be public servants? What about the guy who boots your car? Lew and others in the office wrestled with one hypothetical in particular: Would cleaning up cemeteries count as national service? On the one hand, it's like doing environmental work in an urban park; on the other hand, it looks a lot like an ordinary job (not to mention the dreary symbolism). The process of choosing could be dicey, and possibly political. (One might envision the labor union representing the city coroners asking to be included: "We dissect the dead, so that others might live.") Under the Bumpers plan, it would be extremely difficult for the federal government to guarantee quality. Someone could easily end up redeeming a voucher at the Parks Department, even for raking leaves or picking up gum wrappers. "We felt you couldn't just say, 'Go out and do something meaningful,' " Sagawa said. "You had to have a carefully designed program."

Carefully designed by whom? Segal knew one thing for sure, he didn't want "another CETA." The Comprehensive Employment and Training Act, a job program of the 1970s, was tremendously unpopular and was eliminated in the 1980s. Segal told legislators at every opportunity that national service would not "repeat the mistakes of CETA." In order to learn just what those mistakes were, he asked Robert Gordon to write him a paper on it. Gordon reported back that CETA had been *too decentralized*. It had become rife with patronage and pork, not because of a bloated federal bureaucracy, but because the government had given the money to local mayors, who then gave their nephews jobs in the parks department—raking leaves and picking up gum wrappers. Federal "oversight" usually came after the projects were completed.

Designing national service, it was turning out, was like solving a Rubik's Cube. Each time Segal and his team matched up the colors on one row, another two would go out of alignment. He wanted a small federal bureaucracy. That meant, by definition, relying on the states. He wanted to avoid "another CETA," but it turns out that CETA failed because it relied too heavily on the states.

Indeed, the memory of CETA seemed to haunt the Office of National Service, like some Ghost of Programs Past who issued ominous warnings at pivotal moments. Give the money to the mayors? CETA showed they couldn't handle it. Give it to the governors? CETA showed they would vindictively try to rip off the cities. The ghost of CETA taught Segal's team that, while Washingtonians think governors and mayors all look alike, on the state level they usually hate each other. Bill Ford let Segal know that he despised the Republican governor of Michigan, and that the feeling was mutual. Chicago mayor Richard M. Daley sent word to Segal through Daley's brother William, who had just started working for the administration, that the governors should not be allowed to control the program. And no one trusted the mayors either. "We came to realize: We're not going to have better programs if we hand out the money through the mayors," one administration official said.

After studying history and listening to experts and politicians of all stripes, Segal and his team concluded that the program couldn't be controlled by the feds . . . or by the governors . . . or by the mayors. Who did that leave? The sewer authority?

Lew and Sagawa proposed a mixed structure. Half the money would be given out by an independent federal corporation whose directors would be appointed by the president but couldn't be fired by him. The other half of the money would go out through fifty independent state commissions modeled after the successful Commission on National and Community Service. Each would be appointed by the state's governor, but would operate independent of the governor's influence. These commissions would give out grants by competition to local nonprofit groups.

The idea of having grassroots organizations run programs is a "new" idea that gets rediscovered every four or five years, despite a fairly poor track record. The Community Action Program in the War on Poverty gave grants directly to private groups, which often would alienate the local government by staging protests, filing lawsuits, or otherwise embarrassing city hall. VISTA was established under Lyndon Johnson with the same hope that using bootstrap programs would guarantee efficiency and creativity. But as illustrated in Jonathan Rowe's hilarious account in *The Washington Monthly*, this structure did not ensure high quality. In the late 1960s, Rowe joined a nonprofit group called Mobilization for Youth, which organized rent strikes, picketed construction sites over union hiring practices, and verbally attacked public school principals. MFY assigned Rowe to a summer program called Neighborhood Youth Corps, not to serve as a mentor to kids, but to help staff figure out a computer problem that had fouled up the group's payroll system.

> This was not exactly the sort of work the VISTA posters and forward-looking logo had suggested. But since New York was overwhelming and I had no idea how else to wage war on poverty there, the punch cards were at least a way to keep busy and feel like I was contributing. . . . We sat in the classroom, correcting card upon card, while "Whiter Shades of Pale" came from Tito's radio on the window sill. There was no shortage of administrators, who seemed to issue forth from the inner sanctums of PS 82 like clowns from the Volkswagen in the old circus trick. What they all did, I never quite grasped. I began to suspect that the Neighborhood Youth Corps was intended to provide summer employment not just for ghetto youth but for high school guidance counselors from Brooklyn as well. There was also, of course, a generous provision for MFY's administrative expenses.

Clearly, having a program run locally or by nonprofits wouldn't guarantee that it would produce real work.

Still, Lew had faith in the nonprofit sector. For one thing, the size and quality of these local groups had grown enormously in the past decade. From 1982 to 1992, the number of nonprofit organizations doubled, and new ones included such highly entrepreneurial programs as City Year and Teach for America. These groups were often far more efficient than the government, but held public-interest motives that private corporations might not share.

What's more, Lew had developed a backup system, a way the feds could ensure quality in these local enterprises. In the spirit of the administration's "Reinventing Government" drive, which aimed to make government work more like the private sector, he built in competition at every turn. The federal government could give money to local nonprofits like City Year, national nonprofits like the Red Cross, or even to other federal agencies—but no one would get it automatically. If the Interior Department wanted to set up a forestry corps, they would have to apply and compete against perhaps the Agriculture Department or the Red Cross.

The same went for the state commissions. Any given state could count on getting only 60 percent of its allotment automatically. The rest would be parceled out under an unusual bonus system: each state would have to compete with *other states* for extra cash. If Alaska had fantastic service programs and Texas didn't, Alaska would get the bonus money. In addition, the federal government could veto any single project it didn't like.

Lew showed the plan to lobbyists for the states—who thought it stank. The federal government having line-item veto authority over each state would be burdensome and intrusive, argued Ray Sheppoch, the lead Washington-based staffer for National Governors' Association. Staffs for governors Zell Miller of Georgia and Roy Romer of Colorado called Segal and Lew to urge a greater role for the states.

Lew consulted David Osborne, author of *Reinventing Government* and a consultant to Vice President Gore's task force on reforming the federal government. Osborne warned that if the administration put too many restrictions on the states, the governors would not feel "invested" in the success of the program. If that happened, the governors could find thousands of creative ways to quietly sabotage the local projects.

Lew offered the governors a compromise: Instead of the feds having veto power over projects, Washington would appoint someone to each of the state commissions. Lew thought the states would reject this, too, since it amounted to Uncle Sam having a spy on each commission. "We want to hear about problems before they hit the local newspapers," Lew explained. In early April, to Lew's surprise, Sheppoch agreed to the deal.

But in late April—just days before the plan was to be announced —the governors came back for more. Roy Romer, chairman of the NGA, sent word to Segal that still *more* of the money should go through the states, and more of it should be given automatically on the basis of formula. The governors wanted two thirds of the money if they were going to endorse the bill.

This posed a great dilemma for Segal. He wanted the program to be loved by governors around the country—and by one ex-governor living in the White House—but feared he would lose control of the program if too much money went through the states.

That cow's out of the barn, Lew argued. If the states screw up, the program will be doomed whether they have 50 percent of the money or two thirds. Might as well give them two thirds and get them more invested in the programs' success.

The most ardent opponent of giving so much to the states was Robert Gordon. Shy and forever vigilant not to be disrespectful to his elders, Gordon rarely made his pitch in meetings. But Segal usually knew that within a few days of any particularly significant internal debate, he would find a memo from Gordon on his desk. Gordon had the most hardheaded view of service in the office, because he had actually served. He had run a program that tried to get Boston junior high school students interested in government by introducing them to local politicians and setting up mock congresses. He had taught tennis to inner-city kids for two summers, turning urban playgrounds into makeshift courts. And he had been steeped in the touchy-feely politics of college campuses in the 1990s. At one point, his dormitory at Harvard had gone on a retreat to Cape Cod and, in order to break down emotional walls, played the "shoe game." This is a sensitivity-building exercise in which participants don someone else's footwear and discuss what it felt like. Gordon realized that many local service programs pushed to include "reflection" exercises as part of their efforts. "I came away realizing that limited federal funds shouldn't be spent on the shoe game," Gordon said. He understood that there was plenty of room for garbage in the service movement and regularly reported on service corps that were "mush." Gordon feared that if the federal government ceded too much control to the states—and to local groups— they would end up with a whole lot of shoe games instead of real work.

Segal and Lew didn't like giving up so much control, either. But "with the president being a former governor, you didn't want to go to him and say the National Governors Association is not on board," one White House official explained. They also had become convinced that they couldn't pass a program without the governors' support. Segal saw a silver lining in this latest storm-cloud formation. He believed the real threat to quality was not so much the size of the state share, but the percentage that went out automatically instead of by competition. He decided he would give the states more money if they agreed to have more of it be "bonus money" awarded by competition. Segal recommended that package to Clinton, who quickly approved the deal: one third of the money to be given out by the federal government, two thirds by states.

Even though the federal corporation would directly control only one third of the money, Segal figured it could still have a dramatic impact on the service world—if it acted swiftly and creatively. It could establish model programs, articulate broad themes, and hold states to high standards. That raised another question: Is there such a thing as a federal agency that acts swiftly and creatively? Many in Congress believed that the Commission on National and Community Service, set up by the 1990 legislation, was just such a rare beast. The commission gave out $75 million annually with a staff of twenty. By contrast, ACTION, which ran VISTA and several other War on Poverty programs, needed four hundred staff people to oversee $200 million. Not surprisingly, the Clintonites viewed ACTION as an ossified relic. It "is an old style bureaucracy, heavy on federal personnel with a history of resistance to change," Galston wrote in his secret transition recommendations. Segal decided the new corporation would swallow up ACTION and the commission.

Catherine Milton, executive director of the commission, privately argued that the secret to her agency's success lay in being able to operate outside the normal civil-service system. She was able to recruit talented young people who were interested in brief tours of duty, pay them less than the standard government wage, and get rid of the ones who didn't work out. The proposed new corporation, she pointed out, would be inheriting 90 percent of its employees from bureaucratized ACTION. She urged Segal to adopt flexible work rules, including some dramatic reforms inspired by the Peace Corps. That agency, it was thought, had retained a good workforce by using renewable contracts and adopting a heretical idea known as the "five-year flush," in which many employees got automatically pushed out the door after five years. David Osborne, Mr. Reinventing Government himself, also weighed in supporting the move to a radical new system of private-sector-style work rules.

Segal took the plunge. He proposed that ACTION employees be given a choice: they could waive their civil-service job protection and be welcomed into the new corporation, or they could go somewhere else in the federal government. He adopted the concept of the five-year flush as a means to achieve a constant infusion of new blood and ideas. To Lew's surprise, the national labor unions signed off on this scheme, too. They had their eyes on something they considered more important: regulating exactly what the servers would be doing.

If any Democratic interest group could destroy the service program, it was labor. Over the past decades, unions had resisted many efforts to create meaningful government service jobs. Local service corps working on low-income housing renovation have often run into difficulty with the Davis-Bacon law requiring construction workers to be paid the "prevailing wage."

The unions had some legitimate fears. If you create a government-subsidized environmental job at minimum wage, why should the Parks Department hire someone for $25,000? "It makes no sense to hire the son and fire the mom," said Bob McGlotten, the legislative director of the AFL-CIO. In March 1993, AFL-CIO president Lane Kirkland set up a task force composed of representatives from building trades, teachers, police, firefighters, and the big government employee unions. It was the American Federation of State, County, and Municipal Employees (AFSCME) that proposed a radical solution: The state commissions would have to get "concurrence" from a local union to make sure a project didn't potentially displace workers. In other words, unions could veto the projects!

The White House hated the idea of giving some local shop steward life-or-death power over service projects. But they had a political dilemma. The White House believed they needed not just the acquiescence of the unions, but their active support. Why? They feared that no one else would work aggressively enough to pass the bill. Many interest groups liked service, but few viewed it as their top priority. And despite concerns about giving the unions too much power, Sagawa feared the shop stewards less than the local mayors who, facing budgetary pressure, might try to use service workers to replace municipal employees.

After weeks of negotiations, the White House gave the unions almost everything they wanted. They did not get broad-based veto power, but did get to oppose service grants to programs already staffed by unionized employees. (If a unionized school district got a grant to use volunteers as teachers, the local teachers' union would have veto authority. But if the nonunionized Teach for America got the grant, union approval would not be needed.)

But that's not all the unions got. Labor was guaranteed seats on all of the state commissions, and on the federal corporation board. And perhaps most important, service programs would not be allowed to "displace workers or *duplicate their functions*" (emphasis added). A local program could theoretically be prevented from placing a volunteer as a teacher even if the school district had a shortage—because the server would be "duplicating" an existing function.

Lew and Sagawa knew they were giving unions the statutory tools to make mischief, but they had concluded it was a low-risk gamble. They had been impressed with the experiences of groups like YouthBuild and a few service corps, which had worked closely with unions without diluting the quality of the service. Some unions figured that young people who learned construction trades could later join unions. In Pennsylvania, the state conservation corps became a magnet for retired construction union members. Finally, Lew and Sagawa figured, communities dominated by recalcitrant unions would simply not get funded.

Clinton became directly involved in designing the structure of the national service apparatus on only two occasions all year. First was when he made the decision to increase the amount of money going through the states. The second was at the April 12 meeting during which Segal finally convinced the president that the two-tiered system of scholarships (at $10,000 and $5,000) would not fly. At that meeting, Clinton reviewed Segal's recommendations on all of the "reinventing government" components of the plan—from the state commissions to the union rules. Lew and Sagawa had entered the meeting with some trepidation, unsure how this ex-governor would react to the balance between the feds and localities. Segal had given Clinton a "decision memo" that outlined the responsibilities of the state commissions and the corporation. To the relief of Lew and Sagawa, Clinton said he liked the structure *because* it protected cities from states. As a former governor, he said, he knew full well what mischief governors could make for cities. For the same reason, Clinton said he liked the independence of the state commissions, and the fact that local programs could turn to Washington if they felt shut out at home. Vice President Al Gore chimed in frequently on the importance of these government reforms, and helped to generate an air of excitement about the drive toward innovation. When Segal explained the requirement for a federal representative on the state commissions, Clinton seemed positively tickled.

"I love it," he said smiling. "I love that."

Clinton signed off on the labor provisions quickly, asking only whether Segal's team had run it by the unions. When they got to the most radical section of the bill, the flexible work rules, Clinton seemed pleased. He liked it that the corporation managers would be able to hire and fire with ease, but he wanted to know how it would play politically. "Will the Republicans like it?" Clinton asked.

He grilled the group on the details for about an hour, but in the end signed off on almost every recommendation—with one telling exception. ONS had recommended that the local programs be required to put up one dollar of their own for each federal dollar they received—a "matching" system designed to stretch the federal dollar farther and improve the quality of programs. City Year supported the approach, arguing that having to raise money had forced them to run a tighter ship and build community support for their efforts. To help smaller programs meet the 50-percent requirement, ONS had suggested allowing programs to make an in-kind contribution instead of cash. That meant they could apply what they paid in office rent toward fulfilling the matching requirement.

Clinton picked the proposal apart on two grounds. First, he argued, allowing the programs to use in-kind contributions would encourage them to "game" the system; they would list overhead costs ranging from Xerox machines to refills for the water cooler as "contributions" to the program. "In-kind means higher administrative costs," the president of the United States explained. The participants were impressed. He'd spent a total of about sixty minutes on the national service program's structure, and had already honed in on a facet of nonprofit-world shenanigans that only the most experienced experts understood.

His second objection to the fifty-fifty match was equally revealing, but for a very different reason. He argued that the high match discriminated against poor communities. It's one thing for Harvard Law School alumni to raise money from foundations, but Clinton wanted his program to be available to small neighborhood bootstrap organizations. "Use a figure everyone can meet," he said. It was idealistic, populist—and risky. Lowering the match almost increased the odds that real lemons would get funded.

Clinton seemed fully aware of the pitfalls of relying so much on local groups and governments. Despite all the safeguards, the bottom line was that two-thirds of the money would be given out by the states, not the federal government. The program that Clinton hoped would be his abiding legacy would be largely shaped by the governors, some of whom were political enemies, some of whom didn't give a whit about service, and some of whom couldn't design a quality service corps if you paid them. If the governors allowed volunteers to pick up gum wrappers, Clinton would get blamed. "What people have always said in the past in Washington is if you run a nonbureaucratic, noncentralized, nontop-down, nonrule-oriented program, you will be responsible if someone in state *x* doesn't make people work to earn the benefit," Clinton said to me in an interview. But *wouldn't* he have to take responsibility for those failures? "Of course, but I'd gladly take responsibility for doing it as the price of running a decentralized program, one that's less bureaucratic. I still think it's the right thing to do." Clinton had shown himself to be as much a states' rights federalist as Nixon or Reagan, albeit with one key difference: Nixon and Reagan wanted to turn programs over to the states as a way of shrinking government; Clinton did so to make activist government more effective. Given the reputation he earned as a lover of Big Government during the 1994 health-care debate, it's striking how much more faith Clinton had in the localities than in the federal branch he ran.

Clinton and Segal had genuinely tried to learn from the mistakes of the 1960s and 1970s. But did they learn the *right* lessons? One tends to think of public-private partnerships and local government as inherently efficient, and of the federal government as inherently bloated. Yet some of the biggest failures in social policy have come when the federal government provided the money and the localities spent it: the Community Action Program, CETA, revenue-sharing. And programs in which the federal government has allowed private contractors to spend its money have an even worse history: consider S & Ls, the HUD scandal, nuclear-plant cleanups.

On the other hand, the two programs mentioned positively by the focus group that so impressed Segal—the Peace Corps and the space program—were both federally run. So too, of course, was the CCC. While states and cities may better understand local conditions, when spending federal funds they often act irresponsibly for a simple reason: *It isn't their money.* A basic tenet of human nature that gets lost in the federalist impulse to decentralize is that people are more careful with their own money than with that of others.

Segal later explained that they addressed many of these problems by instilling so much competition into the funding process. But the problem with trying to apply the principles of market economics to government is the irksome question of politics. What happens if, come, say, November 1996, Alaska's programs seem much better than California's? Would Eli Segal really give the bonus money to Alaska?

In drafting their plan, Segal and his team took several steps that risked undermining their goal of producing real work. They included the "duplicating functions" provision (to appease the unions); they refused to focus service on one or two issue areas (to appease everyone); and, most importantly, they gave two-thirds of the money to the states (to appease the governors).

But the plan Clinton approved on April 12 also took some gutsy steps: the right to hire and fire, appointment of a federal spy on the state commissions, and a strong rhetorical insistence that programs be able to measure quantifiably their work output. Clinton and the Segal team had shown some intellectual courage. It remained to be seen whether they would show political courage.

9

The Unveiling

As I sat in the landing craft looking out at Omaha Beach, the sound of waves grew thunderous in my ears. I knew that some of the men around me I would never see again. But before I could contemplate the implications, the front side of the vessel collapsed. The group scattered out onto the sand like a spilled bushel of crabs. In a matter of minutes, it was all over, and we went on to the next exhibit.

I was standing in the strangest museum I'd ever visited: the Robert R. McCormick military history museum outside of Chicago. It is housed at Cantigny, the estate of McCormick, the former publisher of the *Chicago Tribune*. He served as a colonel in World War I, commanding an artillery battalion in the U.S. Army's First Division, which fought one of its greatest battles in the French town of Cantigny — hence the name of his homestead. (Good thing he hadn't fought in the Battle of the Bulge.) McCormick turned the mansion into a war museum, featuring re-creations of Vietnamese jungles, a Sherman tank, and World War I bunkers (the Omaha Beach landing was a simulation included in a section on great battles of the past). The overall effect was of a Disney World designed by the editors of *Soldier of Fortune*.

Cantigny was symbolically the perfect site for the conference I was attending on national service on April 21 and 22, 1993. Charlie Moskos, the Northwestern University professor who had been so influential in giving Clinton the national service bug, referred to the event as a gathering of the "stalwarts." Actually, it seemed a bit like old-timers' day at Yankee Stadium—a collection of great men who had once inspired, but now had little impact on the game. In addition to Moskos, there was Don Eberly, the grand old man of national service, who had set up a demonstration program in Seattle in the 1970s, and who first got Hubert Humphrey interested in the Peace Corps idea. (It was Humphrey, not Kennedy, who introduced the first Peace Corps legislation in the U.S. Senate.) No single individual had spent more of his life pushing the cause of national service than Eberly. David Roosevelt, the grandson of FDR, attended. So did Admiral Stansfield Turner, Jimmy Carter's CIA director, and Neal Creighton, a retired two-star general.

At first I thought, as I do whenever I happen to catch a baseball old-timers' game, that these guys couldn't hit today's pitchers. At the opening dinner, Turner, Moskos, Creighton (still sporting his military crew cut), and Richard E. Friedman, the program's organizer, sat literally trading war stories. They compared ranks, gossiped disapprovingly about gays in the military, engaged in some friendly verbal jousts about the marines versus the navy, etc. Midway through the meal, I realized I was the only person at the table who had never served in the armed forces. At first I felt vaguely superior to the old geezers, so mired in the gauzy past. Then I began to admire them. I could write about literacy programs and environmental cleanups all I wanted; these guys had really served their country. I felt ashamed, and wondered whether Bill Clinton felt this way when he first met the Joint Chiefs. Eventually, though, I grew excited because their presence showed that they saw civilian service as comparable to what they had done—that it *was* national service.

Cantigny made me wonder: Why wasn't the military playing more of a role in planning the national service program? Officers did, after all, have quite a bit of experience dealing with eighteen-year-olds from different backgrounds. As the military dwindled, a lot of drill sergeants would be looking for jobs. What a natural resource.

Charlie Moskos's speech, "National Service: Save Us from Our Friends," proffered one theory. He argued that service had been captured by "softheaded" liberals who cared more about the server than the served, and who in some cases had a left-wing advocacy agenda.

"To succeed, to become truly national," he said, "it must make an appeal to the sons and daughters of the American Legion as much as it does to Ted Kennedy's staffers. And so far it's been sort of geared toward Ted Kennedy's staffers rather than the sons and daughters of the American Legion." He then read from a statement by the Young People for National Service, a small group of recent college graduates that formed to lobby for the legislation. Their statement described how service could "challenge our generation, build a sense of community spirit or involvement, offer opportunities for experimental education, work against racism, sexism, classism and homophobia by building bridges of understanding." Moskos stopped there, and said, "Well I'm not sure the pro-gay agenda has to be an essential part of a national program." He then held up *Visions of Service*, a collection of essays about service, and said of the activists who contributed to the booklet, "I doubt if one of these voted for George Bush or Ross Perot."

Service programs will live or die by the service performed, Moskos argued, and he set a simple standard of measure: "If the youth server disappeared, would he or she be missed?" He complained that so little consideration was given to the idea of having a centrally run service program. "Sixty years have passed since the CCC was formed, and people still probably have a better memory of the Civilian Conservation Corps than they do of any of the contemporary local youth corps."

It struck me as I listened to Moskos that the ideological stereotypes had been turned on their heads. The liberal activists favored federalism, a decentralized approach relying on local programs; the DLC conservatives favored a centrally controlled national program. During twelve years of Republican presidents, liberals had come to realize that while they would only occasionally occupy the White House, they would almost always run the major cities. Moskos, coming more from a military background—the one institution that must be federal—was dismayed by this decentralized approach. "It's like postmodern national service—no boundaries or anything. We're going to have private corporations, public work, local cities, old people, young people—all mixed together."

To carry Moskos's postmodern analogy one step further: The White House had put a big hunk of clay on the table and allowed input from several hundred artists. In the future, many more artists would be allowed to participate. The problem was that the White House had no idea what, in the end, the sculpture would look like.

At the very moment the stalwarts gathered at Cantigny, Clinton's presidency was in the midst of a defining moment. The Republicans had mounted a successful filibuster against Clinton's economic stimulus package. Minority leader Bob Dole had jolted the administration into a realization: The White House could create, but the Republicans could destroy.

Segal and Lew had been working closely with the Democratic staff in both the House and the Senate, earning rave reviews for consulting Congress much more thoroughly than had the arrogant group Jimmy Carter brought to town. But Segal's team hadn't worked at all with Republican staffers. Starting about a week before the White House was to submit the legislation, it had begun scouring Capitol Hill for Republican co-sponsors. Normally, co-sponsorship of legislation is not terribly important. In this case, it was. If the administration failed to get Republican co-sponsors, it would signal that national service was a "partisan issue."

In the House, the White House turned to Christopher Shays of Connecticut, a former Peace Corps volunteer in Fiji who had proposed his own national service bill, and Steve Gunderson of Wisconsin, another moderate Republican. Shays set up a meeting with twenty House Republicans on April 29. The members said they liked it that the plan would encourage service and require only a small federal bureaucracy; but they had enormous problems with the price tag. They wanted *more* money to pass through the states, instead of the federal government. Ten billion dollars over five years, at a time of fiscal austerity, seemed way out of line. Segal assured them that the program would only grow that fast if it succeeded and won over public opinion. Someone in the room (no one remembers who) suggested a solution: In the legislation, instead of listing big, specific authorizations for each year, why not simply say "such sums as may be necessary"?

It was a classic case of a few words that meant nothing to the outside world but carried enormous importance within Congress.

"Such sums" meant that a Republican congressman could tell constituents: "Yes, I voted for national service but I'm not locked into some Big Government spending spree. It will only grow if it deserves to." Literally, it meant that each year the congressional appropriations committees would decide how much the program should get.

How could the White House agree to that? It had fought so hard to get that $3.4 billion authorization in the third year of the president's budget. The Office of National Service press releases had ballyhooed the massive commitment of this $7.4 billion program. The change seemed like a screeching political U-turn and possibly a colossal sellout. But Sofer told Segal that it was a shrewd compromise: it got the Republicans *without* actually giving up anything. Remember the difference between authorization and appropriations, Sofer said. An authorization establishes the law so that Congress can legally spend *up to* a certain amount. It is the appropriation that actually provides the money. So even with the original language—a $3.4 billion authorization in 1997—the White House would have to convince the congressional appropriators to give up cash. Either way, Sofer argued, the program would grow if it became popular and shrink if it didn't. Segal agreed to the change.

Technically, Sofer was right. The problem was, the Office of National Service had been misleading in trumpeting Clinton's $7.4 billion commitment back in March. Staffers had emphasized the big number when it served them, and hid the cost when it didn't.

The change made a difference to the moderate Republicans. Gunderson and Shays spent the next week working to drum up co-sponsors so that the administration would be able to claim bipartisan support when it unveiled the legislation April 30. Two days before the scheduled announcement in New Orleans, Shays stood behind a desk in his tiny office—junior House Republicans don't get palatial work spaces —with his sleeves rolled up and, on his desk, a list of phone numbers of Republican congressmen.

"Look, is there any issue you've had a hard time with?" he asked a colleague.

Money, the other congressman replied. It's too much money.

"Well, I'm on the budget committee, so I'm very sympathetic to that," Shays assured him. "I've voted for cutting *more* spending," he added. His silver hair, virtually shoulder-length, made him look slightly out of place in the Republican caucus. He was forever having to reestablish his bona fides.

He then whipped out the new weapon the White House had given him. Look, he told the Republican congressman, this program is going to start small and if it doesn't work it will stay small. "I'm not talking billions!" he yelled. "I'm talking four hundred million!" He practically left his feet as he talked into the phone. "That's *very* cost-effective."

"They changed the whole presentation," Shays later explained. "That seven billion may never happen."

Shays and Gunderson would produce a remarkable "Dear Colleague" letter—"National Service: A Republican Idea"—which argued that the White House had used sound conservative principles in fashioning the program.

Segal too began working intensively on Republicans. He had called on the president of the American Red Cross to gain that organization's endorsement. Such a prominent, blue-blood organization could carry real weight on Capitol Hill, especially since its president, Elizabeth Dole, was married to the Senate Republican leader. Segal and Dole discussed the details of the legislation during a private lunch in her office. As aides cleared the china from atop a white linen tablecloth, Segal stressed the reliance of the system on well-established, high-quality nonprofits, like the Red Cross. She seemed receptive, but said she would get back to him with a more specific response. To keep the pressure on, Segal had Richard Schubert, the president of George Bush's Points of Light Foundation, call her. Segal waited anxiously, knowing how important an endorsement from Elizabeth Dole could be.

On April 28 and 29, national service supporters worked overtime to find co-sponsors. Representative Bill Ford had decided that if they could get more than 218 co-sponsors—a majority of the members— by the time the bill was introduced, the legislation would take on an air of inevitability. Ford concentrated on members of the Education and Labor Committee. Representative Dave McCurdy of Oklahoma recruited conservative Democrats and, along with Shays and Gunderson, moderate Republicans. Representatives Major Owens of Brooklyn and John Lewis of Atlanta tried to round up black support. By April

30, there were more than two hundred co-sponsors, including sixteen Republicans, and virtually every member of the Congressional Black Caucus.

Along the way, the White House learned of a dilemma that tested all its skills of political etiquette. McCurdy wanted to be listed as the prime sponsor of the legislation in the House. He had, after all, introduced the DLC plan that had formed the basis of Clinton's proposal, and he'd single-handedly brought in thirty Republicans and moderate Democrats as co-sponsors. This put the White House in a terrible spot. It was grateful to McCurdy for his work, but did not want to irritate Ford, who, as chairman of the Education and Labor Committee, would customarily be the prime sponsor. McCurdy wasn't even on the committee, after all. The question went all the way up to Clinton, who decided it would be extremely unwise to snub Ford. So White House aides told McCurdy he could not be the sponsor.

But Ford wasn't going to let McCurdy go unpunished for his power play. He decided to mess with his head. To demonstrate that it was Bill Ford who decided sponsorship and not some blow-dried DLC congressman like McCurdy, the chairman capriciously threw the honor to Matthew Martinez, the *seventh*-ranking member of the committee. And he chose Martinez over another congressman by flipping a coin.

Preparations in the Senate were not going as well—and that was where Republican support mattered most. Because the Senate has no rules regularly limiting debate, as the House does, any senator can stall legislation by continuing to use debate time. This is, of course, known as a filibuster. The only way to shut off debate is to vote "cloture," a process perfected to stop the anti–civil rights filibusters in the 1960s. Cloture requires sixty votes. There were fifty-six Democrats in the Senate; four Republican co-sponsors should make national service filibuster-proof, Segal figured.

On April 27, just three days before the plan's unveiling, Segal finally met with Senator Nancy Landon Kassebaum. The leader of the charge against direct lending would also be the chief Republican negotiator on national service, yet until that point, neither she nor her staff had been consulted. To bolster his credibility with the Kansas

Republican, Segal brought with him Ray Chambers, the businessman who helped run the Points of Light Foundation, and Nick Lowery, a place kicker on the Kansas City Chiefs who had been volunteering at ONS. (It would not go down as one of history's greatest lobbying moves: to Kassebaum, who wasn't a football fan, Lowery just looked like an unusually large bureaucrat.) Segal expressed his strong desire for bipartisanship, but Kassebaum said she was unlikely to co-sponsor his legislation and quickly changed the subject to direct lending. She told him she had serious problems with the loan reform, and urged that Clinton separate the student-aid and service programs into two pieces of legislation. Direct lending, she warned, would almost surely drag national service down.

Segal feared Kassebaum was right. He had never cared as much about pay-as-you-can loans as national service, and he shared Kassebaum's assessment of the political risks of keeping them linked. Sure, loan reform would be nice, but Segal viewed his sole concern as getting national service passed.

He wanted the bills split. After conferring with House Speaker Thomas Foley and OMB director Leon Panetta, Segal again made the case to Clinton—but this time he used a procedural argument. As a practical matter, Segal reported, it would be impossible to introduce service and loan reform as one piece of legislation because of the peculiar rules governing budget bills. They had no choice but to introduce them separately.

Finally, Clinton agreed. From that point on, the college-loan and national service plans would have separate bills, hearings, markups, and floor fights.

Segal hoped that jettisoning student-aid reform would help get Republican co-sponsors for the service legislation. The most obvious target was David Durenberger of Minnesota, a moderate Republican who had supported service-learning programs in his state's high schools. He had voted for the national service bill of 1990, and had shown willingness in the past to break from his Republican colleagues. Segal had intended to meet with Durenberger on April 1, but the senator had to cancel when he found out he would be indicted the next day on two counts of criminal fraud. Segal and Durenberger managed to have breakfast in the Senate dining room on April 28. Two days later, the senator's policy development director, Jon Schroeder, sent Segal a private memo detailing what it would take to get Durenberger on board. It turned out Durenberger *liked* direct lending, but distrusted Clinton's approach to service. The senator wanted more of an emphasis on "community" over "national" service. Easy fix: Segal changed the name of the legislation on the spot. It would now be the National *and Community* Service Trust Act. Durenberger also worried that national service would replace Pell grants. Segal responded that the administration wanted to increase Pell, too. Durenberger loved service learning; Segal said he couldn't agree more. On Monday, May 3, Durenberger agreed to co-sponsor the legislation.

The White House needed more than Durenberger, though. Segal thought they would be able to get James Jeffords of Vermont and John Chafee of Rhode Island, both liberal Republicans like Durenberger. But the White House wanted at least one *real* Republican.

Their best shot seemed to be Arlen Specter of Pennsylvania. As the chief interrogator of Anita Hill during the Clarence Thomas hearings, Specter had certainly earned the hatred of liberal interest groups and some respect from the conservative wing of his own party. He could bring middle-of-the-road credibility. What's more, Pennsylvania had many active service programs, and its other senator, Harris Wofford, was among the national service's most fervent supporters.

The White House turned to Don Mathis, director of the Pennsylvania Service Corps, which had gained some national attention in February 1993 when it sent twenty-three members to Homestead, Florida, to help rebuild low-income housing destroyed by Hurricane Andrew. A blunt, bearded man who talked in a sarcastic monotone, Mathis called an old friend who used to work for Specter and asked him to put in a good word. "How many pins could we put on a map of Pennsylvania to show service programs in the state?" the friend asked. "And how many more could we put on if national service passed?" Mathis said he could show that fifty-five of Pennsylvania's sixty-seven counties could benefit.

Mathis then called a Specter aide, who peppered him with questions, all about the bill's effect on Pennsylvania: What programs existed in the state now? How could they be expanded under Clinton's plan? How would Specter's support for such programs pay off for

Pennsylvania? Mathis had answers for all of them. That morning, Ted Kennedy cornered Specter at a Senate Judiciary Committee hearing and Wofford talked to him on the floor of the Senate. By the end of the day, Specter called Kennedy and asked to be listed as a co-sponsor.

———

The Office of National Service was in chaos leading up to the proposal's unveiling. For starters, it needed a date. The White House had promised all along that, given the importance of national service, the program would be announced in the first one hundred days. The only problem was that the administration wanted to unveil all of its other essential priorities within the first one hundred days, too. Campaign-finance reform was scheduled to go, and welfare-reform advocates wanted to make a splash. It took quite a bit of wrangling for Segal to get April 30, the one hundredth day, as the date for Clinton's big speech. They decided to do it in New Orleans to coincide with the Democratic Leadership Council's conference—as a way of emphasizing the plan's roots at the DLC. The date and location did turn out to be problematic for Jack Lew, who needed to attend this event but, as an orthodox Jew, had to be home in Washington by sunset that day for Sabbath. Segal arranged for Lew to fly back on Air Force One so he could be back in time.

Then there were questions of packaging. A few days before the announcement, Gene Sperling, deputy director of the National Economic Council, had seen the press materials put together by the ONS. He noticed the materials placed little emphasis on the student-aid reform, and didn't explain the pay-as-you-can loans in a user-friendly way. He feared that once again the press would miss the importance of that feature of the program. On April 28, Sperling dashed off a memo to Stephanopoulos, Kunin, Galston, and David Dreyer, the deputy communications director who was in charge of message management for the event. "The President's income-contingent loan program is one of our most important domestic initiatives," Sperling wrote. "While the discretionary domestic caps put pressure on all of our initiatives, the income-contingent loan proposal is our one major opportunity for the President to offer a tangible benefit to every middle-class and poor family while also demonstrating our commitment to economic growth through investing in people. Therefore we must ensure that this is presented in the most visible, comprehensive and memorable fashion."

He had several practical suggestions for this presentation: It should include a summary sheet with five or six key bullets, an example of how the loans would work "for John and Jane Average," and a list of common questions and answers ("What will happen if a rich person borrows and then never works?"). Also, there should be "a few top people with credibility in Congress and the education community ready to take calls from reporters." Most important, the loan program needed a name—a catchy title that would make it easily recognizable and "associated with the President."

"I don't care what it is, but it needs something," Sperling wrote urgently. The existing term, *income-contingent loans,* was "an awful and bureaucratic sounding term." He suggested referring to them as individual "accounts."

The night before the event, Sperling walked around the cramped offices of the west wing of the White House, polling friends on the name. He suggested "Invest Accounts" to George Stephanopoulos, who thought they had overused the term *invest* while promoting the president's budget. Sperling came up with "EXCel Accounts" (EX-Cellence in Education), but other staffers thought that the capital letters looked too cute. They agreed on "Excel Accounts."

Around the same time, a squabble had broken out anew within the White House over the relative importance of student aid versus national service. Political consultant Mandy Grunwald and pollster Stan Greenberg had come to believe the proposal's popularity stemmed from its ability to tap into middle-class anxiety about college costs. Grunwald and Greenberg went directly to Clinton. They urged that, in unveiling the proposal in New Orleans, he ought to stress college access whenever possible. "For most Americans, having access to college is a much more powerful concept," Greenberg said. Stephanopoulos cautioned against overemphasizing college access, since no one knew how much the legislation would actually help students and, consequently, they needed to be somewhat careful about the grandiosity of claims. Privately, Segal and Rick Allen tried to convince Greenberg that service was really at the heart of the president's proposal. But

Greenberg was not persuaded. "The [polling] data supported the power of loans," he said later. Greenberg took his case to David Dreyer, who agreed. To the consternation of the ONS staff, he ordered up an enormous banner to stretch the entire wall of the gymnasium at the unveiling, declaring, SERVICE MEANS EDUCATIONAL OPPORTUNITY.

By Friday morning, April 30, despite the pandemonium, everything seemed finally to have come together. They had a good site for the event, a large auditorium at the University of New Orleans. The press packet was brimming with clear, helpful information about "the national service trust," the "Excel Accounts," and the "One-Stop Direct Student Loans." There were separate fact sheets on each component, a nine-page summary of the national service proposal, and a twenty-six-page section-by-section analysis of the legislation. To make sure there weren't any points of confusion, Galston and Jack Lew flew to New Orleans on the press plane to answer questions.

There was only one remaining problem with this glorious one-hundredth-day-in-office event.

April 30 was the 101st day.

10

The Grass Roots

Joe Clayton was eating dinner in an Italian restaurant on Capitol Hill when he saw his opportunity. Two tables away sat Bob Kerrey of Nebraska—a key senator in student-aid politics. The thirty-one-year-old Clayton was director of government affairs for Dan Cheever's American Student Assistance Corporation, which had stepped up its efforts to block direct lending. Clayton already planned, of course, to give a copy of the Coalition for Student Loan Reform's alternative plan to one of Kerrey's staffers, but the odds of that aide telling Kerrey about it, let alone getting him to read it, were slim. Still, the idea of interrupting Kerrey's dinner to give him a lobbying document seemed unconscionably rude. Midway through the meal, Clayton got a break.

Kerrey visited the men's room.

Clayton thought for an instant about passing it to him over the urinal—what a great story that would make—but quickly discarded the idea as unseemly. So he waited outside the john. When Kerrey emerged, Clayton introduced himself and handed Kerrey a press kit containing a copy of the neatly printed twenty-page plan.

The student-aid fight showcased all the colorful species of lobbyists in the special-interest aviary. There were the young ex–Capitol Hill aides like Clayton; former Clinton insiders peddling their expertise, such as Jerry Hultin of Sallie Mae; special-constituency lobbyists like Bud Blakey, who represented black colleges; and former politicians like Bill Gray.

In 1993, fifteen thousand people worked as lobbyists; many had passed through the "revolving door" from government to the private sector. This oft-noted practice is truly one of the most significant forces in Washington. The press has reported odious examples of experts cashing in on friendships or knowledge of the system (as in the case of a U.S. trade representative who went to work for the Japanese government). While this certainly happens, the higher-education community involved in the student-aid reform battle illustrates a subtler variant of the phenomenon—what might be called the "cousins-marrying syndrome."

There's often something to be said for cousins marrying. They have similar backgrounds, overlapping guest lists for the wedding, etc. But society discourages inbreeding because it spawns kids with three eyeballs. The problem with a community like higher education—where staff moves regularly from the Hill to the Department of Education to trade associations—is not corruption but, potentially, stale thinking and stasis. Objectivity in policymaking becomes more difficult. For instance, is the Hill staffer who knows he some day wants to work for the college association going to deny it money in the legislative process? Does the Education Department staffer who knows he'll be having drinks at the Front Page that Tuesday night with the college lobbyists want to sign off on a policy that will hurt the organization represented by his pal near the nachos? Was the department so focused on direct lending—as opposed to pay-as-you-can loans—because the higher-ed lobbyists were? And vice versa? Were they living in an echo chamber, hearing only their own voices?

The industry lobbyists, meanwhile, were meeting regularly themselves under the auspices of John Dean. But these meetings tended to illustrate the divisions within their ranks as much as anything. Sallie Mae's Hough came to conclude that they mostly helped the lobbyists run the meter on their clients. "They all got in a room, shared information, and went back and called their clients to prove they had this great depth of knowledge when actually they didn't know much," he said. Hough had hit upon another phenomenon of modern lobbying: lobbyists milking their clients as well as the taxpayers.

The most significant lobbying trend of the 1990s, however, is not the revolving door or influence peddling or the cousins-marrying syndrome. It is organized grassroots lobbying. The phrase conjures up images of Ralph Nader interns in cutoffs and solar energy T-shirts pounding on doors during their summer vacations; but in the 1980s and 1990s, private industry borrowed the techniques pioneered by environmental and public-interest activists to generate massive issue-oriented political campaigns. Even big Washington lobbying firms, such as Patton Boggs & Blow, or Hill and Knowlton, have developed "grassroots capabilities."

Primitive grassroots campaigns involve mobilizing the members of a group, as when the Consumer Bankers Association sent alerts to banks on the Kassebaum amendment. But many grassroots campaigns focus on getting credible, disinterested third parties to lobby for the client—a political bank shot. The major players in the student-aid industry realized they had little credibility, so they had others make their case for them. Who had the most credibility? Financial aid administrators, the grunt-level men and women who actually gave out the aid, dealt with students, and would have to implement a direct lending system. Sallie Mae sent "self-tutorials" to three thousand schools, so that they could estimate how much aid reform would harm their colleges and universities. Teams of technical experts visited dozens of schools and held misleading seminars with one thousand financial aid officers on the effects of direct lending. They whipped out studies they'd done that, lo and behold, determined that colleges would have to hire extra staff, buy computers, open new offices—at an average cost of $219,000 per year.

The blitz worked. On March 24, the Iowa Association of Student Financial Aid Administrators wrote colleagues, urging them to oppose full-blown direct lending. On March 31, the Florida aid officers joined them, and soon so did their colleagues from Kansas. By April 6, the Southern Association of Student Financial Aid Administrators had endorsed a go-slow approach on behalf of officers in nine Southern states. Joe Russo, the financial aid director at the University of Notre Dame, circulated a daunting paper called "Ninety-five Questions to Help Plan the Direct Loan Program." The financial aid director at the University of California–San Diego, Tom Rutter, launched an aggressive campaign to enlist fellow officers in opposition; he eventually signed up more than one hundred, from schools ranging from Southern Methodist University to the Baptist Bible College in Missouri. In many cases, the financial aid administrator at a college opposed full-blown direct lending, while the president of the same school supported it. Even families were divided. Joe Paul Case, the financial aid director at Amherst College, wrote a letter strongly supporting direct lending, while his wife, Judy Case, who had the same job at the University of Massachusetts Medical School, fought against it.

What would prompt the lowly financial aid officer to buck the president of his or her own school? College lobbyists grumbled that it was a case of simple corruption: the aid officers had been bought off by Sallie Mae, the guaranty agencies, and the banks, which often helped finance the aid officers' annual conventions. To prove that claim, the lobbyists faxed around leaflets showing that USA Group, the largest guaranty agency, sponsored the "Fiesta of Spicy Cuisine & Mariachi Music" at a San Antonio convention of aid administrators. Tom Rutter didn't help his cause by faxing a slew of letters from Sallie Mae's offices in San Francisco, with the result that some grassroots missives from the "independent" aid administrators arrived in legislators' offices with "Sallie Mae" printed in tiny letters along the top.

The aid officers had developed loyalty to the industry players for practical reasons. As colleges cut financial aid office budgets, it was Sallie Mae and the banks that often came to the rescue with new computer software and training programs. The aid officers looked at it this way: Maybe direct lending would work, maybe it wouldn't. But if it didn't, the results would be catastrophic for students and schools, and aid officers would be the ones to get blamed—and this time they wouldn't have Sallie Mae to back them up.

The industry efforts to recruit credible allies reached a high point, or actually a low point, in May 1993, when the National Consumers League issued a report criticizing direct lending. When the report hit Bob Shireman's desk in Senator Simon's office, he was speechless. Why would NCL—a respected consumer group—be opposed to, or even care about, direct lending? Shireman immediately called the group's director, Linda Golodner. He asked how she had become interested in the subject. She told him she'd become alarmed after hearing the concerns of a much-admired liberal group—the United Negro College Fund. Trying not to leap out of his chair, Shireman asked slowly if she remembered the names of any of the lobbyists who had visited from the United Negro College Fund.

"Well, yes," she said. "Bud Blakey."

As Shireman had suspected. Do you realize, he asked gently, that Blakey is a law partner at Clohan & Dean, the firm representing the banks, which are opposed to direct lending? Golodner seemed stunned. She hadn't. In the end, because of Shireman's intervention, the National Consumers League never did the mass mailing of its report.

This was not the only time that an interest group's effort to recruit surrogates backfired. In April, ads began appearing in college newspapers around Ohio from a group called Students for Loan Reform. THE GOVERNMENT NEVER ASKED FOR YOUR OPINION, BUT DON'T LET THAT STOP YOU, said the headline. The ad stated that the new loan program "could mean increased tuition, reduced student programs, and more government red tape. (Maybe even the IRS collecting our loans.) What's worse, if the program fails, you could be without means of getting money for college." The ad listed an 800 number; students who called it were patched immediately through to their senators' offices. It turned out that Students for Loan Reform was set up and financed by the Ohio Student Loan Corporation, the secondary market in Ohio, and one of John Dean's clients.

Around the same time, Shireman heard that a student was claiming to have been paid by Sallie Mae to lobby against direct lending. Shireman quickly contacted the young man, a University of Wisconsin–Madison student named Robert Kraig. Sensing a golden opportunity to make industry lobbying the issue once again, Simon's aide David Carle organized a May 25 press conference featuring Madeleine Kunin, several congressmen, and, of course, Robert Kraig. As visuals for the cameras, they set up enormous posters that listed the names of Washington lobbying firms representing the loan industry, and compared the compensation of the top five Sallie Mae officials to that of the president of the United States.

Kraig told his story, which, it turned out, was not exactly in a league with Iran-Contra. He and another student had been flown to Washington by Sallie Mae; there, they had met with the company's executives, who briefed them on direct lending. Nonetheless, legislators moved before the bundle of microphones, attacked the lobbyists, and bemoaned their own underdog status. "We can't possibly compete with this onslaught," said Representative Rob Andrews of New Jersey, as a half dozen TV cameras recorded his words. "All we can offer is lower interest rates and better access." Simon pointed to the poster that used tall piles of green coins to symbolize the pay of various Sallie Mae executives, and added, in his goofy baritone, "That little coin at the bottom is for the president of the United States."

There was one embarrassing moment. After Simon and company had attacked Sallie Mae for flying the student to Washington to lobby, one reporter asked how this young man had been able to afford to attend the press conference. The answer was that the Senate Labor and Human Resources Committee had flown him out to testify at a hearing that day—at Simon's request and taxpayers' expense. Few reporters noticed the irony, and again they got great press coverage. The brilliance—and craftiness—of the Simon team's strategy was clear: to orchestrate a massive lobbying campaign attacking the industry for massive lobbying.

Shireman knew that the best way to counter the industry's grassroots efforts was to organize his own. In the modern legislative process, senators regularly push their own legislative agendas by generating political activity in the states of other senators. They realize that their colleagues would more likely listen to constituents than to a senatorial golf buddy. On May 26, Shireman brought a dozen key education lobbyists to a conference room in the Dirksen Senate Office Building to plot how to "reach" each senator.

"Let's go through the Senate Democrats by state," Shireman began. "Heflin and Shelby. I met with Heflin's staff a few days ago. He's close to the banks in his state. He's worth some contacts. Does anyone have any ideas?"

"There are two black colleges in Alabama," said Joyce Payne of the National Association of State Universities and Land-Grant Colleges (NASULGC), which represents many large state universities, including public Historically Black Colleges. Payne had taken on the job of counteracting the influence of the United Negro College Fund, which represented private black schools.

Shireman nodded and took notes, recording the interests of each senator. On his green index card for Senator Herb Kohl of Wisconsin, for instance, he noted a May 18 conversation he'd had with staffer Sherry Hayes: "Don't assume he'll support. Deficit and debt issues are key. He's a fiscal conservative." About John Glenn, Shireman noted: "So many lobbyists and lawyers from all over Ohio; campaign manager types." About Frank Lautenberg of New Jersey: "PS should talk to him @ luncheon or grab on floor."

Shireman continued: "DeConcini in Arizona?"

This time the report came from Tony Calandro at the Career College Association, which represented trade schools. He explained that DeConcini's "biggest concern is whether the department can handle this." The CCA, he reported, would do "some limited advertising and PR in Arizona" to light a fire under DeConcini.

"The three public schools in the state are opposed to direct lending," reported Sean Tipton from NASULGC. "But," he added dryly, "we've convinced them to keep quiet."

"Wendell Ford of Kentucky," Shireman continued. "Sallie Mae is putting a lot of pressure on him. We'll keep working that. That's not in the bag. Breaux [of Louisiana] is very close. His staff people sound positive."

Nick Littlefield of Kennedy's staff cut in impatiently. "Yeah, but unless we've heard from *him* it doesn't count."

"Mikulski of Maryland," Shireman continued, trying to ignore Littlefield's critical interjections. "You can't tell by talking to her staffers."

"We've got a meeting with twenty Maryland college presidents," said Jane Wellman, the representative from the private colleges, the National Association of Independent Colleges and Universities, or NAICU.

But Shireman knew that one must take the utmost care when pushing a senator's buttons. He warned Wellman not to have Johns Hopkins University take a lead in the effort. "She doesn't like them," he said. "She likes Villa Julie or something," he added, referring to a small community college in Stevenson, Maryland. "Is Villa Julie going to be there?"

"Yes. We're getting the dinky ones to call her," Wellman assured him.

Shireman continued down his list. "Bingaman. He's another unpredictable one."

Suzanne Ramos from Kennedy's staff pointed out that there might be a way of getting Hispanic pressure on Jeff Bingaman, who represents New Mexico. "If HACU is in on this," she says, referring to the Hispanic Association of Colleges and Universities, "we may want them to call Bingaman too."

Tipton from NASULGC reported that there was an internal fight at the University of Virginia over the school's position. The financial aid officer wanted to oppose direct lending, but the school's lobbyist wanted to support it. "I talked to the government-relations person, and his full-time job is quashing the financial aid officer," he said.

Leahy of Vermont. "Put him down for a Kunin contact," Shireman said, making a note on the index card.

"The Culinary Institute has hosted a number of dinner fund-raisers for him," reported Calandro of the Career College Association. "We'll call him."

At one point, Senator Simon entered the room, wearing a red bow tie, and sat next to Shireman. "I'm glad you're doing this," Simon said. "We have to understand that our friends on the other side are doing the same."

Simon rattled off a few suggestions on how to pressure particular senators. He suggested getting Bill Danforth, president of the Washington University in Saint Louis, to call his brother, John Danforth, the Republican senator from Missouri. "I know him real well," Simon said, "but it really ought to come from you [at the colleges]. The more grass roots you can generate, the better."

With his anachronistic gait and his aw-shucks speaking style, Simon seemed pure self-caricature. Yet Simon is no dope. He won his Senate seat in part because his farm-boy integrity immunized him from the inevitable suspicions that he was beholden to the Chicago Democratic machine. Similarly, he could get away with slashing attacks against the banks because he had such a squeaky-clean image.

Of all the higher-education groups, the most sophisticated at lobbying was the Career College Association, which represented the trade schools. CCA emphasized bank-shot lobbying: it got the companies that *hired* their students to contact legislators in support of direct lending. At the CCA's request, McDonnell-Douglas and USAir wrote to senators in support of direct lending.

Most importantly, CCA also made a conscious effort to educate its own members on *how* to lobby. In fact, they held a seminar at their national conference in Washington on May 12. Of course, *sophisticated* might not have been the first word that would come to mind when watching the warm-up exercise for this tutoring session. It consisted of a group of businessmen walking around a room with index cards taped to their backs, playing "Who Am I?"

"Am I, sort of, an organization?" Dave Goehring of the New Castle School of Trades in Pulaski, Pennsylvania, asked, trying gamely to catch the spirit of the exercise. His goal was to guess the vocabulary word on his own back by asking questions of other grumpy businessmen.

The man he was speaking to shook his head.

"Am I part of the legislative process?" persisted Goehring, whose school trains people to be auto mechanics and air-conditioner repairmen.

"No, but you're around all the time," the other man said. After a few minutes, one of the young former congressional staffers running the workshop called time, and Goehring saw that his word was *lobbying*.

The CCA staff then began to teach what that word meant. "One way of having influence, used to be paying one person to get what you want," Phillip Robinson, CCA's Southern coordinator, explained to the group. "That day is over. CCA is now working from the grassroots level up."

Lesson number one of "How to Be a Lobbyist": Build relationships with the members of Congress and their staffs. "The key is serving *their* needs," explained Margo Pave, another CCA staffer. "If you call and say, 'Oh my God, Congressman—help!' that won't work." Pave suggested that her listeners sit on advisory committees set up by the legislator; attend town hall meetings; host coffees with the congressperson and other local dignitaries; bring them on a tour of the school—anything to make themselves known to the legislator.

And it doesn't hurt to turn your school into a political machine at the disposal of the politician. "We've turned over our facilities as phone banks around Election Day to our congressman, and we provided students who were interested" to help make phone calls, recalled Jan Friedheim, who owns a string of secretarial schools in Dallas. "And we volunteered students to put out yard signs—just a little thing, but it really helps."

After the workshop, the school owners fanned out to practice what they'd learned on real-life legislators. One group met with Senator Specter of Pennsylvania. "If we could share with you what this means to students," said Deborah Dunn of the Restaurant School in Philadelphia. Then, remembering the key phrase, she added, "Students in Pennsylvania." She and other businessmen told Specter how local banks refused to give loans to their students. "We don't think that's fair," Dunn said.

To reinforce the effect of the visit, Dunn mobilized the students at the Restaurant School. Seventeen men and women dressed in white chef outfits gathered a few weeks later in a classroom to listen to her call to activism. Standing below an enormous overhead mirror—slanted down from the ceiling so students in regular classes could see what the instructor was cooking on the stove—Dunn gave her pitch. "President Clinton has come up with a plan called the direct lending program. It means everything will go through the schools. It may mean one hundred to one hundred fifty more dollars for you. . . . We want direct lending to pass because you guys will be out in the cold otherwise."

"Are you suggesting the banks will stop lending?" one student asked.

"From everything we've seen in the past, it will not surprise me if they stopped lending. . . . The bankers spend a lot of money to lobby, *a lot* of money to lobby."

She urged the students to fill out postcards to Specter—"that's S-P-E-C-T-E-R"—right then and there if they wanted to preserve their aid. And in case the self-interest appeal didn't work, Dunn offered a more altruistic motive. "When you write to your senators, you're assisting the people behind you, the student who comes next."

"It is," she said, "one of those really community-minded things."

11

Ford's Pooch and Pell's Spine

On May 11, students at Fenton High School in suburban Chicago witnessed the president of the United States, leader of the free world, attacking some obscure entity called Sallie Mae. "No sooner had I even mentioned changing this system than Congress was deluged with lobbyists," Clinton said, drawing on information provided by Simon. "The biggest organization, Sallie Mae, alone, that's supposed to be in the business of helping you get money to go to college, has already hired seven of the most powerful lobbyists in Washington to try to stop this process from changing." Actually, the briefing material stated that the financial-aid industry as a whole had hired seven powerful lobbyists. Clinton may have been anxious about embracing direct lending, but once he made the decision to go with it, he did not hold back.

Why would the president want to get so far into the muck on direct lending? One reason was H. Ross Perot. This issue gave Clinton an opportunity to bash a special-interest group, a way to appeal to discontented anti-Washington Perot voters. "With direct lending, you have both conflicts and villains," one White House political aide said. "Sallie Mae and the banks—the 'money changers in the temple'—are the villains."

But there was a more immediate reason. The House Education and Labor Committee was scheduled to mark up the student-aid legislation the next day, and, amazingly, Clinton didn't have the votes.

Education Department strategists had assumed they would run into trouble in the Senate—they had almost lost on the Kassebaum amendment, after all—but were counting on a dunk in the House, and a 360-degree, windmill slam dunk in the committee. But on May 11, the committee's top staffer, Tom Wolanin, counted only seventeen solid Democrats. Clinton needed twenty-two. The Republicans would vote as a block against direct lending just to give the president a defeat. A loss in this committee would be disastrous for Clinton. If direct lending went down, so would pay-as-you-can loans, and so would IRS collection.

———————

Bill Ford, the chairman of the committee, seemed like an unlikely savior. A longtime protector of the banks, he was in fact married to a former Sallie Mae lobbyist—which put him literally in bed with the agency. Ford also seemed temperamentally at odds with the new hyperempathetic president. A former labor lawyer elected in LBJ's 1964 landslide, Ford is gruff, sharp-tongued, and sometimes vindictive. But Ford had taken a liking to the new president, in part because of six campaign visits by Clinton to his southeast-Michigan blue-collar district. Ford won by just seven percentage points in 1992, and credits Clinton with helping him win, particularly in the University of Michigan area of Ann Arbor. Ford loved to tell about Clinton's first speech to the 256-member Democratic caucus, when the president-elect called on each person by name. "He feels very smitten," Wolanin said. "Clinton's a politician's politician." Early in the administration, Ford told Riley that he would be Clinton's footsoldier on direct lending and national service. "You hum a few bars, and we'll write it for you," Ford had said.

The Department of Education did give Ford a solid piece of legislation with which to work. Once the careerists had become engaged, they came through for Riley and Kunin. They had assuaged the concerns of small schools by allowing banks or other companies to run the direct lending program for the colleges—interview the students, disburse the loans, keep track of the payments. The legislation also offered students several new repayment options for their loans. A student could start with the pay-as-you-can formula but then switch to a regular fixed-payment plan once he or she earned more income. Or the student could choose a plan designed around smaller initial payments, with larger ones coming at a later date.

Ford and the administration quietly revised the legislation to avoid controversy and ease passage. Buried on page 59 of the "chairman's mark" was a one-sentence change that almost no one on the committee noticed, and no one in the press reported—yet it signaled one of the most significant retreats of the entire legislative process. A few weeks before the markup, the staff of the House Ways and Means Committee, which oversees the IRS, had read the Clinton administration's proposal for IRS collection, and, to use a common legislative expression, freaked out. The Ways and Means staff informed Ford and the White House that if anyone was going to change the responsibilities of the IRS, it would be Ways and Means, thank you very much. The administration could feel free to do "a study," and if the study favored IRS collection, the White House could make a recommendation to Congress. Then, and only then, the Ways and Means Committee would decide. The White House backed down quickly. "It was made very clear to us that the opposition to going farther was staunch and unlikely to be moved by acts of persuasion," Bill Galston said. "It sounded awfully convincing to me."

The problem was that the White House was relying on Ways and Means chairman Dan Rostenkowski to push through much of Clinton's controversial economic plan. White House staffers didn't feel that they could butt heads with him over something this small, so they agreed to the change. "We had to make a cost benefit judgment on pressing this, given the perilous state of the economic program," Galston said later. "Remember the atmosphere at this time: the fate of the administration was hanging in the balance." While that is true, neither Galston nor anyone else in the White House even raised the issue with Rostenkowski. Ford's Education and Labor Committee was happy to drop the provision too, fearing—in the tradition of petty jurisdictional feuds—that if Ways and Means got involved, it would eat the whole national service–student loan enchilada.

Galston felt they could probably implement pay-as-you-can loans anyway by having the IRS share borrower income information with the Education Department or some other entity doing the collecting. But congressional advocates believed direct IRS involvement was crucial. They argued that the IRS cannot give graduates' income information to private contractors without breaking privacy laws. And the technique promised by Clinton in the campaign—some kind of automatic withholding—could only be pulled off by the IRS. "It was a lousy cave-in," said Joe Flader, staff aide to Representative Tom Petri, a Republican congressman who had long pushed for pay-as-you-can loans. "This study is a pathetic retreat on a crucial element of the whole thing."

The administration's direct lending plan had applied almost all of the savings to the deficit, making it hard to cast the plan as "pro-student." Wolanin, a rumpled, taciturn former political science professor, had been doing student aid for twenty years and knew how to solve that problem. Sitting at his desk in the Rayburn House Office Building, periodically lighting a well-worn pipe, Wolanin went through the legislation; he nipped, tucked, and found roughly 100 million dollars in extra savings. He gave most of it back to students in the form of a few hundred dollars off the fee they pay when they get the loan.

Even with these adjustments—the weakened IRS provision, the extra savings to students—Ford still feared he might lose. So he readied two bold tactics. He gave the Democrats on his committee near-total political "cover" by agreeing to bring the controversial bill to a voice vote rather than a member-by-member roll call. There would be no record of how anyone voted. In the unlikely event that a congressman was attacked back home for supporting direct lending, he or she could simply deny it; there'd be no proof otherwise.

The second idea came from Rob Andrews, a junior member of the committee from New Jersey, who had written a direct lending proposal the previous year. Smart, aggressive, and media-savvy, Andrews was typical of the modern breed of young congressmen who accumulated influence before gaining seniority. Working with Ford, he devised a plan to put the banks on the defensive. The financial players had begun offering alternatives to direct lending, but Andrews figured they were creating a trap for themselves. The banks had proposed cuts in their own subsidies to save the federal government money—which meant they were implicitly conceding tremendous waste in the student-loan system. "Either they're wrong now, or were wrong then," Andrews said.

He proposed a phase-in of direct lending *and* a cut in the subsidies for loans already on the books—the worst of both worlds for the industry. What's more, Andrews prepared to offer a massive tax on the industry as restitution for its past gouging. To seed panic, he leaked word of the idea to a reporter for *Education Daily,* and, by Tuesday "rumors" were shooting around the lobbying community. They had the desired effect.

"It doesn't say much about Rob Andrews's qualities as a human being," said one enraged banking lobbyist. "It's just mean-spirited."

In the weeks before the May 12 markup—at which the committee would actually amend and decide whether to approve the legislation —the administration intensively lobbied the committee. Each time Wolanin heard about a wavering congressman, he passed the information on to the department, which was holding weekly strategy sessions. After assessing the intelligence, the department and congressional staff would decide which members needed a visit from Madeleine Kunin and who needed to be contacted by a technical staffer. Clinton's speech in Chicago also helped. "Rumors had been floating around that Clinton really didn't care about direct loans—he cared about national service," Wolanin said. "To have him take on the bad guys certainly dispelled any such suspicions."

The day of the markup, Clinton's allies girded for battle. Wolanin had his notes about the extra savings to students. Ford had his voice-vote plan. Andrews was ready to go with his scare amendment. The strategy: If the Republicans offered an alternative to direct lending, Andrews would offer the bank-bashing tax.

When Andrews walked in to the Education and Labor cloak room a few minutes before markup, clutching his preprinted amendments, he was pumped.

"Withdraw your amendments," Ford told him.

Andrews was stunned and a bit disappointed, like an adrenergic athlete who's discovered the other team has forfeited.

Ford explained that, in the previous twenty-four hours, the Republican opposition had fallen apart. Representative Bill Goodling, the ranking Republican, had been undermined by bickering within the financial aid industry over whose subsidies should get cut the most. What Goodling didn't tell Ford was that the Andrews strategy had worked. The Republican had figured that if he offered his plan, he would lose; that would prompt Andrews to offer the industry-bashing amendment—which would win. The industry would be better off if Goodling held his tongue.

The hearing room was packed with lobbyists from both sides of the issue. As at many big markups, the hallway looked like a box office the night before Grateful Dead tickets go on sale. Many of the lobbyists had hired place-holder services that send bike couriers or college students to get in line in the wee hours of the morning. The couriers stand in the congressional hallways, and, a few minutes before the event begins, they are replaced by freshly shaven men with fine leather briefcases, and perfectly coiffed women with expensive silk business suits and cellular phones.

After Goodling leveled some harsh criticism at what he deemed the phony savings estimates of direct lending, Ford took the microphone and gave a stunning "confession." "As I have talked to people about this program," Ford said, starting quietly and gradually increasing his volume, "I was forced to admit that nobody on this committee had more to do with getting us into that mess than the present chairman. The same people that are out there condemning this committee now, came crying to us every time somebody wanted to cut the cost of the program at their expense—and we protected them. We spent a whole decade piling on bribe after bribe after bribe.

"We did not start out here to create a banking system," he exclaimed. "We started out to find a way to help young people to go to college."

A few minutes later, it was all over. "All in favor say aye," Ford said. "All opposed say nay. In the opinion of the chair, the ayes have it, and the motion is agreed to."

The president's loan reform had taken another crucial step forward. Still, the opposition had shown itself, once again, to be formidable, and had come close to victory when it was supposed to have had no chance.

After the vote, Wolanin went up to Winkie Crigler, one of Sallie Mae's top lobbyists. A classic steel magnolia—simultaneously tough and flirtatious—Crigler's prime job was reconnaissance: to find out who was doing what to whom. Her smile was withering.

"So how many arms did you break?" she asked Wolanin, mockingly jerking her right arm behind her back. Wolanin grumbled. Never losing her wired-tight grin, she pressed Wolanin for information on what to expect next. He grumbled again, noncommittally.

"Oh, come on, Tom, *please*," she said coquettishly. Again he said little, so Crigler abruptly switched gears.

"So how's that big boy of yours?" she asked, referring to Wolanin's new dog. It sounded like small talk. Why, as a matter of fact the dog had chewed through every toy he'd gotten, Wolanin responded. Then Wolanin heard why Crigler had turned to this subject.

"You know, when the chairman's dog is [staying] with me," she said matter-of-factly, "I have that problem, too."

This was Washington lobbying at its most exquisite, where every word is spoken with political intent. "The chairman," Bill Ford, was Wolanin's boss. That Crigler took care of his pooch meant she was close to the Ford family.

Wolanin's interpretation: "Don't fuck with me too much. I know the chairman personally."

————

Dan Cheever at the American Student Assistance Corporation in Boston was fully aware of the loan industry's credibility problem. Several of the key industry players had asked Cheever to be the spokesman for the Coalition for Student Loan Reform, because, as a former college president, he was thought to be the most believable among them. Of course, a spokesman is only as good as his air time. It was the Widmeyer Group's job to get him some. The Washington public-relations firm suggested a classic hook: a public opinion poll. Editors love polls, which provide a simple news peg, and allow them to say that someone or something is winning or losing. Widmeyer paid Penn + Schoen Research to conduct a survey on public attitudes about direct lending. The results were trumpeted in a May 24 news release from the Coalition for Student Loan Reform: MAJORITY OF AMERICAN PUBLIC, EDUCATORS SUPPORT CURRENT COLLEGE LOAN SYSTEM. Such polls will not win a Nobel Prize for their scientific rigor. On issues like this, for which public ignorance is high, the phrasing of the questions basically determines the answers. In this case, only 14 percent of the respondents had even heard about Clinton's loan reform. Yet, the release declared, "By a 68 [to] 8 percent margin, Americans say shifting management of the program to the federal government will mean more bureaucracy." The question that elicited this response had asked whether shifting the program from "the private sector" to "the federal government" would mean more bureaucracy, less bureaucracy, or have no effect. The fact that "the private sector" included a hilariously bureaucratic network of banks, guaranty agencies, and secondary markets—all bankrolled by the federal government—was not mentioned.

There was more "good news" for the industry. "Forty-four percent of Americans think direct lending will make it harder for students to get loans, while 28 percent think it will make it easier." The release didn't disclose that 23 percent believed it would have "no effect." In other words, 51 percent believed direct lending would be better or neutral, while 44 percent thought it would be worse.

Finally, the Coalition for Student Loan Reform reported that "about as many people strongly approve of the IRS's involvement as strongly disapprove, 30 [to] 20 percent respectively." (Only in public-relations land does a three-to-two margin count as "about as many.") But if one added together the "strongly approve" and the "somewhat approve" responses—as most reputable pollsters would—57 percent *favored* IRS collection, while 42 percent disapproved.

Nonetheless, local TV stations loved the poll and used only the numbers cited in the press release. Widmeyer sent the release to stations in key congressional districts, and at least thirty did stories. Channel 5 in Nashville, for example, carried a split-screen interview with Cheever and a local anchorwoman. "Well, a couple of national polls were taken recently on the direct lending system," the anchor stated. "What were the results of those?"

"The results were very supportive of our position," Cheever reported, deadpan. "Seventy-five percent of the American people do not believe that the federal government can run a student-loan program better than the public-private partnership which has worked for thirty years."

The anchor listened thoughtfully on the left side of the screen, and then "asked" Cheever: "Your coalition has an alternative to the government's plan, I see."

After Cheever explained his alternative, the anchor wrapped things up: "Okay. Quickly, is there anything that students or future students themselves can do to make their opinions heard? They're the ones it affects."

"Absolutely. Both bills have some benefits for students but the key issue for students is to make sure their loan funds don't get interrupted because direct lending turns out not to work. So they should call their representatives and senators."

———————

Cheever figured his biggest chance to influence legislation came in the Senate on May 26, when the Labor and Human Resources Committee had scheduled a hearing on student-loan reform. For several days, Cheever, Clayton, and other ASA staffers worked into the evening, preparing testimony to explain why direct lending would fail and how Congress could make the current bank-based system work better. When Cheever arrived in Washington, however, he learned that hearings aren't for persuading—they are shows choreographed by the majority to help its cause. Cheever and the other opponents were placed on the last panel, which came up about three hours into the hearing, after most reporters and all but two senators had left. "The whole process was disgusting. It was like this old eighteenth-century Court of Saint James—a complete show," Cheever said bitterly. "Everyone was doing their special dances, the gavotte and the minuet, a little flick of the fan, a bow—and no one listened. I kept thinking this was our big chance. When I was there I felt so *irrelevant*." The low moment for Cheever was having to politely listen to Senator Paul Wellstone of Minnesota imply that direct lending would solve the problem of students' "selling plasma to pay for books."

Despite the careful scripting, the hearing did produce one dissonant sound: the barely audible statement of the seventy-four-year-old senator from Rhode Island, Claiborne Pell.

Pell mumbles so meekly that many assume he is senile. His gaunt neck makes his threadbare three-piece suits seem two or three sizes too large. While listening to witnesses, he often sits with his mouth open, looking as if he might drool at any moment. His bearing earned him the cruelest nickname in the Senate—"Stillborn Pell." During his 1990 reelection campaign, he prompted questions about his mental competence when he was asked during a television debate what bills he had proposed to benefit Rhode Island, and responded, "I couldn't give you a specific answer. My memory's not as good as it should be."

But Pell chaired the Senate subcommittee on education; the main student-aid grant program bore his name. Other senators might not want Pell managing their reelection campaign, but when it came to education matters, his views did count. Pell was as much a symbol as a senator.

For months, he had been expressing concerns about shifting from a "private sector"–run to a government-run loan system. He knew the current system was complicated, but the bottom line was kids got their loans. In discussions with his top aide, David Evans, he had even considered putting together some sort of alternative to the president's plan. That would have been devastating to Clinton. If Pell came out against direct lending, opponents would immediately have "cover." Democrats with concerns could publicly oppose the White House without being labeled traitors; Republicans could oppose the plan without seeming like partisan obstructionists. The White House knew that Pell had influence, but it assumed he was not the sort to bolt from a newly elected Democratic president. Pell was a sweet, loyal old man, not a rebel.

Not everyone was so optimistic. Direct lending supporters on the Hill kept imploring Bill Galston to have President Clinton call Pell before the senator put an alternative plan on paper. Once Pell issued a plan, he wouldn't be able to back away. "They've let it slide and let it slide," one frustrated congressional staffer said. "They've ignored our pleas."

But Galston had decided it was premature. He viewed his job as trying to resolve this issue *without* distracting the president from any of his other tasks. The strategy for now would be to have Kunin and other officials stroke Pell continuously.

At the May 26 hearing, though, Pell surprised the White House. Reading from a written statement without looking up, Pell said, "We cannot and should not move from one program to another until we are sure we have all the safeguards in place to protect student accessibility to loans."

"Students and families," he added, softly, "simply cannot be put at risk."

Direct lending advocates were stunned at the strength of Pell's statement. During the first week of June, congressional aides again urged Galston and Kunin to get the president to call Pell. The Senate committee markup was coming up the next week. Again the White House and the Department of Education said no. "A presidential phone call is not something you just *do*," Galston said. "The situation has to be ripe."

On June 2, speaking to financial aid officers in Rhode Island, Evans unveiled the "Pell compromise." It was a lethal threat to the president's initiative—a carefully wrought plan devised by Evans, immediately more credible than any of the industry-crafted proposals. Instead of going to full-blown direct lending, the department would slowly phase in a pilot program until 30 percent of the schools had converted to direct lending. A commission would then study its success and Congress would vote whether to continue. To top it off, Pell's plan included immediate savings for students—a cut of $100 in fees for someone taking out a $2,500 loan. Evans figured he might be able to draw support from other senators, perhaps even Ted Kennedy, if the Pell plan gave something to the students. After focusing for months on blocking Republicans and scores of industry lobbyists, the White House had made a tactical blunder—it failed to manage one genial septuagenarian.

Part of the problem was that the White House had concluded that Pell was a "highly staffed senator," meaning heavily reliant on staff. That was true. Evans, Pell's education aide for sixteen years, was so influential that people sometimes referred to him as "Senator Evans." A balding, flamboyant man with a dog named Ruggles that sat in his office all day, Evans knew what people said about Pell behind his back. He was forever watchful of signs that his boss—and he—weren't being taken seriously.

As soon as Evans unveiled the Pell compromise, intense negotiations began between him, Galston, and Kennedy's equally pugnacious aide, Nick Littlefield. Littlefield had been chief counsel to the Senate Labor and Human Resources Committee for three years, having made a name for himself in the early 1980s by helping to prosecute high-profile drug cases. A fifty-two-year-old with curly brown hair, Littlefield had done a bit of off-Broadway acting and actually had one line in the Broadway production of *Kismet*. Not surprisingly, he brought both a prosecutorial and histrionic bearing to his congressional negotiations.

The talks between Evans and Littlefield proceeded for several days ("I'd pay good money to watch those two work together," one aide said), with each offering small concessions related to the speed of the direct lending phase-in. At Littlefield's suggestion, Galston proposed naming the blue-ribbon study commission after Pell, an idea Evans considered patronizing and proof that the White House viewed his boss as "dumb as a stone." "The assumption was that we were going to cave," Evans said ruefully, "that when push came to shove, Pell would be the good soldier."

Back at the Department of Education, officials tried to determine how to deal with Pell. They could try to beat him, but they might lose on the floor; even if they could win, Kennedy clearly didn't want to "roll" his friend. They could try to cut a deal, but that would be unfair to people like Simon, Durenberger, and Ford, who had gone out on a limb to support direct lending. "We're trying to figure out whether it's time to deal or not," said David Longanecker, the Education Department official in charge of college aid. "I think a lot of Claiborne Pell. He's the father of a lot of these programs. On the other hand, he hasn't been helping us on this program. . . . Pell is clearly being influenced by the existing forces in the program."

Was that it? Was Pell in the pockets of the industry? What was motivating Pell? One widely held theory was that he had been convinced by Paul Quinn, one of Pell's oldest friends and his first administrative assistant back in 1961. Quinn now worked as a counsel for Fleet Bank, the largest student lender in Rhode Island. Quinn did indeed talk to Pell regularly. But former Pell staffer Sarah Flanagan rejected the theory. "Everyone asks me, 'Is it the banks?' No. It's exactly where he has been all along. He's seen this system work for twenty years. It has bugs in it, but the most important thing is, when the students need the checks, they can get them. He is somebody who feels the most important thing in the federal government is student aid. This is, in very many ways, his legacy. When he gets his mind set on something it's not easy to change his mind."

On Thursday, June 3, a week before the Labor Committee's student-aid markup, Kunin called Pell at his estate in Newport, Rhode Island. The next day, Galston called Evans to see if there was any other area for compromise.

Then Evans offered one small hint of flexibility. "Now I haven't talked to Pell about this," Evans said, "but since you think thirty percent is too low, and we think one hundred percent is too high, maybe something in between would work. But I'd have to check with Pell to see if he would mind fifty percent." Evans, in fact, had been willing to go to 50 percent all along, but wanted Kennedy and the White House to think they were forcing a compromise.

After further negotiations, Evans finally agreed that 40 percent of the schools could go to direct lending in the third year, 50 percent "at a minimum" in the fourth. That phrase, *at a minimum*, was key to the deal for the White House, since it basically gave the administration carte blanche to jack up to full direct lending, kicking out the banks without any further congressional approval. (Referring to the unexpected toughness of Pell—and then his decision to give in at a critical point—one direct lending critic said, "He had been fitted for a spine, wore it for a while, and then shed it.")

The night before markup, Evans briefed the staff for Senator Kassebaum and the other key Republican, James Jeffords of Vermont. Both Republicans urged Kennedy, Pell, and Galston to take out *at a minimum*. "Three small words and you'll get bipartisan support," Kassebaum told Galston.

Galston said no. The president wanted to send a strong signal that full direct lending *was going to happen*. Galston feared that, if the commitment weren't rock solid, "various actors would try to sabotage the transition"—in other words, lobby against direct lending for three years. In that case, schools might be reluctant to switch over to direct lending.

The Democratic senators knew the script for the markup that Wednesday morning. Pell would declare victory and Kennedy would praise the compromise. As for Simon, who had gotten most of what he wanted: "We'll say we're disappointed," Shireman confided before-hand. "They'll say they won, and everyone on the floor will feel more comfortable because they'll think we were all forced to make a huge compromise."

At first, the markup proceeded according to plan. Kennedy pledged, "If the program works well, then we can move toward full direct lending." Pell said he still had reservations about direct lending, but that the legislation "no longer required that we go to one-hundred-percent direct lending. That's very important."

Simon dutifully played the unhappy warrior. "Frankly, I'm not completely happy," he said. "Putting in a fifty-percent goal—the lob-bying effort is going to be incredible. Nevertheless, I will support the compromise."

But Kassebaum was not appeased. She again said she wanted to remove those three naughty words—*at a minimum*—and raised the stakes by hinting she would fight them on the Senate floor. And to Shireman's surprise, two Democrats, Chris Dodd of Connecticut and Barbara Mikulski of Maryland, went off-script and criticized the agree-ment. "Some of these cost savings border on those *National Enquirer* ads where you eat twelve Big Macs and lose twenty pounds," Mikulski said. Many schools in her state were quite worried about how direct lending would work, she said.

Simon then made a gross tactical error; he suggested that the Mary-land schools were objecting only because the paid lobbyists were telling them to. Mikulski shook her head angrily, like a mother who'd just heard her children insulted. Simon had broken two cardinal rules of Senate politics: Don't impugn the constituents of a colleague, and don't imply, publicly anyway, that a senator is caving in to special-interest pressure. While Simon's bank-bashing had muted the indus-try's voice, it was beginning to erode his credibility with other senators.

Kennedy adjourned the markup without a vote, and, that after-noon, convened a crucial private meeting of Riley, Kunin, and the Democratic senators to reexamine their position.

Pell quietly made his case for removing the phrase *at a minimum*, to get Kassebaum's and Jeffords's votes. "We have a twenty-year his-tory of bipartisanship," he mumbled. "My own strong advice is to do that."

"But if fifty percent is a cap, then the banks will lobby for three years on it," Simon told his old friend Pell.

Then Dodd spoke, and turned the course of the discussion. "We'll get lobbied *anyway*," he said. "The question is, What do we get *politically?* Nancy [Kassebaum] says the Republicans would go along. President Clinton could use a strong bipartisan victory. And without this, there's a danger of losing on the floor.

"In my view," Dodd concluded adamantly, "take it and run."

Kennedy added that other Democrats had problems with direct lending. And if they're going to have to compromise eventually to get Republicans, he said, "It's better to do it now, so they don't feel we're screwing them—that we only want them when we're in danger." This was an important point to Kennedy, who, despite his reputation as a Democratic brawler, has become effective precisely because he stitches bipartisan coalitions. He had an eye on the Democrats' future legislative agenda—controversial issues like health care and school reform—in which he would need Republican help.

As the group was talking, Littlefield handed Kennedy a piece of paper. It was a vote estimate—and it was not good news. By staff's count, the President would win 50–48, but at least five Democrats were expressing strong anxiety. As each Democrat in the room looked at the list, they realized that, to win on the floor, they would have to enter into a bloody public battle with Kassebaum—a battle they could very well lose. Evans didn't say anything, but his own vote count showed prospects even worse for Clinton: forty-three for direct lending, forty-seven against it, the rest undecided.

As the mood of the group moved toward accepting the Republican offer, Kunin asked what the Clinton administration's posture ought to be. She was particularly concerned about not making Bill Ford think they had abandoned the direct lending position after he had fought for them.

"Your position must be that you support the House position," Simon stated.

"You can live with that?" Kunin asked. The Senate Democrats were, in effect, suggesting that the White House publicly side with the *House* Democrats. Yes, the senators agreed.

Riley then reiterated that a halfway compromise would enable the interest groups to pick away at the program. But without saying so explicitly, he indicated that the senators should feel free to make the deal, and the administration would feel free to express disappointment.

The next morning the committee convened again. Kennedy explained the compromise, emphasizing the fact that Congress would reauthorize higher-education programs anyway in 1997, so they would get another whack at it.

"I believe it puts us irrevocably down the road toward direct lending," Kennedy said diplomatically. "There are others who may have different views." Both sides could claim victory, in other words; it was the model of a good compromise.

The moment of truth came a few seconds later, when the senator from Kansas spoke. "I appreciate the time and effort the chairman and other senators put in," Kassebaum said. "It's really a step forward."

"I am less than enthusiastic, to put it mildly," Simon said, this time sincerely. "Real candidly, I hope in conference we can come closer to the House position."

In the end, all of the Republicans joined with Pell, Dodd, Mikulski, Wofford, and, yes, Paul Simon. Senators Harkin and Wellstone voted no, feeling that the Democrats had given in too much. The final vote was 15–2. Kennedy had compromised significantly, but had won over the Republicans—and would avoid a floor fight.

The one thing as interesting as the debate on direct lending was the total lack of debate on pay-as-you-can loans. All the political and bureaucratic interests pushed toward a massive confrontation over direct lending. What got lost in the process was the part that crowds had loved during the campaign. Not one senator discussed pay-as-you-can loans at the hearings or markups.

Several forces pushed toward keeping the flexible repayment reform out of the legislative spotlight. The more Kunin and her team delved into the details, the more they realized that pay-as-you-can loans could be anything from Marxist redistribution of wealth to hardhearted social Darwinism, depending on how it was set up. Within the Department of Education, there was sharp disagreement over how to construct the program. Some experts wanted to forgive the remainder of a loan after twenty-five years of payments. Others objected that it didn't make sense to wipe out a loan just as the debtor was getting to peak earning years. Kunin believed that students should keep paying for as long as forty-five years. That would mean that Heather Doe could pay well into retirement if she took that job at the Head Start center. Kunin believed it wasn't fair to make the successful—those who pay off before the forgiveness period—subsidize the unsuccessful.

For Kunin, there was some political advantage to offering a less-detailed proposal. Pay-as-you-can loans and IRS collection clearly had potential to stir great controversy. Politically, the department would be better off if everyone focused on direct lending and gave the ad-ministration a blank check on IRS collection and the Excel loans. So the department left all of these issues unresolved in the legislation it submitted to Congress. The bill said merely that the secretary would set up the "Excel program." It did not say what the formula would be, how many years students would have to pay off their loans, or how the department would handle the serious problem of compounding interest.

The ambiguity illustrated the extent to which the department still didn't fully buy into the importance of flexible repayment; it viewed direct lending as a major reform, and pay-as-you-can loans as a minor convenience. In fact, Galston and Sperling, at meeting after meeting, warned department officials that Excel accounts were as important as direct lending. They viewed pay-as-you-can loans as a major reform and direct lending as a minor convenience.

The only substantive legislative discussion about flexible repayment occurred among a few Senate staffers in the week before the markup. Aides to Kassebaum and Jeffords suggested that no student should have to pay off a loan for more than twenty years. Shireman and the other staffers agreed. Although the discussion took about ten minutes, the long-term consequences of the change could be enormous. If Heather Doe graduated with $20,000 in loan debt and then worked as a day-care assistant—earning low wages her entire career—she might pay off only half her debt by year twenty. At that point, under the new plan, the government would retire the remaining $10,000. *Poof* —these Senate Republican staffers had made the reform dramatically more progressive, establishing a much stronger incentive for public service than Clinton's own Department of Education.

There was similar quiet over the issue of IRS collection. Kennedy and Littlefield feared that once the IRS started collecting student loans, the Senate Finance Committee might assert jurisdiction over the entire student-loan program. Senate Labor and Human Resources Committee staffers had searing memories of how the Finance Committee had usurped their domain over the crucial Medicaid and Medicare programs. But Shireman and Durenberger's staffers Susan Heegaard and Jon Schroeder argued that for their bosses, IRS collection was essential. Without it, they said, the pay-as-you-can loans couldn't work. Reluctantly, Kennedy's staff agreed to keep in a stronger provision allowing the administration to establish IRS collection.

On June 25, the full Senate passed the student-aid reform as part of the budget bill. The House had done the same on May 27. The controversial student-aid reform had moved faster than the National Service bill. But the two college-loan bills were very different. The House gave the president 100 percent direct lending; the Senate 50 percent. The House squelched IRS collection; the Senate authorized it. The House left a blank slate on pay-as-you-can loans; the Senate, based on ten minutes of discussion, prescribed a potentially radical plan. The fate of Clinton's student-aid reform would be decided by the House-Senate conferees meeting in July. In large measure, it would be decided by a clash between two formidable men: Representative Bill Ford of Michigan and Senator Edward M. Kennedy of Massachusetts.

12

Action

Banks have their ways of preparing to lobby. Trade-school owners have theirs. And earnest community service groups, well . . .

"Okay, everyone close your eyes," said Ellie Falk Young, a coordinator of Volunteer Maryland!, one of the local service programs that had sprouted up during the 1980s. "I want to do an exercise." Around her sat representatives from forty groups, ranging from the Girl Scouts to City Year to the Delta Service Corps. They were gathered, on May 7, to plot strategy for getting Clinton's national service package through Congress.

Everyone closed their eyes.

"Now think about why you're here on a beautiful Saturday," said Young, a thirty-year-old redhead in a knit sweater and a long Laura Ashley peasant dress. "Think about who you represent and what they're all about. Now say one word that sums up what you're *feeling* now."

"Opportunity," said one participant.

"Blast off," another offered.

"Impact."

There it was: the quintessential nineties moment. Zen and the art of interest-group lobbying. Funneling positive healing energy toward a successful markup. At first glance, it seemed, these service boosters couldn't be more different from the financial industry's advocates. Sallie Mae hired expensive K Street lawyers; the community service groups did stretching exercises "to get people smiling." More striking than the differences were the similarities. When Ross Perot talks of "special-interest groups" the public thinks of tobacco companies, the gun lobby—or banks—and of PAC money bulging from their lobbyists' suit pockets. But being a special interest is less about money than a state of mind. Special interests distort American politics because they impose an ever-narrowing perspective on all policy deliberations.

Consider the fifty state commissions, those powerful "independent" bodies that would distribute two thirds of the money to local service programs. The White House proposed that the commissions have between seven and thirteen members. To assuage the unions, one of the commissioners had to represent labor. To mollify localities worried that the governor might stack the commission, a guaranteed seat would also go to a representative of "local governments." To reassure the community groups that no one type of service would be favored, three slots would be set aside for representatives from "a national service program, such as a youth corps program, a service program for school-age youth, and a program in which older Americans are participants." Add to that the federal representative—*aka* the spy—and you're up to seven preordained slots.

Once the community service groups saw that the White House was passing out favors, they lined up to demand equal treatment. Young People for National Service got a quota for a person between the age of sixteen and twenty-five. Senior citizens groups got a guaranteed slot for an elderly person. State public school officials got the Senate staff to include someone from the "state educational agency." Senator Kennedy's staff inserted language requiring the presence of a service-learning advocate. The commissions now had eleven set-aside slots.

And that was just the Senate. The House had its own interest groups to appease. To balance labor's spot, the House added a business representative. Plus, it required "an individual with expertise in the educational, training, and development needs of youth, particularly disadvantaged youth" and someone from community action agencies (requested by NASCC).

Add up the members demanded by White House, Senate, and House, and you have fourteen groups guaranteed a place on a thirteen-person commission. Oh, and the legislation specified that, of course, each state commission had to be "bipartisan" and "diverse" with respect to "race, ethnicity, age, gender and disability characteristics."

Congressional staffers realized this could be a problem (How many ninety-two-year-old Republican labor organizers *were* there?), but devised a typically courageous solution. They increased the size of the commissions to twenty-five.

Clearly, the sum of legitimate narrow interests does not equal the public interest. Each one of those groups could make a reasonable case for inclusion, but together, they produced a farce. Interest groups concentrate on protecting their memberships and, consequently, rarely advocate a broad agenda. Since there was no National Association of People Who Prefer Small Commissions, no one pressed the case that a twenty-five-member body would no longer be an efficient deliberative panel. While legislators required seats for seniors and labor, they did not include an advocate of racial integration or, for that matter, someone with experience in the military.

While the commission-stacking provided the clearest illustration of an interest-group spiral, it was hardly the only one. It seemed every service group was asking for some special treatment. At one point, Kathleen Selz at NASCC was pushing for a special funding set-aside just for the youth corps in her association; this prompted Shirley Sagawa to write back, "Frankly, we are resisting percentage earmarks because there are so many different interests seeking them."

Two other instances of special-interest influence, however, were most significant. First was the success of the National Governors' Association in shifting the plan's funding—and control—toward states. The second revolved around the crown jewel of the White House's "reinventing-government" effort: the ability to hire and fire at the new national service corporation. Segal and Lew had gotten approval for their flexible employment rules from the two key national unions: the American Federation of Government Employees and the American Federation of State, County and Municipal Employees. But Segal's office made one miscalculation. It assumed that since it had gotten thumbs-up from the national AFSCME union, it also had support from the local unionized employees who worked for ACTION and VISTA in Washington and in field offices around the country. Catherine Milton at the commission had warned Segal that the unions "will force the corporation to absorb" all the ACTION careerists, but Segal apparently had thought she was overreacting.

She wasn't. ACTION workers erupted in anger when they learned that under the president's plan, the new corporation would place the ACTION staff under a new personnel system: managers could hire and fire with relative ease, base salaries on—gasp!—performance, and invoke this strange "flush" rule, kicking people out after five years.

Just two weeks before June 16, the scheduled day for markups in both the House and Senate, the local union representing the ACTION employees began a massive lobbying campaign. At a hearing on ACTION's role, local union president David Gurr told several surprised Education and Labor Committee members, "We were very excited to hear about President Clinton's ideas. When we read the legislation, however, excitement was replaced with gloom." White House allies seated in the audience shook their heads in amazement as Matthew Martinez—the number-one sponsor of the president's legislation—*agreed with Gurr.* "This committee ought to have real grave concerns about this," Martinez said. "I don't know why I didn't realize this." He didn't realize it because the administration, hoping to sneak it through without a fight, had not flagged it for Martinez.

Representative Major Owens, also a prime co-sponsor, asked Gurr, "If you had not been covered by civil service when a hostile administration came in, what would have been the result?"

"I believe many of them would have been fired," Gurr responded.

Over the next two weeks, Gurr mobilized his members. He issued a bulletin warning, "Employees transferring to the new corporation will not have the option to take their civil-service status with them." Another message stated, "If you haven't sent in your letters, do so immediately." More important, Fran Butler of the National Association of Foster Grandparent Program Directors energized a sophisticated network of volunteers and staff from VISTA, the Foster Grandparent Program, and the Older American Volunteer Program. They activated telephone trees to generate hundreds of calls and letters in support of the ACTION employees. Butler had convinced the local programs that the flexible work rules would enable the new corporation to eliminate ACTION and, along with it, the friendly ACTION staffers.

Sagawa was livid. Here they were trying to shepherd through a new service bill against inevitable Republican opposition, and they were getting slammed by, of all people, the employees at the existing service programs! The ACTION employees claimed they supported the bill as a whole, but Sagawa believed that the message they were sending was, "This is a pretty good bill, but it would destroy civilization as we know it." She urged Segal to get the president to appoint a new ACTION director to keep this open rebellion from sabotaging the president's plan. "It seems to me that you must move on the ACTION appointments," she wrote in a private memo. "We really need someone **loyal to the President** (and therefore the ONS agenda) to move the agency into place. . . . All of the problems we have now with the union and disgruntled employees could be dealt with if there were a Director who could bring some discipline to the staff." Time was running out, she warned, to whip ACTION staff into shape.

Segal began to worry that the ACTION issue could sidetrack the entire bill. "The whole thing is very tenuous," one anxious administration official said. "The whole thing could fall apart."

The Senate Government Affairs Committee staff initially sided with the union and scolded White House officials for their naïveté. Kennedy had to convene a meeting, off the floor of the Senate, with Vice President Gore and John Glenn, the chairman of the committee, and several other key senators. "What will it take to get this done?" Gore asked. Glenn talked about the need for an inspector general, audits, and other quality-control mechanisms. The White House quickly agreed. More significantly, the White House threw overboard its idea of a five-year flush, figuring it didn't matter as long as the corporation retained the flexibility to hire and fire.

But the House would not be so easily appeased. Bill Ford, himself staunchly pro-union, turned the issue over to the House Post Office and Civil Service Committee, which he used to chair and which had always protected civil-service rules. The ACTION employees worked the committee hard. "Most people [in the House] do not have an interest in this being a vehicle for reinventing government," said Ford aide Gene Sofer. The initial response from Bill Clay, that committee's chairman, was devastating: The entire corporation would have to work under traditional civil-service rules.

Lew and Segal were despondent. Ford, a close friend of Clay's, set up a meeting in Clay's office on June 10 with key staff and congressmen. "They were the meetings from hell," one participant said. Segal and Lew tried to argue that the change in work rules was essential to their efforts, but ultimately they didn't believe they had much leverage—and Ford could not roll his pal Bill Clay. Clay said he was willing to allow new rules for new employees but insisted on rigid protection of existing employees.

The White House gave in. The four hundred ACTION employees would be guaranteed civil-service safeguards. They could not be fired or reassigned without going through an elaborate civil-service process that can take years. If the corporation wanted to abolish someone's unnecessary job, that employee would retain "bumping rights," and could take the job of one of the new young tigers the corporation had just hired. Only the part of the corporation that absorbed the Commission on National and Community Service would work under the flexible work rules. "The White House just caved," one participant in the talks said. "No backbone."

Segal viewed the concession not as cowardice, but as shrewd pragmatism. He always viewed the civil-service reform as nice, but not essential. It was a bargaining chip he was all too happy to give away to move the bill forward. "National service was *not* about reinventing government," Segal explained later. So, with Segal's acquiescence, the House stripped much of the innovation from the legislation.

On June 16, just six days after it had passed the student-aid reform, the Senate Labor and Human Resources Committee marked up the national service legislation. The staffs of Kennedy, Wofford, and the White House had worked intensively on a few Republicans to generate a big win in committee. They had discovered, to their great delight, that the college roommate of Senator Dan Coats of Indiana was Jim Kielsmeier, a key national service advocate in Minneapolis. Coats heard from Kielsmeier as well as from the presidents of Indiana University and the University of Notre Dame. To impress Republican Judd Gregg of New Hampshire, the committee invited to its hearings members of the New Hampshire Service Corps and the CEO of Timberland Shoes, a company based in that state. Gregg and Coats, both conservatives, voted with the Democrats, as did Republicans Durenberger of Minnesota and Jeffords of Vermont. On June 16, the committee voted 11–3 to send to the floor S. 919, the National and Community Service Trust Act of 1993. Kennedy and Wofford got it through without any fundamental attacks on the premises of the legislation. An impressive win.

The White House was not so lucky in the House Education and Labor Committee, which marked up the same day. In addition to putting out the ACTION fires, the administration had to fight off a blizzard of Republican amendments, some of which struck at the core of the president's proposal.

To shore up support among Democrats, Representative Ford and Gene Sofer accepted scores of "friendly" amendments, many designed to appease particular interest groups. Again, the most influential group was the National Association of Service and Conservation Corps, which produced a list of 33 specific legislative changes, mostly designed "to further emphasize low-income participants." With the administration's avoidance of integration issues and NASCC's aggressiveness, the legislation had begun to resemble a classic antipoverty measure instead of a service bill designed to appeal to a broad range of people.

And this was all *before* markup. Representative Bill Goodling of Pennsylvania, the committee's leading Republican, tried to take the bill one bold step further in the antipoverty direction. Since Clinton said this was a student-aid program, why not treat it like a student-aid program? Why not target it to the needy? Goodling proposed applying the same "means test" used for other financial aid programs, so that families with incomes over $70,000 would get few or no benefits.

The Republicans were attacking from the left.

Goodling almost got an endorsement from, of all people, Bill Ford. The liberal chairman was quite sympathetic to Goodling's arguments and, in the weeks before the markup, went through a political calculation of the amendment's merits. "We had to figure out who we'd pick up and who we'd lose," Sofer said later. If Ford agreed to means testing, he could pick up Goodling and maybe some moderate Republicans on the floor. The amendment could also appeal to liberal Democrats, but Ford already *had* them. No gain. On the other hand, he could lose thirty or more moderate or conservative Democrats who wanted the program to attract middle-class kids. Even before he factored in the White House position, Ford leaned against supporting the amendment.

When Eli Segal heard the details of Goodling's idea, he decided it would destroy the program. "I learned in the sixties that when programs become identified as antipoverty programs for a narrow segment of society, they lose their broad-based support," Segal said. The White House this time sent a clear message: no means-testing amendment. Ford would have no choice but to destroy it.

Ford was as improbable a savior on national service as he had been on student-aid reform. Since he arrived in Washington in 1964 on Lyndon Johnson's coattails, Ford had been a traditional labor-union Democrat. He had attacked the original Nunn-McCurdy plan as an assault on the poor, and had even called Bruce Reed during the campaign to scold him about the program's cost. At one point, he had called the DLC bill "Stalinist."

But Ford now viewed his role differently. He was not the leader of some ideological movement, but Bill Clinton's field lieutenant. "I don't know how much the issue of national service resonates," Sofer had said back in March, "but he desperately wants Clinton to succeed." Clinton appealed to Ford's inner politician, and the urge for action, progress, victory.

Clinton seemed to touch something even deeper in Ford. Listening to Ford talk later about means testing, one got the sense that his switch was perhaps not entirely political. He talked about how he had left the auto assembly line during World War II to go into the navy, where he had met people of many different backgrounds; how he had gone to college on the GI Bill and discovered, "Christ, I'm just as smart as these rich guys. It changed my whole life." Ford began to see Clinton's New Democrat approach as a return not to the party of JFK but to the party of FDR and Truman, the party of old World War II movies in which Joey Brooklyn learns to love Tex Hayseed because he throws himself on a grenade.

Finally, the chairman's position came about after a calculated effort by Segal and Clinton to, in Segal's words, "suck up" to Ford. "A great deal had to do with his affection for Clinton but a lot of it had to do with the fact that he was courted," Segal said later. "He knew he was important, and he performed because he knew he was needed." Working assiduously on Ford, Segal explained, "has nothing to do with being nice; it has to do with being smart."

The president would flatter Ford by asking for his political advice on a range of matters. "He calls me down and picks my twenty-nine years of experience," Ford said. "He asks a lot of questions. He wants to know how to make this thing run." Even though their personality types differ dramatically—Clinton gushes, Ford growls—the chairman came genuinely to like Clinton. "He's so smart it scares you," Ford said, adding the highest form of praise he could muster: "When you work with him, he's like Lyndon Johnson."

Ford agreed to work against the Goodling amendment, but the White House feared that might not be enough. Liberals on the committee were extremely nervous that national service might take money from the poor, so the means testing had great appeal. As Segal lobbied the members himself, he tried to undercut the means-testing argument by saying national service was *not* a student-aid program and shouldn't be treated as one. Unfortunately, Segal knew he couldn't hit that argument too hard in public, since Clinton himself had, in fact, been selling it as a student-aid program. (Remember, Clinton unveiled national service standing under the words SERVICE MEANS EDUCATIONAL OPPORTUNITY.) The spinmeisters' insistence on selling national service as a student-aid program was now jeopardizing the entire effort.

Just as it had taken Nixon to open China, Segal knew it would take a great liberal to tackle means testing—someone with impeccable credentials on the left, who could give cover to Democrats to vote against means testing. Segal needed a person, in fact, who could argue that means testing would be *bad* for the poor. Segal knew there was just one such person: Marian Wright Edelman, president of the Children's Defense Fund and longtime friend of the Clintons. No one carried more moral weight among liberals than Edelman. "At its heart, national service is not an education program," *she* was able to write in a letter to Bill Ford. "It is an effort to restore American citizenship and rebuild American society. While the services that participants provide should be targeted at those who need them most, the participants ought to be as diverse as America itself."

The White House had refused to push the class-mixing vision as it was writing the legislation and selling it to Democrats. But now that it was under attack from Republicans, the administration rediscovered that the integration goal was at the "heart" of national service. Edelman stated it more clearly than anyone in the White House had done since Clinton's election: "National service can bring Americans of varied backgrounds together in the shared experience of working for a common good, building a community of citizens that goes beyond economic or racial lines," she wrote. "Strict limits on eligibility jeopardize the breadth of participation that is critical to the proposal."

When Segal told Clinton what Edelman had done, Clinton sat down and, on the spot, wrote a thank-you note. They sent the letter Edelman had written to each member of the committee.

Representative George Miller, another influential liberal, joined the effort by working on the freshman Democrats. Segal personally lobbied nearly everyone on the committee. His basic message: Forget about the substance of poor versus middle class; this is a Republican trick to kill national service.

At the markup, Ford did not use the World War II class-mixing argument. That was not the most effective pitch for this liberal committee. Goodling was hitting from the left; Ford decided to hit back from the far left. He argued that the particular needs-analysis formula Goodling had devised actually would *reduce* aid to low-income students. "This amendment took me completely by surprise because it does exactly the opposite of what you want," Ford said in mock shock. "You're penalizing the very people you were concerned about."

The assault left Goodling flustered, shored up support among liberals, and didn't suffer at all from the fact that it was untrue. Goodling's amendment did not penalize Pell recipients. It was quite responsibly written. But Ford insisted it was so, and he was the chairman.

"I'm sure you will persuade everyone," Goodling said with deep, uncharacteristic bitterness. "But it is a total misrepresentation of what I said."

The committee voted 29–12 against Goodling's amendment. Ford held every single liberal on the committee. After the vote, a giddy Eli Segal waved his hand at the members of the committee and declared, "These *are* New Democrats!"

For the rest of the day, Ford used a similar combination of trickery, bullying, and stunning oratory to beat back a variety of Republican amendments attacking the size, structure, and purpose of national service. The House Education and Labor Committee, by voice vote, then approved H.R. 2010, the National and Community Service Trust Act of 1993.

Later that day, Segal visited Clinton and told him the results. The House Education and Labor Committee had voted *against* means testing—against targeting the money toward the poor. Clinton clenched his fist and pumped it in the air.

13

SOS

In public-relations terms, Summer of Service couldn't have been more glorious.

"Distancing themselves from the kind of self-indulgence and apathy that marred the 1980s," the *Philadelphia Inquirer* wrote, "1,475 young people began training yesterday in President Clinton's Summer of Service program, vowing to help rebuild their communities and the nation."

"The pay isn't great, but Alton Marcello expects to get more satisfaction helping immunize poor children than delivering pizza," began the Associated Press.

The *Los Angeles Times* carried the headline: GORE PROVIDES THE SPARK: AMID CHEERS AND HIGH HOPES, VICE PRESIDENT HELPS LAUNCH SUMMER OF SERVICE PROGRAM.

It was, in the words of one administration official, "the most undeserved press coverage we've ever gotten."

Contrary to the image of harmony presented by the media on kickoff day, the Summer of Service training week in San Francisco—timed to coincide with congressional consideration of the service bill—was a near disaster. The retreat, from June 19 through 25, quickly took on the appearance and sound of any 1990s college campus dominated by "identity politics." Young people broke into African-American, Hispanic, and gay-lesbian-bisexual caucuses. One of the African-American groups debated whether whites should even be allowed to attend its meetings. And some volunteers lashed out at the Clinton administration, which had brought them there. At its lowest point, one administration official remembered, "I almost thought we were going to have a riot."

What went wrong?

President Clinton had announced Summer of Service during his March 1 address at Rutgers University. The goal for the administration was primarily political: to give the media some living, breathing examples of service as Congress considered the legislation. The White House turned to the Commission on National and Community Service to run the pilot. On March 8, the commission sent out a request for applications from local groups around the country; the request stated that the commission would prefer programs whose participants were "from diverse racial, economic and educational backgrounds." The Summer of Service staff was ecstatic about the quality of the winners, which were based in Los Angeles; New Orleans; Newark, New Jersey; Baltimore; New York City; Boston; Atlanta; Oakland; Philadelphia; Delaware, Ohio; and Red Lake, Minnesota. Most had established special partnerships of community groups just for the Summer of Service. Together, they promised a wide range of activities, including, in the words of the press release, "immunizing children, tutoring and mentoring young students, providing housing assistance for homeless families; revitalizing urban landscapes and school playgrounds; and testing for lead paint." Summer of Service got strong cooperation from the military, which let the groups use the Treasure Island Naval Base as the site for the training. Everything seemed to be going according to plan.

On Saturday afternoon, June 19, Catherine Milton went to the parking lot at the naval base to greet the busloads of participants. Milton grew excited that after all the planning, real human beings—enthusiastic and ready to work—were finally arriving. But as they poured out of the buses, she noticed something surprising. They were mostly minorities. In fact, 75 percent were black or Hispanic. Milton was nonplussed: so many programs had promised integration, yet so few seemed to have produced it.

Part of the first day was, as the press accounts said, uplifting. City Year led the group in its patented physical training exercises, and ex-

citement grew about the arrival the next day of Vice President Gore.
But shortly before he arrived, the organizers had a major crisis of political correctness. To form the backdrop for Gore's scheduled speech,
Phil Caplan of the Office of National Service and Don Gips of the
National and Community Service Commission had randomly pulled
120 students representing all of the different programs. Some were to
sit in the center bleachers behind Gore, others in the bleachers to his
side; the latter group was to provide a "cutaway shot"—a second, visually interesting image for cameras. As the participants filed into the
seats, an African-American man in the audience pointed out that the
rows directly behind Gore were fifty-fifty white-black, even though
the program on the whole was 75 percent minority. He protested that
organizers were not accurately representing the "people of color" at
the retreat. Caplan turned down his request to scramble the seating,
but Milton feared that they might have a major blowup just as the
vice president arrived. In an extraordinary moment in the annals of
image management, a Gore aide asked whites to move farther back,
blacks and Asians to move up to the center bleachers. As this was
happening—just forty-five minutes before the vice president was to
arrive—a Native American went up to Caplan and complained that
no one in *his* group was in the center bleachers. Caplan tried to explain
that there were some Native Americans in the "cutaway" bleacher,
but his argument seemed to lack moral heft. The irate volunteer ended
up in the front row.

Ironically, that evening, at the "cultural diversity" workshops, some
African-American students *complained* that the organizers had moved
blacks up to the front of the bleachers. "They felt they were being
used to diversify the group that was already there on stage," said
Heather McLeod, a reporter for *Who Cares* magazine who observed
the training. "That led to a feeling of objectification on their part, that
they were being treated as token 'coloreds.'"

Small groups gathered outside the barracks, arguing fervently about
the training. Some griped that the organizers were trying to enforce a
midnight curfew, and weren't allowing volunteers enough time to min-
gle and meet. The irritation was compounded by logistical problems.
A few programs didn't submit their rosters until the last minute, so
organizers had to scramble to assign people to the proper bunks, and

there weren't enough blankets. There was no bottled water for the first day. No one had arranged meals for the vegetarians.

Tuesday, the participants were scheduled to do mini–service projects in the Bay Area. Some, like painting buildings in the Valencia Gardens housing project in San Francisco, went quite well. One of the groups, however, was supposed to do environmental work at the Presidio, a former military base on prime San Francisco real estate. One group of inner-city volunteers resented doing what amounted to lawn manicuring. So they laid down their tools and walked off the site.

When the servers went back to the barracks that night and exchanged notes, some complained about being used as a prop in an administration photo op. Many questioned whether Summer of Service would do useful work. Some argued that service had to include political advocacy, like tenant organizing. That led to discussions about whether they could improve society without overturning the power structure. "It looked like there'd been a radical takeover of Summer of Service," said one team leader, tongue only partially in check.

The Latino caucus worked until sunrise, putting together a document about what needed to change. The groups from Newark Summer of Service, Buildup LA, and East Bay Conservation Corps drafted letters as well. They complained about the lack of color in the leadership, the stage-managing of the Gore event, and the tendency of the naval base residents to refer to them as "kids," even though many were in their early twenties.

Those in the thick of this found it exhilarating, empowering, and sometimes frightening; a tension pervaded the base. On Tuesday night, the situation almost exploded over a pickup basketball game. Some "tough" volunteers from Newark and LA began feuding because one player had bumped into another without apologizing. This meaningless accident led to shouting and emotional arguments back at the barracks. At one point, a car with a siren was heard pulling up. At first, people thought it was the police coming, and "this led to the sense there was a rumble and they should be in there with their buddies," one observer remembers. As it turned out, it was an ambulance that had come to help an epileptic. But it was clear that the Summer of Service was just minutes away from, in one participant's words, some "impending violent confrontations."

The staff launched heroic personal efforts to rescue the event on Tuesday and Wednesday. Catherine Milton, Jennifer Eplett Riley, Greg Ricks, and other team leaders stayed up until three or four Tuesday and Wednesday in the morning talking with young people, trying to convince them they were all in this together. Milton encouraged them to be constructive, and to apply their energy to making the program effective. The team leaders worked with private companies to help solve some of the logistical troubles. They brought in several thousand bottles of water to prevent dehydration and on Wednesday night ordered six hundred pizzas.

It was into this swamp of emotion, resentment, and soul-searching that Eli Segal walked obliviously on Thursday morning. In two sessions of 750 participants each, Segal tried to give an inspiring talk, calling on the idealism of youth. The crowd chewed him up. One by one, servers took the microphone and berated Segal for the sins of government, the Clinton administration, and authority in general. One person complained that organizers had not taken into account that he was an abused child. Another charged they'd ignored the needs of gays and lesbians. Servers gave Segal a hard time about gays in the military and the failure of the program to organize the poor. In smaller groups after Segal's speech, participants continued to rail against him and the Clinton administration. One volunteer declared, "There is no place for them in our movement."

The organizers began to see that their 1960s notions of integration were antiquated. These students came from an environment that emphasized separatism: Afrocentric studies and Malcolm X, not Freedom Summer and Martin Luther King. The organizers didn't know how to handle them. "There were too many high-concept liberals who didn't know what it was like to be tough," said one observer. The organizers did not feel they could put down the ethnic politics or kick out the troublemakers. White House officials lived in dread that some scandal in San Francisco would spill into the news and jeopardize the legislation.

By the final day, tempers had cooled among the young people— who had lowered their expectations and begun to focus on the service projects ahead of them. Reverend Cecil Williams and the comic Sinbad gave inspirational speeches that helped bring people back together. In fact, most young people reported that, in the end, it was one of the most profound and exhilarating experiences of their lives.

But Segal was furious. The Summer of Service training week was like a bucket of ice water dumped on his head during a photo op.

That Friday, at a board meeting of the Commission on National and Community Service, Segal sat quietly as the staff reviewed what went wrong and right. Wayne Meisel, a thirty-one-year-old commission member and former campus activist, sided with some of the young people. "I don't mean to be irreverent, but I think in some ways, some of the things that happened made some people feel very disaffiliated, or disconnected to the vision of the president. We need not only to have a diverse group of trainers, but we need to train people in diversity. I mean, what's happening with these young people is: we have three hundred fifty years of animosity dumped on their heads and they're supposed to deal with it in a weekend. I don't think this country has enough quality people that can really deal with this issue to survive a weekend like this, without a massacre."

Frances Hesselbein, president of the Drucker Foundation, pointed out that what happened was quite similar to the "sense of rage on campuses and how some campuses are so politicized that it's very difficult to get any work done." Indeed, 70 percent of the SOS volunteers were in college or had graduated recently, and many of the most radical ones were middle class.

After an hour of evaluations and mea culpas from the group, Segal began talking. "I wish I could walk away as bullish as people in this room are," he said. "And I want to be persuaded, but I keep on thinking two words: Newt Gingrich." In other words: *Imagine how Newt Gingrich could use this frenzy of political correctness against us.* Segal was being a realist; he'd run the potential headlines through his mind. The House and Senate would be considering the service bill on the floor in the next few weeks. If the American people found out what had happened at the Summer of Service training, their reaction could destroy support for the legislation.

Segal made it clear he would not be mau-maued by the young people. Energy and enthusiasm is one thing, Segal said, but the program won't work "unless they're prepared to be more civil, less self-indulgent. . . . Those of us who lived through the sixties and who have remembered those awfully intense, exciting, but ultimately failures of the late sixties and early seventies, have got to be very nervous about *who*, in fact, is empowered to improve our communities."

Segal had thought he'd have a lot in common with these young people. After all, he had been a college activist himself—an antiwar protester, a McCarthy organizer, for God's sake. But, he told the meeting, what he saw in San Francisco had opened his eyes. "I was profoundly disappointed by how antipolitical, in the best sense of the term *political*, this group was. Both how there was a chip on their shoulder and about how ignorant they were about it. I asked a lot of people, perhaps some of the people in this room, what part of the participants do they think really voted? You would have to think that a service community percentage would be in the nineties. I would bet—I'd bet any amount of money—that the voting participation of this group was less than a third. There was a real [mood of] almost contempt for the American political systems that now exist, enough so that I would say that we went out of our way to keep the administration—which, frankly, is not going to play a small role in this as we go forward—with as low a profile as possible."

"We used the word *diversity* today," Segal continued. "When the president of the United States talks about diversity, he was not talking about the group of people who were here. I'm not talking so much about race now, but I think he was talking about perspective." The problem, for Segal, was radicalism; so few of the volunteers seemed to have what he thought of as middle-class values. These were not the people that Clinton's national service plan had appealed to during the campaign.

"I don't enjoy being the representative of three hundred fifty years of white colonialism," he said. And, he added, he was much more understanding than senators—or, for that matter, the White House political team—would be. If James Carville had been at Treasure Island, he would have argued for dumping the entire national service project right there. "I hope my colleagues at the White House will also be tolerant and comfortable and prepared to understand that this is not going to be as easy as a speech on 'It's the economy, stupid.' This is really deep stuff."

In a way, this was Segal's finest moment of the year. He was the only one in the room who seemed to be applying the political lessons of the sixties as seen by the majority of Americans. He had witnessed the ugly side of left-wing politics up close twenty years earlier, and the thought of those same dynamics destroying national service made him heartsick.

The Summer of Service training was a blessing for Segal because it alerted him to problems before the main program rolled out. He no longer suffered any illusions about this being simple. "I walk away," he said, "humbled and sobered."

The training was, of course, only one week in a nine-week program. The young people fanned out to dozens of programs throughout the country. Some programs continued to have problems, but most worked quite well. In fact, despite the rocky start, the participants gave one of the strongest demonstrations yet that service could be extraordinarily useful to communities. Eighty-eight VISTA "summer associates" got 105,000 children immunized in six Texas communities. Working with the Texas Department of Health, they fanned out door-to-door, educating parents, describing the location of the nearest clinic, and, in some cases, arranging transportation. In Waco, the number of kids using the clinics increased sixteen-fold. Governor Ann Richards was so impressed she created a Texas Health Corps, which continued to boost immunizations rates and reduce waiting times in health clinics. Twenty-five members of the New Hampshire Conservation Corps went to Van Buren County, Iowa, which had been devastated by that summer's Mississippi River flooding. Together with local residents, they removed thirty thousand sandbags in one day. SOS volunteers working at Clark Elementary School, in a low-income neighborhood in Atlanta, set up an after-school program that regularly attracted more than 250 kids. Before the volunteers arrived, only fifteen children were showing up.

The most promising legacy of Summer of Service was that a lot of the anxiety and conflict that marred Treasure Island evaporated when the young people actually got to do work. This is a central premise of national service: Boundaries break down when black and white become mutually dependent.

Still, the organizers got their first sense of how difficult it would be to make diversity a central element of national service. The White House's assumption that race- and class-mixing would just *happen* turned out to be deeply mistaken. Asked how he would feel if the full program had the same makeup as Summer of Service, Clinton said, "I would be disappointed if we didn't have a lot of white kids, middle-class white kids in there, too. And I think we will. I think we'll get a lot of upper-class white kids, who may be doing it for the service experience and not the educational benefit."

Clinton seemed quite comfortable with his thoughts on race- and class-mixing in the program—but, interestingly, his staff at the Office of National Service did not. "You're not going to use the line about getting more white kids, are you?" Diana Aldridge asked me, fearful that Clinton's comments might offend minorities. Similarly, Segal later came to regret his comments about the radicals at Summer of Service, and prayed that they would not get widespread distribution for fear they would be interpreted as antiblack.

This raised a delicate question: Did Segal and his team have the courage to take on the issue of race?

———

Segal had one thing going for him. Of the dozens of reporters for major media outlets that wrote about Summer of Service, not one highlighted the difficulties. How could the same press corps that had been overly cynical in March be uncritical in June?

For one thing, it wasn't the same press corps. Different communities sustain different media cultures. While the Washington news circle emphasizes irreverence, local papers and TV news shows love soft feature articles. Editors assigned Summer of Service as a spot news story. Few were given the task of finding out what really happened in the programs. "We have not been asked detailed questions," said Melinda Hudson, who handled press for the commission. "I'd get questions like, 'Could you get me a gang member I can quote?' Some reporters [just say], 'I need a smart minority.'"

It's always difficult to determine the effect of *not* reporting something. The media's low interest in national service and student-loan reform clearly made the issues seem small and unimportant. In other ways, though, the press's apathy helped the White House. The lack of coverage of the diversity issues in the bill enabled the White House to avoid a volatile debate. The failure of the media to write about pay-as-you-can loans allowed the legislators to concentrate on direct lending, a more winnable battle for the White House. The lack of interest in IRS collection enabled the White House to cave in on a campaign promise with impunity. And the media silence on the Summer of Service might mean the difference between national service passing and being defeated—assuming, of course, that the Republicans didn't hear about it on their own.

14

A "Bad Off-Off-Broadway Play"

National service made it to the floors of the House and Senate just five weeks after the White House introduced the legislation—lightning speed in the era of gridlock. But so far, the White House had been shadowboxing. Segal's team was primed for a real fight in the Senate, but couldn't quite see the enemy. By the middle of June her features began to be visible. The prime antagonist, it appeared, again would be Nancy Landon Kassebaum, the ranking Republican on the Senate Labor and Human Resources Committee who had led the assault on direct lending. She posed a serious threat because she was viewed as a sensible, moderate Republican; other senators would assume she must have real concerns if she opposed the legislation.

At the national service markup, Kassebaum had mentioned she would have amendments when the bill hit the floor. What the White House hadn't realized was that she didn't plan merely to tinker. She assigned three staffers to work full-time for a month to analyze Clinton's bill. Her chief service expert was Kimberly Barnes-O'Connor, who had worked for twenty years in the field, having run volunteer programs in Illinois, Connecticut, and Tennessee. She had developed strong opinions about the need for the federal government to stay out of the way and not burden localities with excessive rules. As decentralized as the White House plan was, Barnes-O'Connor felt it still gave Washington too much control. She wrote Kassebaum a memo in early May outlining the main weaknesses in Clinton's legislation.

First, the postservice benefit—the scholarship—was way too high. She suggested requiring the White House to run several pilot projects to decide the best amount.

Second, despite the rhetoric of "reinventing government," the Clinton plan created another "large bureaucratic structure." It did nothing to consolidate any of the existing seventeen service-related programs scattered around the government, such as the National Health Service Corps or the Department of Education's Student Literacy Corps. She warned that the White House failure to dissolve ACTION would mean constant warfare between the old ACTION state offices and the new state commissions. "They're going to be at each other's throats. They'll be fighting for the best volunteers, fighting for the best sites, fighting for the most federal dollars. I'll put money on that." She recommended a radical reorganization that would place all existing programs in one of two categories: national service (stipended), or volunteer services (unpaid).

Finally, she wrote, the program was to expand too rapidly. Going from 15,000 volunteers currently in the field to 150,000 by 1997 would represent a tenfold increase.

While she agreed with Barnes-O'Connor's legislative analysis, Kassebaum had two other reasons—one political, the other philosophical—for opposing the Clinton bill. Only that year, Kassebaum had become the ranking Republican on the labor committee and was determined to prove herself an effective leader of the opposition. Moreover, she held a strong distaste for paid "volunteerism." "True service is that which is freely given because one wants to make a real difference in improving the quality of community life," she had written. "Financial reward should not be seen as the incentive for offering service." Kassebaum had come to these views through some memorable life experiences. In the early 1960s, before she was a senator, she signed up as a VISTA volunteer, and saw what she thought was tremendous inefficiency and waste. She was sent around to junior high schools as a mathematics tutor even though she was horrible in math, and remembered the coordinator's urging her to bill the government for mileage. But she had fond memories of starting a volunteer program to get parents to teach reading after school.

After discussing it with Barnes O'Connor and Susan Hattan, Republican staff director for the committee, Kassebaum decided to offer not just a few amendments, but a completely new program. It would give Republicans and worried Democrats the ability to vote against Clinton's plan while still voting *for* service.

On June 15, Kassebaum introduced S. 1212, a 194-page bill incorporating most of the suggestions from Barnes O'Connor. It slashed the education benefit from $5,000 to $1,500; gave out four fifths of the funds rather than two thirds, through the states; allowed states to set their own priorities; and cut the spending authorization from $389 million to $98.9 million in the first year. In a June 23 "Dear Colleague" letter, Kassebaum wrote that Clinton's legislation was "too costly, too bureaucratic, too prescriptive and it misdirects education resources."

She personally delivered her "Dear Colleague" letter to several Democrats who had refused to sponsor Clinton's legislation, including Bob Kerrey of Nebraska, Herbert Kohl of Wisconsin, and Richard Shelby of Alabama. She pitched it at the regular Tuesday Club luncheon of Republican senators and staff. She kept emphasizing price tag and bureaucracy.

The Office of National Service scoured the bill for flaws, and for hints about Republican strategy. The good news was that Kassebaum had put together a thoughtful bill designed to improve the program, not merely to make mischief. The bad news, of course, was likewise that Kassebaum had put together a thoughtful program—which could not therefore be dismissed as a Republican effort to make mischief. In fact, the bill could very well give a fig leaf of respectability to those who might be interested in causing trouble.

Neither the White House nor Kassebaum thought her entire substitute would pass. But she promised that if her bill were defeated, she would split it up into amendments—and, like a cluster bomb, spread shrapnel in many directions. At a July 1 strategy meeting, the Democratic congressional staff implored the community service lobbyists to recognize the gravity of the Kassebaum threat. Sarah Flanagan, then an aide to Senator Chris Dodd of Connecticut, warned that even pro-Clinton Republicans could switch to the Kassebaum plan now that they had political cover. The political dynamic had changed. "With every hour, they are getting more and more," she warned in her sharp

New England accent. "Call right away those Republicans—and shore up the Democrats too. At best we have fifty-three votes to beat the substitute." She walked through the Republican strategy like a field marshal outlining the likely battle plans of the enemy. "There will be a series of amendments. The goal will be to divide and conquer." Most people, she said, cared passionately about only a few segments and would be happy to compromise on the rest. Kassebaum therefore could piece together winning coalitions on several amendments. "The cumulative effect will be: Clinton's plan will win, but it will look more like a Republican bill than ours."

The congressional aides feared that the fractious community service groups would play right into Republican hands by failing to put up a united front. Sure enough, when service groups gathered as the National and Community Service Coalition, they at first divided on how to respond to Kassebaum. "The Kassebaum substitute is very ingeniously drafted in a way that could seriously dilute our strength," warned Tracy Sivitz, a thirty-year-old from People for the American Way, who was one of the coalition's leaders. "It's ingenious because they can pick apart this coalition piece by piece."

Some of the community groups would have been perfectly happy to adopt the Kassebaum approach. "I have to point out," said Toni Schmiegelow of the City Volunteer Corps in New York, "that for the CVC, the administration's track record hasn't been good." The Commission on National and Community Service had given CVC a relatively small grant in the previous round. "We could live with this," Schmiegelow said of the Kassebaum plan.

But John Brisco, who ran the Pennsylvania State Service programs, warned the group not to romanticize the new proposal. "We've put this together through a careful process. All of a sudden comes this cockamamie scheme out of the blue that hasn't been debated—no hearings, nothing."

Sivitz brought things back to political basics. She said that their Democratic Senate patrons may very well take some of Kassebaum's suggestions, but if community service groups showed signs of division, the Republicans would do much more than make a few changes. "We should not be going in saying we support sixty percent of it. We have to be more resolute to force *her* to compromise."

With that, Roger Landrum of Youth Service America called a series of votes on the most significant potential Republican amendments—cutting the funding of the program; targeting the scholarship to the poor through means testing; and shrinking the size of the scholarship. The group voted to oppose all of them. Despite differences, the coalition was holding together—so far.

———

At the White House, Jack Lew and the rest of the staff prepared for the House and Senate floor action by trying to anticipate every possible scenario.

That can be hard because senators do not have to announce if they are going to propose an amendment. Based on the debates over the 1990 National and Community Service Act and the committee votes in 1993, the White House staff predicted twenty amendments, some aimed at the fundamentals of the program (scholarship, stipends), others dealing with perennial add-ons (prohibiting a server's health-care coverage from paying for abortions, requiring random drug testing of participants, banning homosexuals in programs working with children). On each controversial issue, a staff member, usually Robert Gordon, had written an "attack and response" sheet to help senators. A typical one:

ARGUMENTS AGAINST HOMOSEXUAL PARTICIPATION
* Homosexuals are more likely to abuse children, and homosexuality is aberrant, immoral behavior that is not accepted by the majority of society.

* Young children without adequate role models are particularly impressionable, and if they are exposed to homosexuality and taught that it is acceptable behavior, they may engage in it. . . .

ARGUMENTS AGAINST BANNING HOMOSEXUAL PARTICIPATION
* The morality of homosexuality is irrelevant. The real concern is that child participants not be sexually abused, and there is no evidence to suggest either that homosexuals are more likely to abuse children or that children exposed to homosexuals are more likely to become homosexuals.

* According to the American Psychological Association, in most cases of male homosexual child abuse, the man is in no way identifiable as a homosexual; therefore, excluding admitted homosexuals would not reduce the likelihood of children being sexually abused.

The prep kit also provided to the troops: a breakdown of the costs per server; positive newspaper articles, including those on Summer of Service; letters of endorsement from Marian Wright Edelman, Republicans Shays and Gunderson, the National Governors' Association, the police and firefighters unions, and the Girl Scouts; a list of other endorsing organizations, such as Big Brothers/Big Sisters, the YMCA, and the United Way of America; a list of endorsing college and university presidents; a list of endorsing corporations, including Archer Daniels Midland, Dow Chemical, and the Ford Motor Company; a list of all 223 House co-sponsors; a detailed comparison of civilian versus military benefits; sample op-ed pieces generated by the service groups; and a list of corps that were right then helping victims of the Midwestern floods. (The Commission on National and Community Service, in close coordination with Segal, had surveyed the youth corps in the areas damaged by the deluge and approved emergency grants for flood relief in Iowa, Minnesota, and Wisconsin.) The most important letter in the packet, however, was an endorsement from the president of the American Red Cross—Elizabeth Dole. Segal's courtship of Dole had paid off. National service, she wrote, would "enlarge the means by which individuals can make a difference."

In the final month, Segal tirelessly stroked anyone and everyone; he was constantly picking up the phone or visiting Capitol Hill. "Everywhere I go, Eli Segal came before me or is coming after me," Kassebaum said during those hectic weeks. Segal showed no concern for status or protocol. "Eli doesn't care if it was some kid three years out of college or a senator, he'll pick up the phone and call," an admiring Senate staffer said. "He's never had his ego in the way." In total, Segal met one-on-one with sixty-seven senators and at least as many congressmen.

On July 14, Segal worked the phones in his spacious office in the Old Executive Office Building.

Segal dialed himself. "This is Eli Segal calling," he told the receptionist of a Democratic senator. "I'm an assistant to the president calling from the White House. If the senator's in, I'd love to say hello."

The senator got on the line.

"How are you?" Segal said. "I missed you back in the state." The small talk lasted just about ten seconds. "I'm essentially calling to let you know where we are and make sure you're comfortable with where we are."

This was Segal at his best. "Are you aware of any major problems we have ahead of us? Anything you want to run through?"

This senator, a liberal, found great merit to the argument that, in a time of scarcity, the government ought to apply a means test to target the benefit to the poor.

"This is not about means testing," Segal said calmly, "it's about getting many different types of people from different backgrounds together." He pointed out that even minority liberals in the House, such as Major Owens and Matthew Martinez, believed means testing would throw the program into a "poverty-program trap. We think that's not a wise way to go."

After hanging up the phone, Segal called in Jack Lew and briefed him on this conversation, so that Lew could keep a running tab on the concerns of particular senators. "He said he has some interest in means testing but he will not offer an amendment," Segal recounted. He uncapped a blue pen and immediately wrote out a note to the senator on White House stationery, which he would send with a copy of the golden letter from Marian Wright Edelman.

His next stop was a meeting of the Sunbelt Caucus, made up of mostly moderate and conservative lawmakers. If the White House lost these Democrats, it could be defeated on several amendments. With this group, Segal stressed the themes dear to the DLC, and tried to assure the caucus that this was not going to be a big, reckless spending program. "Young people have a right to college education, but they have to pay for it," he said. He spoke about how national service would combat "centrifugal forces by enabling people of different backgrounds to work together." He emphasized that he wanted quantifiable results: "How many young people have been immunized? How many acres of land had hypodermic needles removed? What can we do to reading scores?"

"How are you going to guarantee diversity?" one staffer asked. "Do you have a formula?"

Segal said that 50 percent of the money would be set aside for disadvantaged communities. (Actually, it was 33 percent; Segal was still ignorant on that issue.) "But we're hopeful we will achieve socioeconomic diversity."

The staff person wasn't satisfied. "How will you do that?"

"It's a recruitment mechanism," he said, meaning that the administration would *somehow* ensure diversity during the selection process.

"How is this fundamentally different from CETA?" another staff person asked.

Segal boasted about the requirement that programs produce "measurable" results. "We're hopeful," he concluded, switching to "reinventing government"ese, "that this review process will allow us to steer, not row."

––––––––

Since May, Segal, Dave McCurdy, and Republicans Chris Shays and Steve Gunderson had worked diligently to recruit GOP support. The letter from Shays and Gunderson, entitled "National Service—Truly Republican," stated that "national service is a basic Republican idea and that the President's proposal is structured as a Republican would have structured it and . . . it deserves broad Republican support." But House GOP members viewed it as their responsibility to poke Clinton in the eyes whenever possible—and it became clear during the first day of debate that national service would be no exception. "It is more akin to a welfare program for the aspiring yuppies of America," said Representative Dick Armey of Texas on July 13, when the House started debating the "rule" that would govern the rest of the deliberations. He repeatedly called it a $7 billion program, using the cumulative projection the White House had issued in March (before the House Republican co-sponsors convinced the administration to list just a first-year number of $392 million, plus the open-ended "such sums as may be necessary"). Armey's exaggeration quickly took on a life of its own. Representative Craig Thomas of Wyoming rose to denounce the $7.4 billion that would be spent "the first time," implying that the administration would spend $7.4 billion *in one year*. "What is it going to cost a little later?" he asked. An equally misleading portrayal came from Representative Bob Walker of Pennsylvania, who continually referred to the volunteers as "new federal employees": "We are creating twenty-five thousand new federal employees that are now going to have political positions in communities across the country."

(The conservatives had difficulty coming up with potent factual arguments against such an all-American concept as service. At an early national service hearing William Evers of the Hoover Institute set the tone by warning of various unanticipated costs: "Who will bear the cost of the pregnancies and abortions likely to result? In this era of litigiousness, who will pay for the sexual harassment suits?" National service, he maintained, came about mostly because of "older people who resent young people's youth.")

The first day of debate did reveal one line of attack that worried the seemingly imperturbable Gene Sofer of Bill Ford's staff: Clinton's insistence on selling his plan as a key to college access had given opponents a huge target. The Republicans understood this weakness, and intended to exploit it fully. Representative Goodling, perhaps emboldened by the catcalls from the red-meat right, seemed to become more and more hostile. "If we were to enact this legislation in its present form, it would probably be one of the most immoral acts that Congress has ever perpetrated upon the American people," Goodling declared from the floor. "Immoral is the only term I can use, because it is Robin Hood in reverse." Goodling was using the same argument Barmak Nassirian had used at the Front Page, and Bill Gray had used before the American Council on Education. Congress was being asked to spend new money on a program to benefit few students, Goodling argued, while cutting back on other student-aid programs. "You are saying to those who cannot afford an education, over three million who presently receive some funds from the federal government . . . you are saying to them, 'Sorry we don't have money for you. Sorry, we have to cut work-study. Sorry we have to cut state grants. Oh, but we just happen to have fifteen thousand dollars a year to those who are not in need.' " Ironically, the Republicans were doing something for which they always criticized Democrats: trying to foment "class warfare."

Until mid-July, the White House and its allies had been methodical, diligent, and persistent. The speed of the projector would now be turned to fast forward. In one frantic eleven-day frenzy, Congress would decide the future of both national service and student-loan reform.

Tuesday, July 20

On July 20, S. 919, the National and Community Service Trust Act of 1993, went to the floor of the United States Senate. Segal and his team set up a "war room" just outside the chamber in a small office used by the vice president when he presided over the Senate. They each had assignments. Robert Gordon would work on talking points for senators. A rotating cast of young staffers and volunteers would monitor the floor debate on TV. Sagawa would keep track of the dozens of amendments under consideration. Jack Lew would handle negotiations over budget numbers. And Segal would work the senators.

In between the vice president's office and the Senate chamber was an ornate foyer, its walls lined with lush oil paintings of great statesmen, including Bob La Follette and Henry Clay. Cherubs wearing red and blue scarves danced on the ceilings alongside elegant maidens and majestic eagles. All this contributed to a feeling that momentous work was done there. About twenty lobbyists for community groups would gather in this foyer every day of the floor debate to put pressure on particular senators and to make sure nothing against their interests got slipped into the legislation. Several were just out of college and dressed up in their finest duds, hoping to blend in with the ornate room.

Because government ethics rules prohibit the White House from directly organizing grassroots lobbying activity, Segal's team had to use conduits. The most important was Martin Rodgers of Senator Wofford's office. He was only twenty-six, but his narrowly cropped black beard made him look older. Temperamentally he seemed more suited to the first job he'd held, as a management trainee for Aetna Life & Casualty. His voice was so deep and muffled that the lobbyists had to crowd around him as if in a football huddle.

Rodgers came out to brief the community-group representatives. "They take up the Kassebaum substitute first thing in the morning. We have twenty-seven Kassebaum amendments potentially and another fifteen other Republican amendments." Rodgers said the biggest threat would be a "trigger" amendment from Senator Pete Domenici that would deny money to national service until financial aid funding grew. Rodgers had recently learned that Paul Wellstone, the ultraliberal senator from Minnesota, was considering supporting the Domenici trigger amendment or even offering one of his own.

"Paul is just steaming mad," Wellstone's education aide Sherry Ettleson reported to the coalition members gathered off the floor. He had learned that the administration's Education Department budget had cut some smaller financial aid programs like work-study. "How can they be cutting these programs and doing national service at the same time?" she asked. "Don't they know how awful that looks?"

Rodgers began to wonder whether liberals were being asked to cast too difficult a vote. What would it *look* like to vote against the trigger? Rodgers kept asking himself. Could senators be attacked back home for harming the poor? Or local college students? "Does it become a campaign commercial?" he wondered.

Rodgers was particularly nervous, because this was the first time Wofford had helped manage a bill on the floor. Wofford knew more than anyone about the bill; this was part of the reason Kennedy had asked him to be his deputy. But did Wofford know *everything*? He had been so busy with other issues. As a floor manager, Wofford was responsible for anticipating amendments and reacting to them on a moment's notice.

And Rodgers was anxious about his own role. He'd been working for Wofford for less than two years, and this week was the first time he had ever set foot on the floor of the U.S. Senate. He kept breaking rules: he walked up the aisle when a senator was coming down, and accidentally stepped into the "well," the empty space between the senators' desks and the chairman's lectern. But he became aware of his biggest breach when he returned to his office one night to a batch of answering-machine messages from people who had watched the debate on C-SPAN: *Don't chew gum on the floor of the Senate!*

Day one was mostly taken up by opening statements from the Clinton bill's supporters. They were not expected to change any votes, but did reveal something fascinating about the historical moment in which Clinton's proposal emerged: Clinton was not the only one with a personal obsession with service.

The first speaker was Wofford, who had been working to promote service since 1961. When he came to national attention thirty years later by defeating Attorney General Richard Thornburgh in a Senate race, Wofford had already had an extraordinary career. After World War II, he had lived in India studying Gandhism, eventually writing a book, with his wife, called *India Afire*. As a young law professor in the 1950s, he helped convince Martin Luther King, Jr., about the power of using Gandhian nonviolence in the fight for civil rights. As an aide to John F. Kennedy in the 1960 campaign, he convinced the candidate to make his famous call to Coretta Scott King while her husband was in jail for his role in a Georgia sit-in. That helped win Kennedy the endorsement of black leaders, and possibly the election. When JFK took office, Wofford chaired a cabinet subgroup on civil rights, and earned a reputation among Kennedy's inner circle for being a purist —and, to some, a nuisance—on civil rights. Wofford helped set up the Peace Corps, and served as a top Peace Corps official in Africa from 1962 to 1964. When he returned, he pushed the idea of a domestic service program. As president of Bryn Mawr College in Pennsylvania from 1970 to 1978, he set up the campus's first service program. In 1979, he chaired the Committee for the Study of National Service, which, presciently, recommended a national service plan modelled after the GI bill and run by a public corporation. In 1987, Pennsylvania Governor Robert Casey appointed him state secretary of labor; Wofford promptly set up a state service corps. When Republican senator John Heinz died in a plane crash in 1991, Casey appointed Wofford to fill the seat, and, in 1991, Wofford won election in his own right. In an introduction to Wofford's book about the 1960s, broadcaster Bill Moyers said Wofford's "has been the most principled life I've followed over the years."

Wofford smiles less promiscuously than most senators. He is not a dynamic speaker; he insists on using grand historical analogies, usually involving Churchill, no matter what the subject. But he so loves talking about national service that his staffers consider it their primary responsibility to trick him into focusing on other issues. He even tried to make national service a major issue in his senate campaign, but his consultant, James Carville, told him it was "off message." Wofford and Clinton spent hours talking about service during the 1992 presidential campaign, when the senator joined one of Clinton's bus trips through Pennsylvania. Clinton was so smitten with Wofford that he listed the senator as one of the final three candidates to be his running mate.

In his opening statement on the floor on July 20, Wofford summarized his belief in service with a story he had told many times before. He met a young high school dropout who had enlisted in the Philadelphia Youth Service Corps. The man woke up early every morning, jogged around Independence Hall with the corps, then went off to build houses for homeless and low-income people as part of a Habitat for Humanity project. "I said, 'How did you choose this? How did you move from the youth gang you were running with into the Philadelphia Youth Service Corps?' And he said, 'Oh, well, I thought it would be a different gang; I might not die in the end.' And I probed and he saw I was serious, and then he said, 'Well, let me tell you; all my life good people have been coming in to our public housing project to help me. I got tired of people doing good against me. For once, someone asked me to do the helping.'" Wofford tied this to his own experiences in the Peace Corps. "Like so many CCC alumni and Peace Corps and VISTA volunteers through the years, the young man had learned that personal responsibility and self-esteem cannot simply be taught; they have to be earned. And it is a scandal that we have known this, and we have not acted on it." Wofford's tale captured succinctly the secret to service's efficacy: People feel better about themselves, and do better work, when they believe they are needed.

One of the next speakers was Senator Chris Dodd of Connecticut, who served as a Peace Corps volunteer in the Dominican Republic.

"With the exception of my family, no other experience—and I include my service in the House of Representatives and my twelve years of service in this body, of which I am deeply proud—has meant as much to me as those two years as a Peace Corps volunteer. It changed my life." Senator Barbara Mikulski of Maryland, another leading supporter of service, talked about her experience as a social worker in Baltimore. Helping link women prisoners to local churches taught Mikulski that person-to-person contact could accomplish much that a government check could not. Senators Claiborne Pell and David Boren talked about why they had been sponsoring national service legislation for years. The White House had considered support for national service to be "a mile wide and an inch deep." But many of the key players in this legislative struggle seemed to have been shaped by profound experiences in service; the issue seemed to strike a more personal chord.

For no one was this more true than for the senior senator from Massachusetts, Edward M. Kennedy. In his floor statement, Kennedy did not talk about the personal experiences that helped shape his interest in service—the entire world knew about them. "President Kennedy," as he calls his eldest brother, founded the Peace Corps. "Bobby" created the Bedford-Stuyvesant Redevelopment and Services Corp. His sister Eunice founded the Special Olympics. His niece Kathleen Kennedy Townsend ran the Maryland public school system's mandatory service program. And now Ted Kennedy found himself, as chairman of the Senate Labor and Human Resources Committee, in a position to do more for service than any Kennedy ever had. The fate of Bill Clinton's "domestic Peace Corps" would be dependent on the efforts of John F. Kennedy's youngest brother.

It gives one a strange sensation to interview someone as recognizable as Ted Kennedy. It is odd to see the familiar features, his moonscape complexion, the eyelids that turn down slightly at the corner, and those blue eyes. But it is stranger still to see the features that you had never imagined: his nervousness, for instance. When we sat down in the vice president's Senate office, he continually readjusted himself in his seat, and his hands never stopped moving.

But most jarring was his inarticulateness. Kennedy can be among the most inspiring men in American politics, and, in fact, had just spoken eloquently on the floor of the Senate about service. Yet when asked about what influenced his conception of service, he went into a meandering, nearly incomprehensible riff. "And my sister Jean . . . the very special arts program which now is an international . . . in the states which is a program developed out of the Kennedy Center. The concept was very much a part of our lives. The Peace Corps. When I was at Harvard I worked at the Phillip Brooks House. . . ."

People who work for Kennedy get used to interpreting his shorthand; they have a hard time explaining why he can rise to such eloquence in public situations, while his sentences become embarrassingly convoluted during some private moments. But they have come to realize perhaps the most misunderstood point about Kennedy the legislator: his eloquence has nothing to do with his effectiveness as a Senator. Kennedy has become a good Senator because he insists on being well prepared, works hard, has a feel for human relationships, and most surprisingly, is deeply practical. As the torchbearer for modern liberalism, Kennedy has the public image of an ideologue, but in the U.S. Senate he almost always cuts his two pinches of idealism with three cups of pragmatism. After years of fighting losing battles, Kennedy has come to take a longer view: Don't become so obsessed with "principle" that you lose the bill. Aside from wanting to boost school-based service learning, Kennedy did not have strong views on how service programs should be constructed. For him, what passed seemed less important than that something passed.

Bill Clinton had been on *Larry King Live* for almost an hour that night when a caller asked what three or four things he would like to leave as a legacy. First was economic growth, second was health security, and third: "I want my national service plan to pass that will open the doors of college education to millions of Americans." Again, he had used the same wildly misleading pitch for national service; as of that moment, he would be lucky if the plan opened the doors of college to twenty-five thousand. But Clinton stopped his next sentence midstream and said, "Lower-interest loans, and give, many, many of them the chance to work those loans off through service in their communities." It was almost as if he had caught himself and was trying to wrench away from his misleading promise, but he hadn't quite figured out how.

As Clinton was promising college access to millions through national service, Kassebaum's troops were preparing for the next day's full-throttle attack. Joining Barnes-O'Connor to plot strategy that night was Susan Hattan, the chief of staff for the Labor and Human Resources Committee Republicans. A native of Concordia, Kansas, Hattan fits most urban stereotypes of Kansans with her plain style of dress and straight, unstyled brown hair. She talks slowly in a nasal, Walter Mondale-ish deadpan that is interrupted by sudden bursts of laughter.

As floor manager for the minority, Kassebaum was responsible not only for her own substitute bill, but for coordinating all other Republican amendments. Kennedy had expressed willingness to accept several of the amendments, so the Republicans had to figure out their priorities. Most changes to legislation occur through informal swapping of amendments, not through floor votes.

Hattan and Barnes-O'Connor looked over a list of forty-one possible amendments. There was one to remove the federal representatives to the state commissions. Hattan and Barnes-O'Connor viewed this "federal spy" provision as a gross example of federal intrusion, and had intended for Durenberger to propose its elimination. But at eight that evening, Durenberger backed out. They decided to push it anyway with Kennedy's staff. "Durenberger's going to chicken out on this one," Barnes-O'Connor said. "But I think we can win on it."

Republican Senator Paul Coverdell, the director of the Peace Corps under Bush, wanted an amendment requiring ACTION programs to be evaluated every three years.

"Does anyone even read them?" Hattan asked, referring to the government program evaluations.

"No," said Barnes-O'Connor.

"Well, I say leave it out—one less report," she decided. So much for Senator Coverdell's amendment.

Senator Nickles had an amendment that called for means testing of the postservice benefit—much like Bill Goodling's in the House. Surprisingly, Hattan and Barnes-O'Connor weren't interested. It turned out that with all the problems Kassebaum had with Clinton's plan, she happened to agree with him about means testing. It was a lucky break for Clinton, a major reason why this amendment had little chance in the Senate.

Bob Dole had several amendments, including one he was reserving as a nuclear weapon in case the debate got really nasty. It required that anyone who wanted welfare had to do national service. "It would take up all the national service slots with welfare," Barnes-O'Connor pointed out.

Hattan then noticed that Ted Stevens of Alaska, a notorious pork-barreler, had six different amendments increasing money for Alaskan interests. One increased the Indian set-aside from 1 to 5 percent (in some cases); another gave preference to "grants for sanitation systems," which were important to western Alaska. Hattan looked as if she wanted to cry. "Is he going to do *all* of these?" she asked, putting her hands on her head.

As the two women got progressively more exhausted, they began singing a little ditty they had composed to the melody of the "Lamb Chop Play Along Song" from children's TV:

> *This is the bill that never ends.*
> *It just goes on and on, my friends.*
> *Some people started writing it not knowing what it was*
> *and they'll continue writing it forever just because . . .*

Wednesday, July 21

On the morning of July 21, about a dozen community service lobbyists gathered again off the floor of the Senate, where debate was about to start on national service. Someone handed a piece of paper to Marsha Adler of the National Association of State Universities and Land Grant Colleges, the only higher-education lobbyist actively working for national service. She clenched her teeth.

"Have you seen this from those *slimebags*?" she growled, so angry she fused two different insults. It was a letter from her colleagues at the American Council on Education—*supporting* the trigger amendment proposed by New York Representative Susan Molinari, which would prohibit spending on national service until financial aid funds were restored.

The other activists huddled around.

"USSA!" said Sara Hartman of the National and Community Service Coalition, pointing to where the United States Student Association had signed on as well.

"We strongly endorse the goals of national service," the letter stated. "However, we are concerned in this budgetary environment that national service not be funded at the expense of already constrained support for education and research programs carried out by the nation's colleges and universities." It was signed by Robert Atwell, president of the American Council on Education (ACE), on behalf of almost every major higher-education association.

Over on the floor of the House, Gene Sofer had just shown the letter to Bill Ford. "You tell Terry Hartle [ACE's top lobbyist] never to darken my goddamn doorway again," Ford fumed. "Who does he think he is?" Ford demanded a letter from ACE supporting the service legislation.

Upon hearing about the ACE letter, Nick Littlefield dashed into Segal's encampment in the vice president's office. He told them the House seemed to be caving in on the trigger amendment because of the ACE letter. Panic went through the staff. Segal and Lew darted from the office to see for themselves what was happening on the House side. Lew led Segal through back hallways he had learned of while working for Tip O'Neill, until they reached the House chamber. Anxious to know about Molinari, they summoned Sofer from the floor. Sofer was, as usual, completely composed.

"This is going to be a muscle amendment," he said calmly. "It's going to be Ford and Natcher making it happen." William H. Natcher was the chairman of the Appropriations Committee, which viewed triggers as an infringement on its turf. Sofer told them that, after Ford's little tirade was conveyed to ACE, the organization had quickly sent off a second letter clarifying the fact that it still supported the national service legislation as a whole.

"Is there anything we can do to help?" Segal asked intensely.

"If you can, you might want to work on the black caucus," Sofer responded.

"Any sign of them weakening?" Segal asked, almost before Sofer had finished his sentence.

"No, but we don't want to lose any factions," Sofer said. In truth, Sofer was nervous that Bud Blakey might spring some anti–national service assault through the black caucus.

Segal's amiability had disappeared; his eyebrows were locked a quarter inch lower than usual. He rubbed his hands together as he looked back and forth at Lew and Sofer. He had expected some difficulty in the Senate, but the House was supposed to be cake. "You're making me anxious," Segal said to Sofer. "Are you saying we might lose this?"

"No," Sofer responded calmly. "But the margin could be closer." Just when Segal seemed to be relaxing, Sofer added, "The one I'm worried about is Stump." Sofer's casual comment referred to the re-emergence of Clinton's most irksome enemy—the veterans' groups. Republican Bob Stump of Arizona had proposed that the national service benefit be no more than 80 percent of the veterans' benefits. That would again reduce the postservice benefit—this time from $5,000 to under $4,000. Sofer mentioned that even Chris Shays was thinking of voting for that, and that McCurdy, a key liaison with the veterans, wasn't around. "He went to North Carolina for his son's baseball game." Segal rolled his eyes.

When the chair called the roll on the Molinari trigger amendment, Charles Taylor, a Republican from North Carolina, moved to the door of the chamber and began handing out leaflets, as if he were campaigning at a subway stop. "Take this. It's Susan Molinari's amendment," he said. One leaflet prominently cited the support of the ACE. Another announced, "The American Council on Education, which represents 1,700 colleges and universities, supports National Service as well as the Molinari Trigger amendment."

The Molinari amendment lost 247–184. Ford had delivered big. He had conveyed the message: This vote is not about education funding —it's about whether you support Bill Ford and President Clinton.

Soon after, Goodling offered his means-testing amendment, using

Bill Gray's argument that national service "provides economic assistance precisely where we don't need it." In case the message wasn't clear, Goodling added, "Those members who represent low-income, middle-income, I would hope they would look seriously at my amendment." But the Goodling amendment lost 270–156—with the Congressional Black Caucus voting solidly with the White House and against Bill Gray.

The votes happened so quickly that it was easy to miss their significance. Under a Republican president, the amendments—both of which targeted federal money to the poor—probably would have passed. Clinton had managed to unite party liberals, moderates, and conservatives, and beat back powerful liberal interest groups such as ACE and the United Negro College Fund. No media covered either of these battles, but they ought to count as milestones in Clinton's attempts to define the term *New Democrat*. With the help of prototypical Old Liberal Bill Ford, he had briefly changed the rules of what it meant to be a Democrat.

———

Back in the Senate, Kassebaum was beginning to do damage. She brought to the Senate floor an enormous chart showing all the different service programs that already existed. She was followed by thoughtful statements from minority whip Alan Simpson and liberal Republican Mark Hatfield, who praised Clinton's interest in service but said, "The very essence of volunteerism is that it is driven by an individual's desire to give of themselves for the benefit of others, without benefit to themselves." As expected, the Kassebaum substitute was defeated 59–38, with the Democrats solidly opposed. But the Senate then turned to the particular amendments.

Kennedy moved periodically from the floor to the ornate, private Senate cloakroom. As one of the ten most senior senators, he had his name engraved on one of the phone booths in this members-only lounge. He would squeeze himself into the booth, close the door, and call senator after senator with instructions or cajoling: *That amendment you were interested in is about to come up and we need you to speak on it*; or *We have a gap in the schedule so now's the time to offer your amendment*; or *The Republicans are putting us on the defensive about cost, so we could sure use you here to talk about the programs in your state.* On the floor, Kennedy would occasionally organize quick vote counts. When the chamber was full for a vote, Wofford, Dodd, and Boren fanned out, questioned legislators, and reported back to Kennedy. They had identified five Democrats as shaky: Dennis De-Concini of Arizona, Richard Shelby of Alabama, Ernest Hollings of South Carolina, Robert Byrd of West Virginia, and Bob Kerrey of Nebraska.

At one point during Wednesday's debate, Kerrey sat down next to Wofford in the Senate chambers, and they talked for almost two hours. Kerrey had opposed the National and Community Service Act of 1990. He had lost part of a leg in Vietnam, and was viscerally distrustful of any government efforts to define national service.

"This is my flesh and guts," Wofford told Kerrey as the debate continued around them. "This is my blood and soul. You let me know when you have a flesh-and-blood issue like this, and I'll be there."

As the afternoon proceeded, the debate took on a far more combative tone. It began when Senator John McCain of Arizona proposed making soldiers eligible for the same benefits as national service volunteers. He kept referring to the proposal as a $10.8 billion program —taking the exaggerated figure cited by House Republicans and adding another fictitious year of budget projections. Kennedy asked McCain the cost of *his* amendment, but McCain said he did not know. "All I am trying to get is the facts," Kennedy said angrily, "because the senator was very free with facts and distorting the cost of the current bill. He mentioned $10 billion and then, when asked about the cost of his own proposal, he does not have it. . . . I have been around here long enough to understand for those who oppose a particular proposal, their favorite tactic is to distort and misrepresent and put a false price tag on it. That has been done here. . . . We are talking about a national service program of $394 million and such sums in the future." Again the amendment went down, 56–42, with the Democrats holding solid.

The debate continued to turn harsh, as Domenici argued for his trigger amendment to block the "$10.8 billion" service program until education funding was increased. "I'm very, very concerned that what we are going to do is continue down the slippery path of reducing Pell grants and work-study funding," he said.

Kennedy couldn't take it anymore. He rose again and pointed out that it was the Republicans who, in March, had filibustered to death Clinton's stimulus package—which included $2 billion to solve the Pell grant problems. "I am interested in hearing the sense of indignity about this," he bellowed.

The debate ended for the evening without a vote on Domenici's trigger amendment.

When Wofford came off the floor, Segal met him in the lobby to review a good day's work. They talked about some of the highlights, and then Wofford matter-of-factly gave Segal a verbal kick in the gut.

"You know the Republicans are conferencing about doing a filibuster," he said.

Segal looked stricken. His eyebrows tensed again and his optimistic expression was replaced with dread. "On what grounds?" he asked.

"Cost," Wofford replied.

Segal was speechless.

Meanwhile, Kennedy and Nick Littlefield walked down the marble back steps of the Capitol to the senator's car. Littlefield thought the day had gone reasonably well, but Kennedy was uneasy.

"We're in trouble right now," Kennedy said, to Littlefield's surprise. "It's turned into a debate about tax-and-spend instead of about service."

"The chemistry," Kennedy said, "is all wrong."

Thursday, July 22

At 12:15 p.m. on July 22, the Republican senators gathered in Dole's office. Prodded by McCain and New York senator Alfonse D'Amato, the group agreed that in the past forty-eight hours, Clinton's national service program had become vulnerable. The Republicans had been afraid to take on such an apple-pie issue as national service. "D'Amato really shattered that," said one Republican staffer. "He just came out of the blue and said, 'I have forty-one votes.' It kind of caught everyone by surprise." Forty-one is a magic number because it is enough to sustain a filibuster; the Democrats needed sixty to shut off debate with cloture.

D'Amato suggested that the national service volunteers would become political shock troops for Clinton. "What we're going to have is one hundred thousand people going out and working for Bill Clinton," he said. "They're building a grassroots organization." Phil Gramm of Texas agreed, noting that there wasn't much difference between organizing a drive for an environmental cause and for a candidate. D'Amato warned that a victory on national service, coming soon after a possible budget win, would give Clinton too much political momentum. He was about to get his budget passed; they'd better not allow him two major victories before Congress went on recess. "No cheap victories for the president," D'Amato reportedly said.

Durenberger pleaded with them. "I've already gotten them to cut back the size," he said. He argued that much of this was something Republicans should support. Service learning, for instance, was extremely cost effective. But the other Republicans shot him down.

Dole appeared ambivalent. No one loved bloodying Clinton more, but he had some sympathy for the service program. "The biggest impact was Mrs. Dole," recalled Dole aide David Wilson. "When her letter hit the Hill, there was some concern that it might be a turning point. She seemed to have won him over. He seemed to become a lot more supportive."

Kassebaum found herself in an awkward position. She had told Segal she would not support a filibuster, and she did not want to break her word. "What about Coats and Gregg?" she asked of the two other Republicans who had supported the plan in committee. They were willing to go along with the filibuster, D'Amato reported. She decided she would, too, in the hope that it might wring some extra concessions from the White House. As one Senate staffer put it, "You should never, never forget that Nancy Landon Kassebaum is Alf Landon's daughter." In other words, while Kassebaum was temperamentally moderate, her political soul was partisan Republican.

Dole's staff saw four camps within the Republican caucus. There were fifteen or sixteen senators who could support national service if Dole brokered a deal. This group wanted to reduce the size of the program to $1 billion over three years. The administration's bill at that point was $400 million in the first year, plus "such sums as may be necessary." The Republicans wanted a specific spending ceiling and slow growth.

A second group—Durenberger and Vermont's Jim Jeffords—strongly supported the legislation. A third one—including Chafee and Specter—expressed support but were willing to play along with a filibuster. And a fourth faction of hard-liners, including Nickles and D'Amato, wanted to kill the bill or at least embarrass Clinton. Their motives were different, but three of the four camps saw a gain in filibustering. "We were willing to go along with his gambit, knowing that it would give us more leverage," said David Wilson, Dole's aide.

Durenberger came from the filibuster meeting deeply embittered. "The message to me was, 'We don't need you. We've got forty-one votes,'" Durenberger said. "They're all married to people who volunteer for free," he said. "They can't get it through their heads this idea of stipended service. What Republicans do is make money, and have their spouses volunteer. It's something you do for nothing." But Durenberger was disillusioned with Clinton, too. "Everything the president has done and said is an exaggeration," Durenberger said. "He asked for it. The rhetoric is destroying the reality, and the Republicans are taking advantage of it."

———

About forty-five minutes after the Republican caucus decided to filibuster national service, House and Senate negotiators began the conference committee on student-aid reform as part of broader talks on the Clinton budget bill. Conference committees are composed of the senior Democrats and Republicans from the relevant House and Senate panels. In this case, the House team was led by Bill Ford and the Senate team by Ted Kennedy. Both were busy floor-managing Clinton's national service bill in their respective houses, but on the president's direct lending/pay-as-you-can loan proposal, each had his own agenda.

The House, backed by the administration, wanted to scrap the bank-based system and go to 100-percent direct lending within five years. Ford believed that he was in a strong position because the Democrats on the House side were united, plus they had Republican Tom

Petri. Ford was, in any event, not one to be intimidated by the glamour of the Senate. "Ford thinks Pell is asleep half the time, and he's still got a program named after him," said one Senate staffer. "He thinks he knows more than Kennedy and Pell combined. And he's right."

Kennedy had a more complicated task. The Senate wanted to move to 50-percent direct lending. Kennedy supported direct lending and viewed this as his opportunity to impress the White House with his legislative skills. But he had to deal with open rebellion on his committee. He continued to worry about "good old Claiborne." They had been through a lot in the thirty years they had served together. Pell had been friends with JFK; had been one of the first senators to endorse Robert F. Kennedy's presidential candidacy; had helped Ted Kennedy's son Patrick run for the state legislature in Rhode Island. Kennedy wanted to accommodate his friend.

Kennedy was also concerned about two Republicans—Kassebaum and Jeffords of Vermont. Shortly before the conference, the two met with Kennedy and told him bluntly that they expected him to advocate the official Senate position of 50 percent.

"If we get jammed on this I'm going to be very angry," said Jeffords, normally a reserved man.

Kennedy said they would have to compromise some.

"What we did [in committee], Ted, *was* a compromise," Kassebaum said. "We don't want to budge."

What, Kennedy asked plaintively, should he tell the irascible Ford?

"Just tell Ford you ran into a brick wall," Kassebaum replied.

Jeffords had, courageously at times, defected from the Republicans on other issues to help Kennedy, and the chairman felt indebted to him. "I just can't jam him," Kennedy told aides. As ranking Republican on the labor committee, Kassebaum was essential to smooth sailing on future issues. "Being a politician and a gentleman, he understood he couldn't just blow them off," said Kennedy aide Suzanne Ramos. "He felt national service could fall because of direct lending."

Two late-breaking developments also weakened the hand of the pro–direct lending forces. One setback came from a highly unlikely source: majority leader George Mitchell. He had been hearing from the industry and financial aid administrators in his state, and was worried that Democrats were being forced to accept a plan they didn't like. So he wrote a letter to the Senate conferees urging them to go slow with direct lending. The majority leader was telling his troops to go against the position of the White House. "It was a bombshell," Evans said of the letter.

Secondly, there was the nuisance of Representative Bart Gordon. A Tennessee Democrat who had long fought against trade schools, Gordon had decided to make it his mission to stop direct lending. He wasn't on Ford's committee, so he instead offered a nonbinding amendment to another bill on the floor of the House; the amendment attacked direct lending. To the astonishment of the administration, the Gordon amendment passed 397–28. Even Ford voted for it, hoping to thereby convince his colleagues it was meaningless. But Gordon continued to press his case, undermining Ford's bargaining position at the conference.

Lobbyists coated the hallway outside the conference room, just around the corner from the Senate chamber. These were the moments when they earned their pay, or so they told their clients. Most carried cellular phones so they could provide urgent updates.

Still, at conference time, the industry found itself in a weakened position. Shireman's efforts were paying off. "The key to neutralizing us was to villainize us," complained Sallie Mae's Larry Hough. "We were out of the mainstream. The key decision was made to sit down and shut up." Sallie Mae stopped its public relations and advertising and concentrated on quietly persuading key congressional staff to go easy.

Meanwhile, some of the industry coalitions had begun to unravel. The guaranty agencies in Illinois and New York had left Dan Cheever's group to strike their own deals with the Department of Education. "Tempers are high within our coalition," Cheever said just before the conference began. "Everyone's trying to practice cannibalism."

Inside, the legislators sat at four narrow tables linked together to make a hollow square. Bill Ford was elected chair of the conference. He began by pointing out an inconsistency in the Senate's position. Senators doubted the Education Department's ability to run a new program, yet under their fifty–fifty plan—in which half the schools would be under the current system and half under direct lending— the department would actually have to run *two* programs. He stated simply, "I'm here with a strong mandate and a strong personal commitment to protect the House position."

Kennedy responded by saying he had supported direct lending since 1978, but "quite frankly, if we had gone to direct lending [earlier], it wouldn't have passed our committee or the United States Senate. I feel as strongly about our position as you do about yours." This was political code. Kennedy was effectively saying, "Please understand the difficulty of my position." Up until that moment, Ford had thought the Senate might just give in to the House. "We thought, 'We've got the votes, the president's on our side, Kennedy's on our side—it'll just happen,' " Ford's aide Omer Waddles said.

Ford now knew he could not rely on a backroom deal with Kennedy. If Ford wanted full direct lending, he would have to fight hard for it. To increase his leverage, he announced that he'd been told that if they couldn't finish their work quickly, the leadership would simply take the bill away from them. Other committees were busy negotiating on other parts of this big budget bill; the leadership would be damned if they would get held up by student loans. Some on the Senate side suspected Ford was bluffing—and they were right—but in the middle of the negotiations it was hard to know for sure.

Bill Goodling, the ranking House Republican on the committee, began trying to undermine the position of his chairman by mentioning Gordon's amendment. "I think the House overwhelmingly voted to go slow," Goodling said. Expecting this attack, Ford fired back, "You'll remember, I voted *for* it. It was a nonentity. If you think for one minute I would have voted for something that would have limited direct lending, you're wrong."

Thus went the first day's conference. The players had displayed their plumage and clucked their songs. They scheduled the next meeting for Monday. The ritual had just begun.

After the meeting, Ford called Kennedy. The House needs more than fifty percent, Ford said. Be patient, Kennedy responded. He had problems on the Senate side—not the least of which was national service.

In these final days, the fates of the two bills had become linked. The Republicans who wanted Kennedy to go slow on direct lending were also the ones he needed for national service. "Kennedy could not

alienate them in one case and expect to get them in the other," Waddles explained. "The timing could not have been any worse."

———

Kennedy walked directly from the student-aid conference to the Senate floor, where national service was again being debated. The key
order of business that morning had been Domenici's trigger amendment preventing the government from funding national service until
Pell grants were increased. Wofford's team had worked until three a.m.
writing a "Dear Colleague" letter that bore Mikulski's signature; Mikulski was on the Appropriations Committee: her views were thought
to be influential. At eight a.m., Wofford's interns distributed the letters
to each senate office. Perhaps most important, Wofford recruited Claiborne Pell to assure the Senate that Pell grants were not in jeopardy.
The Senate defeated Domenici's amendment 55–44.

Although the vote was a victory for the White House, it was por-
tentous. It showed that Clinton did not have a filibuster-proof majority.
How could that be? The White House had four Republican co-
sponsors—Durenberger, Chafee, Specter, and Jeffords—plus, Coats
and Gregg had voted for the bill in committee. That was sixty-two.
But the roll call on the Domenici amendment revealed that Gregg and
Coats had jumped, and, more remarkably, so had Specter and
Chafee—both *co-sponsors* of Clinton's legislation. It also showed that
despite all of their work with Kassebaum, she would vote with the
Republicans on a filibuster. "We were devastated," one staffer said
later about Kassebaum's vote. "We thought she was the type of person
who would never go back on her word."

Two filibusters—a real one led by South Carolina senator Strom
Thurmond and a fictional one by Jimmy Stewart—formed the modern
public image of the tactic.

In *Mr. Smith Goes to Washington*, Jimmy Stewart led a filibuster to
protest the funding of a dam by a corrupt political machine at the
expense of a "national boys camp" he wanted to create. He stated the
filibuster rules succinctly: "I've been told that if I yield the floor only
for a question or a point of order or a personal privilege, I can hold
the floor almost until doomsday. In other words, I've got a piece to
speak and blow hot or cold, I'm going to speak it."

In 1957, Thurmond stalled civil rights legislation by taking the floor and not yielding the right to speak for twenty-four hours and eighteen minutes.

Most filibusters now skip the colorful grandstanding. In this case, minority leader Dole simply let it be known that he had forty-one votes against national service, which meant he could sustain a filibuster if he wanted to. The modern filibuster can become very abstract, as with two chess masters battling each other twenty moves into the future. The Republicans knew they had the votes for a filibuster; the Democrats knew they knew; and the Republicans knew the Democrats knew they knew. Rather than playing all that out, both sides just made an assumption: the bill is dead as long as the Republicans have forty-one votes. When the Republicans stage such a filibuster, they are careful to continue debating the subject at hand—albeit much more *thoroughly* than they might otherwise. No reading of phone books. This way they can obstruct without being seen on TV as obstructionists. So, the senators continued to discuss national service, yet everyone operated as if a filibuster were taking place.

After hearing about the Republican caucus, Segal called Clinton's office to tell him a filibuster was in progress. He and Lew then turned to keeping the Democrats united. Kennedy, Wofford, and Boren were able to report that the Democrats were so far holding on a cloture vote. Durenberger and Jeffords would join them. So they needed to swing two more Republicans to smash the filibuster.

The hopefuls included: Chafee, an original co-sponsor; Paul Coverdell; Mark Hatfield, a liberal Republican; Coats and Gregg, who voted for the legislation in committee; William Cohen of Maine; John McCain of Arizona; and, surprisingly, Orrin Hatch, the conservative from Utah. Hatch had been a co-sponsor of the 1990 service legislation.

Marty Rodgers, Wofford's young aide, came out to the Senate lobby periodically to update the lobbyists. "Now we need you to do the same thing on the means-testing amendment—a full-court press," he said.

"To the battle points," declared Marsha Adler. Edin Fisher Durbin, a representative of the YMCAs, opened her notebook and reported that she would call the YMCAs in the appropriate states to put pressure on Specter, Coats, Gregg, and Chafee. At Rodgers's suggestion, she added Nebraska, New York, Arizona, New Jersey, and Louisiana, to shore up Exon, Moynihan, DeConcini, Bradley, and Johnston. Lisa Woll from NASCC would have her local service corps call McCain, Danforth, Specter, Durenberger, Warner, Gregg, and Coverdell.

On the floor, Republican Don Nickles of Oklahoma argued that Clinton's statement on *Larry King Live* two nights earlier was proof positive that national service would be a huge program. "As a matter of fact, I heard the president of the United States on *Larry King* the other night and I will read what he said: 'I want my national service plan to pass that will open the doors of college education to millions of Americans.' Wait a minute—millions of Americans. This is only 150,000 and that is by the year 1997. . . . If you are talking about millions of Americans, and I guess two million would maybe count as millions, you are talking about $68 billion a year."

One of the next senators to be recognized was Jesse Helms of North Carolina. His name had not come up before in connection with national service.

"Mr. President, I send an amendment to the desk and ask for its immediate consideration." The amendment was as irrelevant as it was inflammatory: it would grant government patent protection to the insignia of the Daughters of the Confederacy.

What did this have to do with national service? Nothing. Senate rules allow members to amend any piece of legislation; they look for whatever "vehicle" is "moving." National service was Helms's vehicle. On May 6, the Senate Judiciary Committee had voted to deny the patent protection at the request of Carol Moseley-Braun of Illinois, who believed it put a government imprimatur on an organization founded to celebrate Confederate efforts to preserve slavery. Helms proposed overturning the committee action. "Most of these ladies, as I say, are elderly, and are not the kind of gentle souls which the Senate Judiciary Committee should want to offend deliberately, let alone rebuke," he said. Helms and Thurmond then recited many of the good deeds done by the Daughters.

Moseley-Braun, the first black woman to serve in the Senate, moved to kill the amendment, but, to her astonishment, the motion failed 52–48, with six Democrats joining most Republicans. At that point, the tenor of the debate changed dramatically. "In my remarks

I believe that I was restrained and tempered," she said. "I talked about the committee procedure. I talked about the lack of germaneness of this amendment. What I did not talk about and what I am constrained now to talk about with no small degree of emotion is the symbolism of what this vote really means. I have to tell you this vote is about race. It is about racial symbols, the racial past, and the single most painful episode in American history."

Her voice grew louder and emotion choked each phrase. "The issue is whether or not Americans, such as myself, who believe in the promise of this country, who feel strongly and who are patriots in this country, will have to suffer the indignity of being reminded time and time again, that at one point in this country's history we were human chattel. We were property. We could be traded, bought and sold." Finally, she said, "If I have to stand here until this room freezes I'm not going to see this amendment put on this legislation which has to do with national service."

The Republicans had already begun a filibuster. Now Moseley-Braun was threatening to block the bill over Helms's amendment—a filibuster within a filibuster.

The subsequent debate was unusual and historic. The chamber was packed as one senator after another gave passionate speeches, the most notable being that of Howell Heflin, the grandson of Confederate soldiers. He announced he would switch his vote to support Moseley-Braun. "I revere my family," he said in his slow, Southern drawl, "and I respect those who thought whatever they were doing was right at that particular time in our nation's history. But we live today in a different world. We live in a nation that every day is trying to heal the scars of racism that have occurred in the past."

So rare is it that the Senate deals openly with race, that this was a time of great emotion. Inadvertently, the debate highlighted the administration's failure to sell national service as an agent of integration. Speaker after speaker rose to discuss the importance of bridging racial tensions, and no one mentioned national service—even though the Helms amendment was *attached to* the national service bill.

Finally, toward the end of the debate, Wofford rose. "Is there anything that is more the opposite of the bill for national service than the divisive issue we have just taken up?" he asked. "And is not the national service bill itself designed for just the opposite, to bring our country together, rich and poor, North and South, young and old, black and white, cities, suburbs, and farms?" Eventually, the Senate voted again and stripped away the Helms amendment.

When the Senate returned to national service, the debate seemed anticlimactic. The senators defeated an amendment to deny family and medical leave benefits to national service participants. They then defeated a revised version of the Kassebaum substitute. As the debate moved into the early evening, the quality degenerated further. "This bill is a turkey, an absolute turkey," D'Amato yelled from the back of the chamber. He pointed to an enormous color chart showing the cost of a national service slot compared to that of a Pell grant or a student loan. "Here! Look at the cost of the national service program under this bill: $22,600. Incredible! Incredible! . . . And this turkey, that we should shoot, kill it now!" He was really cooking. "Where are we getting the $10.8 billion? Does anyone know? Are we going to get it from veterans? Are we going to close veterans' hospitals? . . . Wait until the veterans find out. Wait until veterans' hospitals get cut back!"

As the debate proceeded, Segal and his team were holed up in the vice president's office calling wavering senators. Segal had grown despondent. He had worked so hard, and the whole thing was unraveling in a partisan drama. "Eli was very shaken," one congressional aide said. "He'd put his reputation on the line. This democracy stuff is very messy." Segal kept thinking about the stimulus package, which had died a slow, agonizing death three months earlier because Dole had forty-one votes.

As they were making calls, one of the staff aides was monitoring the debate on TV. To their surprise, they heard Kennedy on the floor say, "We are glad to try and find some accommodation. The effect of the Kassebaum amendment would be for five thousand Americans. We are talking twenty-five thousand Americans. I would be glad to suggest that we settle for fifteen thousand in the first year, try to double that the next, and then double that for the third year, and stop it if it is not working." This was not part of the script. The administration's stand was 25,000 the first year, 50,000 the second, and 100,000 the third—a cumulative total of 175,000 servers in three years. Kennedy had just offered a total of 105,000—a cut of one third, with nothing in return! Kennedy seemed to be showing signs of desperation.

That evening, party leaders George Mitchell and Bob Dole came to the floor to formalize what was going on.

"I would like, if I might at this moment, to inquire of the Republican leader whether under the circumstances we will be permitted to get to a final vote on the bill or whether under the current circumstances it will be necessary for us to file a cloture motion to terminate debate," Mitchell said. (In other words, "Tell me, old chap, are you filibustering this national service bill?")

"I think if I were majority leader," Dole responded, "I would suggest maybe filing a cloture motion." ("Yes, my good friend, we are now conducting a filibuster, intent on preventing your national service legislation from passing.")

Friday, July 23

On July 23, as the president was preparing to go to the funeral of Vince Foster, his lifelong friend who had committed suicide just three days earlier, he met with Segal for an update on national service. Mark Gearan, the communications director, and George Stephanopoulos were also there.

"How are we doing?" Clinton asked.

"I think we'll win, but it's going to be tough," Segal said. "It may take more than one cloture vote." The Senate leadership had agreed to hold as many cloture votes as were needed to break the filibuster.

Clinton offered to make any calls necessary, then looked over a presidential statement Segal had drafted.

"I think the tone is of disappointment," not anger, Segal said. Clinton agreed.

The president went to the microphones set up on the South Lawn and said, "I was, frankly, disappointed yesterday at the delay in the progress of the national service legislation in the Senate. This is one idea that all Americans should be able to agree on. We know we have broad bipartisan support. Several Republican senators have told us that they like the bill and intend to support it. And I very much hope that next week, whatever considerations were moving the Republican senators toward filibuster will evaporate."

Segal and his team knew, of course, that one presidential statement would not be sufficient. They had to pressure the eight targeted Republican senators. Until now, communications and lobbying strategy had been pretty much left up to Segal's shop. But this Friday afternoon, Segal's team combined forces with the rest of the White House communications operation. They reviewed what was in the works, including a youth rally on Monday to support the legislation. They discussed fitting the national service bill into the efforts to get Clinton's budget through Congress. A consensus emerged that, when talking to the press about Congress's handling of national service, they should use the term *obstructionism* instead of *gridlock*, since *gridlock* implicated everyone while *obstructionism* pointed a finger at the Republicans.

This was a delicate balance. The White House had learned from the fight over the stimulus package that it could not just defeat the Republicans on a party-line vote. It had learned from the budget negotiations, in which each concession had led to demands for another, that it needed to be firm. And yet it couldn't be too combative, because it needed to attract two more Republican votes to break the filibuster. "It was the most interesting chess game I've been part of," Stephanopoulos said later.

The group decided to weave national service into Clinton's address about jobs in Chicago on Monday. In addition, the team decided that, instead of trying a broad media strategy, it would concentrate on stirring up press coverage in the eight states represented by key Republicans. Part of the problem was that the media's lack of interest in the subject was allowing the filibuster to occur. "No one was under pressure," Durenberger explained, "and under those conditions you can generate opposition quite easily."

Segal returned to Capitol Hill and began what he called "the full-court press." He visited Kassebaum. She broke it to him that she still could not promise to vote with Clinton on cloture. They then started talking numbers.

"What about two years?" she asked. Kennedy had mentioned the possibility of a law that would require Congress to reauthorize the entire national service program after two years. The White House bill had a five-year authorization.

A two-year authorization, Segal argued—quite correctly—would not allow enough time for the program to develop. There would be no certainty—for the program or for the servers.

"Okay," Kassebaum agreed, "three years."

Then she put her first offer on the table. "Two-three-four," she said. It was shorthand for $200 million the first year, $300 million the second, and $400 million the third.

"That's just not going to work," Segal responded. "But let's keep on talking."

Saturday, July 24

The Republicans were defining the debate as one about "tax-and-spend." The White House had to figure out ways to make the debate about "obstructionism." Robert Gordon and Diana Aldridge, ONS's public-relations chief, divided up editorial boards. On Friday and Saturday, Gordon called editorial-page editors at the Portland *Oregonian* in the hope that they would pressure Packwood and Hatfield; the Providence *Journal*, the most important paper in John Chafee's state; and the *Bangor Daily News*, to prod William Cohen. Segal and Rick Allen also remembered another possible point of contact for Cohen. The Maine senator had co-authored a spy novel called *The Double Man* with former senator Gary Hart, for whom both Segal and Allen had raised money in 1987. Allen tracked down Hart in a Tokyo hotel and, in his excitement, forgot about the fourteen-hour time difference. Groggy and annoyed about being awakened, Hart nonetheless agreed to call Cohen. ONS staff also phoned newspapers in the states of other key senators: Pennsylvania (Specter), Utah (Hatch), Georgia (Coverdell), Indiana (Coats), and New Hampshire (Gregg). The goal was to have each senator pick up his hometown paper and read an editorial tying him to "obstructionism."

Segal and Aldridge also had lengthy conversations with the editorial boards at the "thought leader" newspapers—*The Washington Post* and *The New York Times*—from which other media outlets take their cues.

Segal went on C-SPAN as well. The message, as Aldridge joked, was basically, "Shame, shame, shame. Shame on Republicans. Bullies, bullies—trying to block the Little Engine That Could for no good reason."

Saturday's papers included brief mentions of Clinton's comments. But the filibuster still hadn't broken into public consciousness.

Sunday, July 25

On July 25, Segal's team got its first bite: a front-page *New York Times* article headlined, FILIBUSTER DELAYS SERVICE MEASURE. The article bluntly assigned tactical rather than substantive motives to the Republicans. "By warring against the bill, whose concept of offering educational grants in exchange for public service is generally popular in the country, the Republicans stepped up their general delaying and harassment campaign against the Democratic legislation. The tactic risks being labeled obstructionism but offers the hope of rendering the new Democratic Administration legislatively impotent." To a remarkable extent in this high-tech media age, *The New York Times* still sets the agenda for what counts as news. Since the *Times* was paying attention to the filibuster, other media outlets would have to as well.

Monday, July 26

The large room in the Dirksen Senate Office Building was packed with about five hundred young people—a third of whom were adolescent girls there to see the featured attraction: actor Andrew Shue, chief hunk on TV's *Melrose Place*. Tom Seegel from Rock the Vote, a youth group originally founded to increase voter turnout, forcefully hailed the "well-crafted bill." Because of the stars and the visuals, there were six TV cameras present, giving this event more coverage than any part of the congressional deliberations had received.

Two speakers inadvertently revealed problems with the legislation. Adam Preskower of the College Democrats of America claimed, "Young people support this because it makes it possible for every person to go to college!" Oops. Gwen Robinson of the Green Corps talked about organizing young people to register to vote and establishing a research project on the Clean Air Act. Barnes-O'Connor went back and told Susan Hattan that some of these service programs seemed to be pushing political advocacy. Hattan told Kassebaum, who raised the issues in negotiations with Segal and Kennedy.

No problem. The reporters weren't paying much attention, waiting as they were for the next two speakers: Shue and Beach Boy Mike Love. Love, wearing a flowery vest and baggy satin pants, declared, with about as much eloquence as you might expect, that the filibuster was "not very fun, fun, fun." Finally, Shue went to the microphone, which prompted nine young girls, mostly congressional pages, to lift their point-and-shoot cameras and begin clicking.

Throughout the day, the senators, staff, and Segal's team worked the phones to scrounge up Republicans for the next morning's cloture vote. Kennedy privately resisted suggestions that the Democrats become more combative and partisan. But the White House strategists believed the time had come to turn up the volume. In Chicago, Clinton went on the attack. "They just want to delay it," he said. "Why? Why shouldn't we send a signal to America's young people that we want you to work in your community to make it a better place?"

———

That afternoon, the House and Senate negotiators met again on student aid. Again, they mostly postured, but after the brief meeting broke up Kennedy, Kassebaum, and Jeffords stayed in their seats— and talked about national service. Surrounded by aides, they began discussing the size of the program—how many participants, how much money, how many years.

"Come on, Nancy," Kennedy said. "Let's work something out."

Kassebaum raised the idea of a study on how to consolidate the programs. Absolutely, Kennedy quickly agreed. They then started throwing around numbers like androids conversing in a special digital language. "Three-six-nine," Kennedy said, meaning $300 million the first year, $600 million the second, and $900 million the third. The White House proposal was for $400 million, $1.2 billion, and $1.4 billion.

"Too much," Kassebaum said. She countered, "Two-three-four."

"Three-five-seven," Kennedy offered, circling the numbers on a pad. He pointed out that that was halfway between her proposal and the administration's original request.

She thought about it for a minute. "Two-four-six," she said finally.

The meeting broke up without a resolution, but all three senators felt that they had made progress. Kennedy called Segal to talk about where Kassebaum stood. What happened next is murky. Either Kennedy misunderstood Kassebaum, or Segal misunderstood Kennedy, because after the conversation Segal came away thinking that Kassebaum had made a solid offer of three-five-seven. So he scheduled a meeting with the president for early the next morning to consider the offer.

Tuesday, July 27

When Diana Aldridge came to work on July 27, she checked the press coverage from the around the country. It looked good. Many papers had carried stories about Republican obstructionism. *The New York Times* ran Clinton's Chicago comments in a front-page story headlined CLINTON ASSAILS GOP DELAYS IN BITTER TONES. An Associated Press story covered Monday's rally and mentioned by name some of those Republicans supporting the filibuster. A *Los Angeles Times* editorial was headlined, IMPERILING A PLAN TO HARNESS IDEALISM. Best of all was an editorial in the *Providence Journal,* the most important newspaper in Senator John Chafee's state. FREE THE SERVICE BILL, the headline read. Gordon was thrilled, not quite believing his phone calls could have had such an immediate impact. The administration's press efforts were paying off.

At 7:30 that morning, Segal and Lew went to the White House and met Stephanopoulos, chief lobbyist Howard Paster, and OMB director Leon Panetta to discuss the three-five-seven offer. Stephanopoulos asked whether this was consistent with the president's basic proposal from April. Segal and Lew argued it was.

How much would you be able to get from the appropriations committees? Panetta asked.

Lew said they didn't expect to be able to get more than $300 million. So it would look like they were compromising without actually giving up anything. "The heart and soul is untouched," Lew said. A consensus emerged from the meeting that the deal could be perceived as a win. Segal, Lew, and Paster then went into the Oval Office, where they were joined by Bill Galston. Segal walked through the numbers for Clinton.

The president was skeptical. He questioned why they had cut the authorization from five years to three. Segal explained that they had been able to get Republican support in the House that way. If they agreed to three years, it would be a sign of goodwill to Senate Republicans, too.

"Will that be enough time to get the program going?" Clinton asked.

Yes, Segal said. That would give them enough time to establish a serious program—and prove its worth.

"How many people are you going to have out in the first year?" Clinton asked.

"We believe we could have twenty thousand young people," Segal said.

Clinton pointed out that that would be more than the Peace Corps at its peak. By the end of the twenty-minute discussion, Clinton felt comfortable that, in Lew's words, "this was his program." He made the decision: Go ahead with three-five-seven.

They went to Stephanopoulos's office and called Kennedy and Mitchell. Mitchell went to the floor to announce that there would not be a cloture vote since negotiations were proceeding productively. Kennedy called a meeting in the vice president's office at ten. It looked like they had a deal. Integral players were there: Kassebaum, Durenberger, Chafee, Nunn, Wofford, and Specter. Kennedy said the White House could accept three-five-seven.

The Republicans left to caucus amongst themselves.

Just outside the office, the community groups were in a slight panic because one of the amendments agreed to by the White House would bar national service money for groups that spent more than 10 percent of their budgets on advocacy. Some of their groups felt they would lose money. Leslie Harris of People for the American Way pressed

Kennedy aide Littlefield, but he became irritated. "It may just have to happen," Littlefield said.

"But that wipes out all the higher-education groups," she said.

Finally, exasperated, he said, "Rewrite it so it's correct."

Littlefield looked frazzled. He thought the whole deal could fall apart, and here were the community groups complaining about their own narrow interests.

"Who drew the assignment of doing Specter?" he scolded. "Let's really work this. Who's doing Maine? Who's doing Chafee? You should get their phones ringing off the hook in the next half hour. We can deal with this other stuff later."

About an hour later, the Republicans marched back into the vice president's office.

"Well, you're a good salesman, Eli," said Chafee, speaking for the group. "You got everything you want. Except we want it to be three the first year, five the second year." In other words, no third year.

No deal, Segal said quickly. Two years would be seen as—would *be*—a pilot program.

Segal was depressed. He had thought they had a deal. He had gotten the president's approval. Now there was no agreement.

The deal had collapsed in part because of division within the Republican caucus. Specter felt that a two-year authorization was crucial. Kassebaum cared more about getting the spending numbers lowered. Durenberger didn't like their insistence on making Clinton cry uncle when the White House seemed willing to accommodate Republican concerns. "We have to remember," he told Kassebaum, "the enemy is Bill Ford, not Bill Clinton."

After the Republicans left, the Senate Democrats and the White House people gathered. They were divided themselves. Kennedy's impulse was to get it done—to make a deal. He thought they should accept the two-year authorization. Wofford, along with Dodd and Mikulski, thought Kennedy and the White House had already compromised too much—or, as one staffer put it, had "compromised with themselves."

Kennedy was "cut and run, cave and run," one Democratic player said. The White House also wondered whether Kennedy had given

away too much, but Segal felt uncomfortable challenging the negotiating prowess of the senior senator from Massachusetts. That task fell
to Wofford, who recruited Mikulski. "I'm already upset about the
three-five-seven," she said. She pointed out that she could have funded
that much without even passing a new bill. Mikulski pressed Kennedy
to hold the line. The Republicans were taking a beating in the media.
They would fold eventually if the Democrats kept hammering. Insist
on the three-year authorization, they said.

Segal and Lew returned to the White House and conferred with
Stephanopoulos and with Paster's lobbyists. All agreed that they
couldn't tolerate the two-year authorization. Three years was the bottom line.

The mood in the room was decidedly different from that on previous days. Before, they had been groping for every possible way to
get the sixtieth vote. Now, at the eleventh hour, they concluded that,
in Lew's words, "It might be better to lose than cut a bad deal." For
the first time, Segal said, "There was a sense that we would win either
way on the cloture vote." If they won, they had their bill; if they lost,
the Republicans looked terrible.

Of course, making the Republicans look bad would be small con-
solation for losing national service.

Back in the student-aid conference that afternoon, Ford made it clear
that his position was not softening and suggested the Senate might
want to compromise.

"I would recognize anyone who has a proposal," Ford said. There
was dead silence. No one offered anything.

Eventually, Kennedy said, "If there's anyone who wants to begin
discussion . . ."

Again, silence. "Now would be a good time if someone wants to
begin discussion." Silence. This was beginning to feel a bit awkward,
like a funeral at which no one volunteered to eulogize the deceased.

Finally, Jeffords said, "I'd like to suggest that the House take a hard
look at the Senate position."

That pricked Ford. "I'm here with a bill passed by an overwhelming
margin," he said. Then he began complaining that the House Repub-

licans were trying to block the president just for political gain. "In all my years this is the first time we've had a party-line vote on this committee," he said. "I'm not about to offer *anything*, frankly. I've got a bill here passed by the House. If you want something other than that, you'll have to suggest what it would be."

There was more quiet—a strange sensation in a room full of professional politicians. Would they just stare at each other until someone started to cry?

"As soon as you shoot out something, we'll shoot back," Ford said.

Finally, Howard Metzenbaum offered a proposal. It would institute direct lending at only half of the country's schools, as the Senate plan stated, but would also add another idea: If the program reached the 50-percent cap and there were still schools that wanted to use direct lending, those schools could apply to the Department of Education. The department wouldn't be *required* to crank the program up to 100 percent, but in Kennedy's words, "We're saying to colleges, if they want to move to direct lending, we're not going to stop them."

Ford gave his response to Metzenbaum's offer. "I don't want you to waste your time, because it is totally unacceptable."

Now it was Kennedy's turn to get angry. "Then you come up with a proposal," he said petulantly, "or we're adjourning!" He stood up and, hands trembling, began gathering his papers.

"With all due respect," Ford yelled back, "*you* cannot adjourn this meeting. You elected *me* the chairman of this conference."

Kennedy sat back down and, hurling his words like spitballs, said, "If you've got some amendment in your hand, fine, good for you."

"You have just offered a senate proposal with a small change from what you had before," Ford said.

They recessed for a while to do some floor votes.

It seemed odd that Bill Clinton's inspirational call to open the doors of college and encourage public service had come to this technical, often petty debate about the phase-in rate of direct lending. There had still been no discussion of pay-as-you-can loans or IRS collection. The senators remained locked on direct lending because they knew that these abstract numbers represented billions of dollars in loans for students. Each compromise they tried to reach seemed problematic. At first glance, the fifty–fifty plan had sounded sensible; Congress could make sure the program was working before going all the way. But Ford, Galston, and the Education Department argued that a half-and-half program would self-destruct. Schools, unsure whether direct lending would be permanent, would be unwilling to invest in new computers and staff to implement it. Banks would maintain their lobbying pressure to dismantle or sabotage it. Then there were the blasted budget implications. The slower the phase-in to direct lending, the less the "savings" to the Treasury, according to CBO. To keep the budget in balance, Congress would have to cut more subsidies from the banks and guaranty agencies. As banks saw profits shrink, they would "redline," jettisoning all but the best loans.

Politically, 50 percent was the line in the sand. Fifty–fifty indicated a "competition" between direct lending and the existing system—and therefore a loss for the president—whereas fifty-one–forty-nine was a "phase-in," a victory. Galston's one message to Kennedy's staff was: Whatever the final compromise, it had to be *above* 50 percent. The industry had to know that, one way or another, direct lending was *going to happen.*

When the conferees returned, Ford responded that the Senate proposal didn't work because it would force too many banks out of the program. "Now I hate pleading for the banks. I'm pleading for them not because I think they've made too [little] money. I'm pleading for them because if you don't pay 'em, they won't play. The only way to get around that," he said finally, "is to get that last number up higher—say halfway between fifty and one hundred. . . . seventy-five!"

Aha! There it was. The previous session of standing up, sitting down, yelling, silence, and insults had all been to soften up the Senate for what Ford always intended to be his counteroffer: that 75 percent of the schools would have to use direct lending by 1997, the final year of the authorization.

"If we can do it so President Clinton can claim a victory, I'm all for it," Ford said. "But if the name of the game is not to give Bill Clinton a win, I want to *freeze this conference.*"

Somewhere in the midst of the bluster, Ford had, in fact, put an offer on the table. Numbers began to fly. Metzenbaum improved his offer to 4 percent of new borrowing in the first year, 30 percent in the second, 50 percent in the third, and 60 percent in the fourth, with an escape clause to go higher if there was demand. By this time, the conferees had developed a shorthand, with a "plus" meaning "to go higher if enough schools want to." The Metzenbaum proposal, then, translated to 4-30-50-60 plus.

Now things were moving. Ford countered. "Well, let's try this on for size. Let's delay going to one hundred percent." He proposed 5-30-60-75-100—full direct lending by the fifth year.

The Pell-Kassebaum group seemed unimpressed. They said they'd think about it and the conference adjourned.

Bob Shireman, who had been watching the conference from a seat behind his boss, Paul Simon, went up to David Tobin of Kennedy's staff and explained a tactical decision of Simon's. "Let Nick know that Paul has not been very vocal or strong *intentionally* because he can't help but get Republicans upset," Shireman said. Better that Simon just keep quiet. But Shireman was growing worried that Kassebaum and Jeffords were having too much influence. At some point, Shireman told Tobin, Simon would have to tell Kennedy, "Look, the Republicans are playing games with you."

Wednesday, July 28

Segal woke up early on July 28, went out to the doorstep of his Georgetown townhouse, and picked up *The New York Times* and *The Washington Post*. Still in his pajamas, he sat in a large leather chair in his living room and began scanning the papers. He liked what he saw. The *Times* ran a story entitled, GOP CONTINUES TO BLOCK YOUTH SERVICE BILL AS DEMOCRATS FALTER, and, better yet, an editorial with the scrumptious headline, PETTY POLITICS ON NATIONAL SERVICE. "The Senate Minority Leader, Robert Dole, seems to be marshaling a filibuster to deny President Clinton a major legislative victory at any cost," the editorial stated. Segal then read *The Washington Post*'s article—SENATE GOP STALLS NATIONAL SERVICE BILL—and its editorial, A CHANCE FOR NATIONAL SERVICE, which concluded, "The administration has gone a long way toward accommodating Republican concerns. Now it's time for moderate Republicans who say they support national service (among them Sen. John Chafee and Arlen Specter) to demonstrate that they're willing to break with pure partisanship in the interest of a worthy program."

The best news of all was the lead editorial in the *Philadelphia Inquirer*. Headlined BLOCKING NATIONAL SERVICE, it read, "Dole's little band has apparently decided to put party ahead of country." The newspaper—the largest in Pennsylvania—singled out Specter as one who had done so. Meanwhile, local papers and radio stations from all the targeted states had been calling the Office of National Service for information. The College Democrats organization (based at the Democratic National Committee), faxed a press release to reporters, which said, in large block letters: DAY 5—HOSTAGE SITUATION CONTINUES. FREE NATIONAL SERVICE.

The momentum had begun to shift. "The drumbeat has begun," Segal thought to himself. While the media had barely covered the national service proposal before, they finally had something they could recognize: a partisan brawl.

That morning, Segal entered the Oval Office and quickly briefed Clinton on what had been happening. They were expecting an eleven-o'clock call from Bob Dole. Segal told Clinton that Dole had supported national service in the past. Clinton took the call, listened, and scribbled, "3-4-5?" He pushed the piece of paper toward Segal and looked at him. Segal wrote "No" next to the question.

Dole made noises about wanting to work something out. Clinton said, "That would be good," and mentioned that he knew Dole had supported national service in the past.

Dole told Clinton that if he wanted real bipartisanship he should not go around behind his back picking off a senator here and a senator there. If Clinton was willing to strike a deal with Dole, the president could get twenty-six Republicans, not five. "You deal with me. You don't deal with peeling six off," he said. "Six is not bipartisan. I'll give you bipartisan."

"I'm hearing a lot of things about this Eli Segal guy," Dole said to Clinton. "Send me Segal."

"He'll be there in ten minutes," Clinton responded.

Segal got into one of the sedans waiting by the White House and went straight to Dole's office.

There, the blunt minority leader told Segal, "You don't have the votes for Thursday."

Segal said he wasn't sure, but they wanted to proceed with a cloture vote anyway.

"Isn't there something we can do?" Dole asked.

"Well, we don't see a lot of movement from us away from three-five-seven," Segal said.

Dole suggested that they pass one lump-sum appropriation, and let the chief executive officer of the corporation decide how much to spend when. That was a good idea, Segal said, but he wanted the number to be $1.5 billion, and "you probably won't want more than a billion two."

Then Dole gave his bottom line: "My members don't want to do more than one billion."

The meeting concluded with Dole saying, "Well, you don't have the votes. You do have Elizabeth's vote. But you have fifty-eight. You're not going to get any more on Thursday. We'd like to work this out."

In the midst of the negotiations to break the filibuster, Segal still had to resolve an equally nerve-racking problem in the House: The veterans were back. Earlier in the debate, Representative Gerald Solomon, a conservative Republican from New York, had accused the Clinton administration of paying for national service by cutting veterans' benefits. He proposed an amendment to shift national service out of the appropriations subcommittee that funded veterans affairs so the new program could not compete with the VA over the same limited pot of money. "The National Service Trust Act finds its funds in the pockets of our nation's veterans," Solomon had declared. "Was it more than mere coincidence that the president's budget called for a cut of more than $340 million in veterans' educational programs in fiscal year 1994 while concurrently seeking $384 million—almost the same amount—in nonmilitary national service program education benefits for 1994?" Solomon had lined up the support of the American Legion, the Veterans of Foreign Wars, the Non-commissioned Officers Association of America, and the Disabled American Veterans. The Solomon amendment passed by six votes.

The substance of the amendment did not worry the White House—it really dealt with internal House procedures—but the vote count most certainly did. It showed that if the White House chose to contest the crucial Stump amendment—which proposed lowering the scholarship level to 80 percent of the veterans' benefit—it would not only have to engage in a messy debate to prove that Clinton wasn't screwing veterans, but it would probably lose. There it was again: Because Bill Clinton hadn't served in Vietnam, the veterans could whittle his national service scholarship to a pittance.

For a while, Clinton had been able to avoid an explicit discussion of whether civilian service was comparable to military service. But, ironically, the means-testing amendments had forced Clinton to articulate his views clearly. Why should rich kids get a benefit? Because the scholarship would be a reward for service, *just as it is in the military.* "You know," Clinton told me, "wealthy people may go into the military but if they do, they're entitled to the GI Bill." That argument had prompted indignant harrumphs from opponents. Dick Armey declared that this bill "cannot even bring itself to decide who deserves the larger monetary reward—college students raking leaves or veterans who have served this nation's flag." Roger Munson, national commander of the American Legion, declared, "We cannot stand by and watch a plan go through Congress that's a slap in the face to all veterans who've served their country during Desert Storm."

Ford knew he had to head off this line of attack quickly. He suggested a compromise: to tie the scholarship amount to 90 percent of the veterans' benefit and do some tinkering with the definitions used in calculating the amount. The national service scholarship would be around $4,700.

Clinton called Ford to say he could accept 95 percent, but not 90 percent.

"Okay, I'll do it, but I don't think it will fly," Ford told Clinton. The problem was that 95 percent came to $4,988. That simply didn't look like much of a compromise. Ford showed it to David Bonior, the

House majority whip, who said, as expected, that it wasn't going to work. Pat Rissler, the staff director of the Education and Labor Committee, then called Stephanopoulos and urged him to cut a deal at 90 percent.

Stephanopoulos said no.

"The headline is going to be 'Congress Debates Clinton War Record' instead of 'National Service Victory,' " she warned.

"We don't care," Stephanopoulos replied. "We have to draw the line somewhere."

Ford was getting pressure from other Democrats not to force a public fight over this. They knew there would be no such thing as a quick, painless discussion on this. They could count on Bob Walker, Dick Armey, and Robert Dornan to rant about Clinton and the draft. Negotiations proceeded for hours between Ford, Montgomery, Stump, and McCurdy.

Eventually Montgomery made an offer to Bob Stump: The White House might be able to accept 90 percent if there was *a minimum of debate*.

Segal and Lew liked the idea. With the redefinitions, the benefit would be $4,725, a reasonable amount, they thought. Stephanopoulos pitched it to Clinton, who, with little hesitation, said yes.

On July 28, the House passed a revised Stump amendment with very little debate.

———

At seven p.m., the House of Representatives voted on final passage of H.R. 2010, the National and Community Service Trust Act of 1993. Few legislators were on the floor when the vote was called. As members came trickling in, Ford's staff, including Gene Sofer, stood looking up at the wall behind the gallery, where 435 names were suddenly flashed like baseball statistics on a stadium scoreboard. Members stuck a special magnetized card into a slot behind the benches and pressed one of three buttons marked AYE, NAY, or PRESENT. Green squares appeared next to the names of legislators who pushed the aye button, red squares next to the names of those who voted no. Sofer was looking up at the scoreboard with his eyes shielded, as if he were looking into the sun. A small sliver of a grin appeared on his face.

Above the chamber, Bill Clinton and Al Gore were standing in the House Rules Committee room. A few minutes earlier they had concluded a meeting on health care, and they were now watching the national service vote on TV. Bill Ford walked in on them just as the monitor flashed "267 Yea." The final vote would be 275–152.

The president went over to the gruff committee chairman . . . and gave him a hug. "Damn good victory," Clinton said, lifting Ford off the floor with his embrace.

———

Just a few minutes after the final passage in the House, Segal received a call from Sheila Burke, top aide to Robert Dole. Dole, Specter, Nickles, and Kassebaum had been conferring, and Specter had come up with another proposal. Segal would be receiving a fax very soon with a new proposal, Burke said. She asked him not to show it to anyone. Segal grew excited with anticipation. The fax arrived.

It was a two-year authorization, "plus such sums as . . ." Segal saw that simple phrase, and for an instant felt as if the administration had won. The Republicans had finally agreed to the construction the White House had been offering for days: a fixed authorization, "plus such sums as may be necessary." But his delight lasted only until he read the rest of the sentence: ". . . plus such sums as may be authorized." Huh? Such sums as may be *authorized*? What the hell did that mean? It *seemed* like progress, and he told Burke, "This is good faith." He then called Kennedy and said he thought he might have a deal.

"Let me hear it," Kennedy said. Segal read the language to Kennedy over the phone.

"No," Kennedy said. "You don't have a deal." Kennedy and his staff were irritated. The Republicans appeared to be pulling a trick. "Such sums as may be authorized" was, for all intents and purposes, a two-year authorization, which the White House had already rejected. "This is so duplicitous and sneaky," one Democratic staffer said. That evening, Segal called Burke back and gave the White House response: no deal.

This would have to be fought out on the floor the next day. The filibuster continued. The cloture vote was scheduled for noon, and the White House still didn't have the votes.

Even though Ford and Kennedy had been working half the day in their respective chambers to get the national service bill through, they were still spending the other half butting heads over student-aid reform.

The senators had caucused and remained divided. "How can Ford ignore all the members who have said they oppose this?" Kassebaum asked in frustration during one of the private meetings. In fact, right before the conference three hundred Democrats had signed a letter, circulated by Tennessee representative Bart Gordon, that expressed concerns about direct lending. Ford did not have a strong hand.

"Ford has three hundred signatures against him in the House. He doesn't have support in the House for any more than a pilot," Coats said during a closed-door caucus. "I don't know what cards he's playing."

They began to take some straw votes. Pell and the Republicans wanted to propose 5-30-50 and hold. (Schools accounting for five percent of borrowing would use direct lending the first year, 30 percent the second year, 50 percent the third.) Mikulski and Dodd were also willing to go against the White House, which insisted on something above 50 percent. The anti–direct lending forces seemed to have a 9–8 vote for a new Senate offer to the House.

Then the unexpected happened. Judd Gregg, the conservative Republican from New Hampshire—a strong opponent of direct lending—raised an objection to an unrelated provision forcing states to bear more of the risk of student-loan defaults. He said if he didn't get these concerns addressed, he wouldn't join his fellow Republicans on this vote. Kennedy told him that the irksome provision was still in there, and then asked Gregg for his vote.

The response was stunning: "No."

The room went quiet. The Pell-Kassebaum forces simply couldn't believe it. They had been on the verge of a victory and, out of the blue, one of their solid Republicans had defected over something unrelated to direct lending. It was a useful lesson to the staff. When all the prep work is done, the vote counts taken, and the memos written, the decision still lies with the United States senator—and the senator can vote however he or she damn well pleases. Kassebaum, who was in charge of delivering the Republicans, looked stunned. "Did I fail in my leadership?" she asked Evans later.

The only thing left was to make the House a more generous proposal, in order to bring other Democrats on board the offer: 5-30-50-50-60. They crossed the magic 50-percent line. The day's action would prove to be a major blow to the student-loan industry.

Thursday, July 29

On the morning of July 29, Specter called Segal several times to plead with him to accept the Republican offer on national service. Look, it's just one line! Specter said. No deal, Segal insisted. He was digging in his heels.

To shore up the votes the White House did have, President Clinton himself called Durenberger and Jeffords to thank them in advance for voting for cloture.

Finally, they held the cloture vote to shut off the filibuster. As senators ambled in, Dole held up his fingers pinched an inch apart. It would be a very close vote. Chafee went over to a staff aide, who showed him a preliminary vote count. Chafee walked toward the desk and voted aye. The White House had gotten Chafee. It now had fifty-nine votes—just one short. Kassebaum waited until the end, and then voted against. She had decided she had to vote to sustain the filibuster, but didn't want to influence anyone else's vote.

Mark Hatfield of Oregon arrived late and was instantly surrounded by senators from both sides. After talking with Durenberger, Nunn, Dole, and D'Amato, Hatfield gave his vote to the clerk. The clerk called it out, "Mr. Hatfield—no!"

The White House had lost.

———————

That afternoon, Jack Lew and Sheila Burke negotiated some more, again slicing and dicing that key "such sums" sentence to try to come up with some arrangement that met everyone's needs. But the bottom line was that the Republicans didn't want the cumulative total to be above $1 billion, and the White House thought that was way too low.

In the course of the negotiations, Burke said to Lew, "You know you don't have the votes tomorrow."

The White House knew that a relative of David Pryor's had died, and that Pryor had to go to Arkansas for the funeral on Friday, so they'd lost his vote. They had tried to keep that a secret from Dole, but maybe the minority leader had found out.

Here's what the Republicans did know: There had been a report on the wire services that day that Cohen of Maine would break the filibuster by supporting the cloture vote. Dole's staff had called Cohen, but Cohen said the report was false. Dole also knew, however, that several of the waverers were about to fold. It was just a matter of time before the filibuster would collapse.

But maybe, just maybe, the White House didn't realize how close it was to victory. Maybe the administration would throw in one or two more concessions. "We were operating on pure bluff," said Barnes O'Connor later.

———

Back at the student-aid conference, rumors were flying. "Did you hear the latest? *Kunin said they could actually take less than 100 percent.*" "Have you heard? *The president says he could support a compromise.*" The tiny, ornate Senate meeting room was packed. About thirty lobbyists lined the hallway outside, afraid to go to the bathroom lest they might miss something. This had the feel of a showdown.

Jeffords threw out an offer: 5-35-50-50. Pat Williams, a congressman from Montana, responded that "it doesn't get the savings." Again, the savings. Again, the budget scoring. They couldn't make a single change without the CBO signing off on it. Each time someone came up with a proposal, a staff member would go call Deb Kalcevic, who would then do a computer run. A few minutes later she would give the verdict: It met the budget goals, or it didn't. She was the invisible referee of the conference.

"I feel like we're in *Alice in Wonderland*," Kassebaum said.

Ford continued to argue that the Senate's half-and-half plan cut subsidies to the existing system so much that it would cause banks to pull out. "If we hit them this hard, we're not going to have a program left."

Jeffords protested: If the approach would be so bad for the banks, how come he had "letter after letter" from banks supporting the *Senate's* bill?

"They'll tell you any damn thing they want to stop direct lending," Ford responded. He was playing a complicated game: protecting the banks by bashing them.

There was so much emotional voltage in the room that it seemed as if any spark could cause an explosion. The posturing, the tugging —it had all frayed congressional nerves. Each legislator felt strongly about his or her position. Finally, one member erupted.

"I've heard the same lecture over and over," said Republican Representative Bill Goodling. "We're not changing anything—let's get it over with!"

"You're also a good friend," Ford said to Goodling, "but nothing I do is going to get you to vote for this."

"Now there you go!" Goodling yelled, like a husband feeling misunderstood by his spouse. "How do you know what I would do?" His voice kept rising. "I've tried to tell you a dozen times, I'll vote the way I think is right!" The rest of the group felt as if it was intruding on a domestic fight.

"Will you vote for the reconciliation?" Ford calmly parried, referring to the president's entire budget plan to which loan reform was attached.

"Talk about my vote *here*," Goodling yelled. "*This* is my responsibility!"

Kennedy tried to cut the tension with a joke. "I thought we had fun on our side . . ."

But Goodling had finally reached the breaking point. He was bitter because Ford had stopped soliciting his support and advice ever since the Democrats won the White House. Under Bush, Ford needed Republican allies; under Clinton, he didn't. "Oh, it was fun when I was *needed*," he said. Spent, Goodling muttered, "Some kind of friendship."

The other legislators in the room tried to shift back to a substantive discussion. Jeffords offered to raise the percentage in the second year. "The problem is you can only move your checkers in one direction to make the savings. It's maddening. The accounting is making policy." He said it would be great if he and Kennedy could change the budget scoring, but that "I have little hope that the combined weight of Senator Kennedy and I . . ."

"Please use a different phrase," the rotund senator from Massachusetts said, cracking up the group.

Panic was turning into delirium. During a break, Shireman leaned over to Kennedy aide Suzanne Ramos and asked if Simon should put something on the table. Kennedy said okay. Shireman wrote down an offer. At that point, Kennedy leaned forward, and like a seasoned bidder at a high-stakes auction, looked at Simon and began discreetly nodding. Only one problem: Shireman hadn't clued in Simon to any of this. As Shireman watched Kennedy nodding meaningfully to the oblivious Simon, time seemed to slow to a comic crawl.

Jeffords reported that if they went up to 35 percent in the second year, that would give them $85 million in savings. With that, Shireman slipped a note to Simon: "Go with higher number in the fifth year as a bone to Ford." Simon moved that the Senate's official offer be 5-35-50-plus 60-plus 60-plus, with plus again meaning the program would be open to any additional schools that want to participate.

Ford again started in about "the moneylenders," prompting Dodd to interject, "Come on! Do you like it or not?"

The group recessed to consider the Senate offer.

Both sides were growing weary. Both now wanted guidance from the Clinton administration. The Democrats on the Senate met again —this time joined by Secretary of Education Riley. This was a crucial moment for Kennedy. He needed to know whether he should fall on his sword.

The day before, Riley and Galston had conferred on strategy. After an education event in the ornate Indian Treaty Room in the Old Executive Office Building, Galston had pulled the education secretary aside. "Now is the time to play the card of compromise," Galston said. Deep down he knew that support for direct lending in the House was weak, as the Bart Gordon amendment had demonstrated. They had pushed as far as they could, given their hand. And the compromise within reach now would meet their goals. It would be seen as a phase-in of a full program rather than an experiment. Riley agreed. The next day he sent the signal to Kennedy. Like a Southern gentleman, he spoke in coded understatement. He told Kennedy he would trust him to do what's best. "We don't want to be saddled with a program that fails, and one hundred is more likely to work," Riley said. "But I leave it to you professional politicians." Kennedy's team viewed that as a signal—he could still work with the Republicans without Clinton viewing him as a traitor.

Ford, meanwhile, retired to a small coffee shop in the Capitol and, after finishing a tuna sandwich, he began chewing on watermelon rinds. At 6:30 Riley arrived at the coffee shop along with Madeleine Kunin. Bill Galston arrived a few minutes later and stood against a pillar, straining to listen to those at the table. Ford lit his pipe and leaned in to hear Riley and Kunin, both of whom have thin, high-pitched voices. This was the only area restaurant open, so lobbyists for guaranty agencies sat at tables nearby, chewing extra-quietly in the hopes that they would hear a few words of the fateful meeting among Riley, Kunin, and Ford.

"This is not looking good," Riley said. He told Ford they had met with Jeffords and Kassebaum, who were not moving from 50 percent. It was time to get an agreement. Ford wanted to press on, but Riley worried that direct lending would hold up the budget conference and antagonize the Republican senators.

"A lawyer can't go much farther than his client wants him to," said Ford regretfully.

At first, when the conference reconvened, Ford did not seem to be any more conciliatory. "I don't want my fingerprints on it," he said. "I guess I haven't been heard here. I have repeated over and over and over. You're hitting the guaranty agencies and the banks too hard—and I don't want to endorse it."

"There's only one alternative," Ford said finally. "Throw in the fifth year, which comes a year after reauthorization. Make that seventy-five percent."

Is this really how policy is made? The numbers flew around in such abstract form; no one really knew what would save money, what would drive banks away, what would be perceived as a victory for Clinton. Yet the stakes for students were great.

"I frankly don't remember who's right anymore," Simon said. "What is clear is we're spinning our wheels here."

Dodd whispered to Wofford that they simply couldn't afford to alienate Jeffords and Kassebaum. If Jeffords and Kassebaum came to believe that the White House was playing nasty, they might retaliate by supporting Dole's filibuster. "We're going to lose national service here," he said. "Jeffords and Nancy are going to quit!"

Again they recessed. As Littlefield walked down the lobbyist-lined hallway, Omer Waddles from Ford's staff reached over and grabbed his arm.

"You've got to move," Waddles said.

"We can't go as high as you want," Littlefield said.

"But you have to go above fifty percent."

"We need to get these guys to talk," Littlefield said of Ford and Kennedy. Littlefield walked quickly over toward Kennedy to keep him from going back into the conference room. Waddles grabbed Ford and said, "I think Senator Kennedy wants to talk to us."

Waddles, Littlefield, Suzanne Ramos from Kennedy's staff, and Pat Rissler from Ford's accompanied the two lawmakers into a nearby anteroom. Kennedy again explained that the Republicans were not going to move. Ford said they'd like to accommodate Jeffords but they needed more savings. Kennedy said he'd make an offer, but it had to be one that Ford would actually accept. They decided to pump up the percentage in the second year: that would produce the necessary savings. Kennedy suggested 5-40-50-plus 50-plus 60-plus.

"That makes sense," Ford responded. They choreographed the next movement. Ramos checked with the Department of Education to make sure it could gear up the program that quickly; in the past it had said it could not. The department decided that, since the number represented a target—no laws would be broken if it didn't quite make it to 40 percent in the second year—it could accept the figure.

At nine p.m. the conferees returned. Jeffords offered 5-35-50-plus 50-plus. After some more argument, Ford moved: 5-40-50-plus 50-plus 60-plus. "This is almost on the button the same savings." An air of relief spread around the room. Peace was in the land. The senators rapidly blurted out their approval, fearful that Ford would change his mind at any moment.

"I would certainly recommend accepting this," Kennedy said.

"I think it's a genuine attempt at compromise," Jeffords said quickly.

"I think it's a very reasonable offer," Dodd said.

"I would accept this," said Pell.

Most of the Republicans seemed satisfied too, since they would have a shot in 1998 at putting a halt to direct lending. They voted. Everyone except Kassebaum supported the compromise. The conference adjourned.

Kennedy, exuberant, called Stephanopoulos, Kunin, and Riley to tell them the final result.

———

Whatever happened to IRS collection and pay-as-you-can loans? The House, you may recall, had a weak provision; the Senate had a strong one. When staff met to hammer out the details on the "minor issues," Shireman was told by house negotiators that they simply could not take on the House Ways and Means Committee. "The IRS made it clear through Treasury, through Ways and Means, they didn't want any part of this—they didn't want the workload," Waddles said. "Ford isn't going to take on Rosty," a Ford aide told Ramos, referring to House Ways and Means chairman Dan Rostenkowski. "We hit a brick wall. It was just not negotiable." Even the Senate Finance Committee had expressed displeasure. Anyway, neither the White House nor the Department of Education had been saying it was important. They had been concentrating on direct lending.

On pay-as-you-can loans, the only issue to decide—since the legislation was mostly vague—was the amnesty period for those with big debts or low incomes. The Senate had said twenty years. The House had no limit. They compromised at twenty-five years. With virtually no discussion, they had limited the number of years anyone would have to make payments. That meant anyone who still hadn't paid off their loan by year twenty-five would get an enormous gift from the taxpayers. The biggest benefit of all would go to men and women who accumulated massive educational debt but then earned low incomes for many years. There aren't many such creatures, but the few that exist include doctors who work in low-income clinics or lawyers who become public defenders—in other words, those doing the public-service jobs Clinton admired. A handful of congressional aides had made Clinton's dramatic plan into a radical one.

The student-aid reform bill would pass as part of the budget reconciliation signed by the president in August 1993. It would not be mentioned on any newscasts, and would rate just a line near the bottom in most articles.

Friday, July 30

On July 30, Eli Segal was awakened by a phone call. It was Jack Lew, telling him to look at the front page of *The New York Times*. VICTORY NOW SEEMS IN CLINTON'S GRASP ON A SERVICE PLAN; GOP FILIBUSTER BROKEN. Cohen had told the *Times* what he told the wires the day before, but hadn't yet told the White House: he would vote for cloture. Segal was particularly gratified that the tie-breaking vote would come from Cohen, who had, indeed, received a call from Gary Hart. With the support of Cohen and Mark Hatfield, who had also indicated he'd defect, the White House finally had sixty votes. Just to make sure, President Clinton called Hatfield and Cohen that morning to thank them for their support. Segal could finally relax. He went to work thinking that today would finally be the day national service passed.

But when Segal arrived at his office, he got a surprise: Cohen had said he would support the cloture vote, but he hadn't said *when*. The senator had gone to Maine—Cohen had skipped town! "It's like some bad off-off-Broadway play," Aldridge moaned. Dole could drag on the filibuster until the next week, making it less likely that the Senate would finish with service before the summer recess.

But the editorial drumbeat had continued over the past two days. *The Washington Post* headline read, ONE VOTE BLOCKS ROAD TO SENATE PASSAGE OF NATIONAL SERVICE BILL. The *Oregonian*, the largest paper in its state, carried an editorial headlined OREGON'S OBSTINATE OBSTRUCTIONISTS: HATFIELD AND PACKWOOD ENGAGE IN FILIBUSTER ABUSE. (Robert Gordon worried that the editorial had gone too far and would make the senators angry. He was informed by others in the office that the whole point of this exercise was to get under their skin.) The ONS staffers were thrilled to see the the *Philadelphia Inquirer*'s editorial announce, deliciously, SPECTER KNUCKLES UNDER. The article began, "Sen. Arlen Specter chose his party over his principles yesterday when the US Senate fell one vote—one vote!—short of halting a Republican filibuster preventing a vote on President Clinton's plan for a national service program. Mr. Specter fell right in line, supporting the filibuster, and, in effect, voting against a bill he *himself* cosponsored."

So even though Dole could have won that day, he decided this had gone on long enough. The filibuster was starting to hurt the Republicans. At 11 o'clock, he met with George Mitchell and agreed to end the filibuster through a unanimous consent agreement. The Republicans were done.

———

On August 3, the U.S. Senate approved S. 919 by a vote of 58–41. It budgeted $300 million, $500 million, and $700 million for the next three years. In the end, after all the effort, only seven Republicans voted for the bill: the four original co-sponsors plus Kay Bailey Hutchison of Texas, Hatfield of Oregon, and Ted Stevens of Alaska, who had gotten those special provisions for his state included in the final bill. Cohen voted no. So, inexplicably, did Coats and Gregg—two conservatives who had voted for it in committee. Coverdell, the former Peace Corps director, voted no. Despite all Segal's efforts, Kassebaum voted no. So did Dole. Democrats Byrd, Exon, Hollings, and Kerrey voted no.

Kerrey's vote provided a nice lesson in politics. The Nebraska Democrat, who had gotten a heartfelt plea from Wofford, voted nay, while Stevens—who had gotten pork amendments for Alaska—voted aye.

———

The White House and congressional allies rushed the bill to conference so they could get it passed before the recess, which was scheduled to begin at the end of the week. Staff went over each item, with Kassebaum managing to knock out some of Kennedy's highly bureaucratic provisions on service learning. But on the most important issues, the staff agreed to a grand swap. If the House accepted the painfully negotiated Senate spending levels, the Senate would accept the compromise over the ACTION employees and the civil-service rules. With little discussion, Segal was perfectly happy to throw civil-service reform overboard if it got the bill finished.

This trade contained an amazing irony. Segal knew that if the House negotiators in conference had insisted on higher spending amounts, it would have jeopardized the final passage in the Senate. He feared that anything above the fragile 3-5-7 pact would provoke another Republican filibuster. But to get the House to go along with the Senate's lower spending numbers, Segal had to give them what they wanted most: preservation of the current bureaucracy. In other words, the net result of the Republican filibuster was the preservation of the stifling civil-service rules pushed by a liberal union!

The actual House-Senate conference, later that day, took about fifteen minutes, since everything had been prenegotiated by the staff.

After the conference ended, Ford went up to Segal. "I have loved watching you learn about the congressional process," he said in total seriousness. "It's horrifying. Time and time again I've seen people come up here with a great idea and only get a little bit. You folks have set a new standard—coming in and getting everything you wanted."

Segal beamed.

Despite the frantic rush to finish by recess, the legislators ran out of time that week. They came back after the summer break and, on September 8, approved the National and Community Service Trust Act as reported out by the House-Senate conference.

The bill had finally passed.

On September 21, 1993, President Clinton signed the bill into law and announced that the new program would, from then on, be called AmeriCorps.

15

Getting Things Done

At 4:30 a.m. on September 12, 1994, Eli Segal was awakened by a phone call. "You're not going to believe this," said White House staffer Judy Green. A lone pilot with a history of substance abuse had crashed a Cessna airplane into the back of the White House—right where the triumphant launch of AmeriCorps was to take place that day. Segal, Diana Aldridge, and the rest of the staff of the Corporation for National and Community Service had worked for months coordinating dozens of activities. The president was going to swear in nine thousand volunteers at sixteen sites around the country via satellite. There would be elaborate torch-passing ceremonies involving military veterans, Peace Corps volunteers, and the first group of AmeriCorps participants. They had made contingency plans in case of bad weather, checked and rechecked the satellite arrangements, reviewed every detail of the staging. "What could go wrong?" Segal kept asking his staff. "What haven't we thought of?"

The plane hit the South Lawn at around 2 a.m. Later that morning, White House staff were told that the area was now deemed a crime site and off-limits. Senior aides like George Stephanopoulos and Mark Gearan gathered to discuss a plan of action. They considered moving the event to the Kennedy Center or even canceling it entirely. In the end, they decided to have Clinton swear in the volunteers around the rest of the country at one o'clock from the Oval Office and have the White House ceremony on the North Lawn at 3:30.

When the time came, five hundred AmeriCorps members crowded onto the driveway in front of the White House. They wore gray AmeriCorps T-shirts and baseball hats with the orange logos printed fashionably on the back side. Segal, Al Gore, Hillary Clinton, and President Clinton came to the podium. "This day is part of a long journey for me personally and for many others who have long harbored the dream that national service embodies," Clinton said. "One of the main reasons I ran for president is that I felt that we as Americans need to make our life journeys together rather than apart.

"We look to you and know that you are no generation of slackers, but instead a generation of doers," he said, before being interrupted by applause. "We cannot go on as a nation of strangers, mistrusting one another because we've never had the chance to work side by side or had the chance to walk in one another's shoes."

Then the president began to deliver the oath, which had been written largely by Robert Gordon. The volunteers raised their right hands. Looking devoutly earnest, they repeated after the president:

> *I will get things done for America—*
> *To make our people safer, smarter, and healthier.*
> *I will bring America together—*
> *To strengthen our communities.*
> *Faced with conflict, I will seek common ground.*
> *Faced with adversity, I will persevere.*
> *I will carry this commitment with me this year and beyond.*
> *I am an AmeriCorps member,*
> *And I am going to get things done.*

National service was now real.

———

A generation from now will AmeriCorps be remembered with the same fondness as Roosevelt's CCC? Will it function like a Swiss Army knife, drawing together people of different backgrounds to perform useful service? The seeds of the program's potential success—or failure—were planted in the law.

The legislation did not assure that AmeriCorps would become a transforming, class-mixing institution. Indeed, members of Congress added provisions that seemed to create just another traditional anti-poverty program dominated by low-income people. The White House negotiators seemed adamantly blasé about that problem. We can deal with that later, they said.

Oddly enough, they did—in the regulations. Segal had appointed Shirley Sagawa to be number two at the corporation (executive vice president), and Catherine Milton to be vice president in charge of dispensing grants. She knew that the regulations were not just for fine-tuning; that, in fact, they could establish important new missions for the program (as long as they didn't outright contradict what was in the law). She pushed hard for language in the regulations that would rec-tify the legislative gaps on race- and class-mixing. Segal agreed. The corporation's rules required that "each program seek actively to engage participants from diverse backgrounds." They spelled out possible ex-ceptions but placed the burden on the programs to show why they *shouldn't* create a mixed group.

By doing this, Segal's team managed to make race- and class-mixing a major goal of the program without ever having a public debate on it. This may prove to be politically brilliant, but just as likely it will be seen as a Pyrrhic victory. Ultimately, real change occurs only when attitudes change, and that happens through public debate. Victories in the dark only pave the way for similarly unnoticed defeats.

To get the legislation through, Segal had also made a number of compromises that undermined the goal of the volunteers performing useful work. He allowed the weakening of the reinventing-government plans, increased the percentage of money going through the states, and accepted restrictions demanded by the unions. After the bill's pas-sage, Segal tried to make the best of the hand he had dealt himself. He intensified his rhetoric emphasizing useful service, adopting as the official AmeriCorps slogan the phrase "Getting Things Done." Again, he used the regulations to rectify problems in the law, requiring that service must provide a *"direct benefit* to the community," be located "physically in the community," and "bring participants face-to-face with residents of the community." In other words, setting up a com-puter system to help with the payroll of a community group will not count. They also prohibited AmeriCorps programs from engaging in political advocacy.

To make the Corporation for National and Community Service more agile than typical government agencies, Segal's team devised a new personnel system that allows managers more flexibility in deciding salaries. Most important, they can hire new employees under renewable contracts instead of giving the lifetime job guarantees of civil service. Segal boasted that this alone made the corporation one of the most innovative in the federal government. The problem was that, under their legislative compromise, they had to insulate the four hundred existing ACTION employees—roughly 80 percent of the corporation's staff—from such innovation. Each individual is protected until he or she retires. Perhaps most troubling, the ACTION state directors were given the assignment of being the corporation's "spy" on the state commissions. A key feature of reinventing government went to the old guard.

A development unrelated to Segal's work gave a boost to one type of service originally mentioned by Clinton during the campaign. The controversial crime bill passed by Congress in the summer of 1994 included $100 million for a "police corps," a program that would provide $7,500 per year for college education of those who agree to become police officers.

One of the biggest questions raised by the legislation is: If one particular program doesn't "get things done," who will be held accountable? The state commission? Not likely. Hard to shake your fist at a twenty-five-person, independent, unelected body. The governor? No, he or she can claim the money was given out by an independent commission. The federal government will probably be blamed, and yet it will be in the weakest position to do something about abuses. By contrast, the CCC of the 1930s was clearly the responsibility of the federal government, and consequently the president took personal interest in making sure it worked. If local AmeriCorps programs begin to give service a bad name, it will be yet another loop in the historical cycle: government screws up . . . "reformers" take spending decisions away from government . . . more failures occur, providing further "proof" that the federal government can't work. Ultimately, real work will happen only if the corporation is willing to de-fund programs that aren't doing a good job. That's a tough thing to do, particularly in an election year.

Did Clinton ultimately meet his goal of radically restructuring the student-aid system? Yes. The Department of Education career staff and White House political aides Gene Sperling and Bill Galston got together and devised a pay-as-you-can loan system that seemed to meet Clinton's objectives. It allowed individuals to make payments equal to 4 percent of their income if they have a $1,000 debt. The payment rate rose as the debt burden got larger. A student with a $30,000 income and a $50,000 debt would pay $345 per month instead of $581 under the standard plan. The formula also revealed the importance of that barely discussed twenty-five-year repayment period slipped in by a few congressional staffers. Someone with a low income and a high debt could end up with a big chunk of loan outstanding at year twenty-five—which the government would then wipe out.

Again, the administration and its allies snuck through that pay-as-you-can language without more than a few sentences of congressional discussion. Tactically, that may have made sense; and one can certainly be glad that the result came out well. But it is highly disconcerting to have such a gargantuan policy shift take place with so little public wrangling.

The one clear defeat for Clinton was his failure to get a major role for the IRS. A year after the bill's passage, the IRS and the Department of Education still had not come up with a plan for IRS collection. So the question remains: Will the administration's political failure on that one provision so hobble the program that the stealth victory of pay-as-you-can loans will be meaningless?

There was certainly plenty of conflict during the intertwined journeys of national service and student-loan reform—but to a great extent it was meaningless conflict. The battles always seemed to center on the least-important elements. Direct lending absorbed 99 percent of the attention of staff, legislators, and interest groups—even though it was far less important than pay-as-you-can loans. With national service, the issue of race- and class-mixing was hardly discussed. And there never really was an explicit debate about how to set up a program that would be most likely to promote useful service.

Why is so much acrimony wasted on things so unimportant? First, the White House and the Department of Education clearly avoided being explicit on controversial issues. It was their political judgment that they could not get either piece of legislation passed otherwise. They may have been right. And that points to a great misunderstanding about "gridlock" in Washington. The problem is not that Congress is incapable of passing laws, but that it is so easy for small groups of people to block or distort legislation that those pushing reform readily agree to self-defeating compromises. And when the White House made concessions, they never seemed to extract much in return. For all they gave the governors and labor, those two interest groups did not push the legislation enough to boost the funding more. So what did the White House gain? Segal's answer: We got the bill passed and AmeriCorps started. The programs themselves, he says, will convince the public of the merits of service far more than some debate in the Senate. That's true—unless their compromises make it so hard for the programs to work well that the public ends up convinced they've wasted their money.

I can't help but think that part of the White House reluctance to raise these issues comes not from shrewd pragmatism but rather from what might be called Battered Liberal Syndrome. Clinton and his team believe in activist government. They believe in class-mixing. They believe it's better for a young person to go into public service than to trade financial derivatives on Wall Street. But they sometimes seemed to have lost confidence in their ability to convince other people. Democrats had been decimated by busing fights over race-mixing; they were not about to carry that torch again. Class-mixing smacked of social engineering; don't want to touch that one. Even Clinton's emphasis on national service as a student-loan program—driven by the polls—showed his lack of faith in the selling power of service. He emphasized the politically safe part, even though it gave a misleading impression of the program.

Interest-group politics also drove the process away from issues of most concern to the broad public. Direct lending became the dominant issue because plump oxen were being gored. The financial industry fought, the direct lending proponents fought back, the press covered the conflict—and important questions of education policy got ignored. On the national service side, advocates of real work shied away from fleshing out what they meant because to do so would have alienated interest groups. If the White House had clarified that they wanted AmeriCorps members to be teachers, not just teachers' aides, the teachers' unions would have objected. If they'd said they wanted to deny money to programs that are predominantly black, the National Association of Service and Conservation Corps would have objected. Somewhere, there's an interest group that will object to almost any strong step. The easiest way to avoid conflict is to be vague.

So many groups in Washington have become infected with cynicism or narrow thinking that the notion of attaining some larger national goal often seems impossible or even laughable. Whether it was the conservation corps pushing a special set-aside for their programs or the governors demanding a bigger share of the spending, the ostensibly virtuous service corps mimicked the behavior of the student-aid industry by emphasizing narrow agendas. This poses a serious problem. When a small collection of special interests pushes members of Congress away from the broader good, the public can at least try to wake lawmakers from the hypnotic spell. But when the petty pressure comes *from* "the public"—in the form of organized constituent groups—it becomes more difficult for a legislator to resist selfish claims. The result, in the case of national service, was a program less likely to work.

The system is supposed to have some built-in checks against this slide toward the parochial. The press, for instance, ought to be watching out for whether the political process is serving the public will. It didn't. Having ignored national service most of the year, reporters became briefly attentive during the filibuster—conflict! sports metaphors!—and then lost interest again. Hardly a word was spoken or written about the essential issues that would determine the success or failure of the program. The press paid even less attention to pay-as-you-can loans.

Sometimes the opposition party plays the role of smoking out the president on controversial issues. But with student aid, most Republicans concentrated on defeating direct lending—largely because Clinton supported it. On national service, there were a few Republican attempts to drive the debate toward real issues, like Kassebaum's plan to consolidate existing service programs and Goodling's amendment to means test the service scholarship. But most of the debate was over substantively peripheral—but politically potent—issues. The Republicans baited Clinton over the veterans or made blatantly misleading claims about the program's costs.

———

It takes several years before one can judge the success of a particular bill. Certainly, the legislative process saddled AmeriCorps with some heavy baggage. The adventures of national service and student-aid reform illustrated the pervasive corruption of the political system. Millions of dollars were spent on phony polls, misleading advertising, revolving-door lobbyists, and artificial grassroots efforts. What's In It For Us has become the operating philosophy of nearly every group in Washington. Even those predisposed toward public-spiritedness eventually conclude they will be taken for suckers if they don't grab their piece of the pie before there's nothing left.

But along with corruption and cynicism (and, alas, comedy) did come some nobility. Those pushing student-aid reform were driven not only by a lust for skewering the banks but also by a desire to improve access to college. In the financial aid industry, pecuniary interests were usually accompanied by genuine convictions that theirs was the best way to help Americans go to college. Similarly, those in the service movement may have had some selfish motives—wanting *their* programs to grow fastest—but most were also guided by mental images of the extraordinary young people who had improved neighborhoods and themselves by working in their communities.

Clinton had promised so much in the campaign that the end result was destined to seem puny by comparison. However, the law passed by Congress did maintain the same basic approach outlined by Clinton in the campaign: Americans would be able to serve their communities in exchange for college aid, and they would be able to pay back their college loans as a percentage of income over time.

Clinton's national service plan is a big idea—in fact, a noble one. It is one of the rare attempts to encourage Americans of different social classes to strive toward some larger national purpose. It stresses commonality instead of differences. And while Clinton muddied the message of sacrifice by emphasizing the college benefit, AmeriCorps is still one of the rare federal endeavors that asks Americans to contribute something other than taxes toward their nation. The program even has a political logic to it that can make it sustainable and real, as it gives the middle class a stake in helping the poor. In fact, Clinton has attempted to do much more in this sphere than his idol John Kennedy. The Peace Corps and VISTA brought a relatively small number of people from homogeneous backgrounds to serve; Clinton asked for something that would attract a much broader variety of Americans and create a new set of weapons in America's social policy arsenal. His college-aid reform ultimately sought not only to put more cash in students' hands but also to change the incentive structure that governs a young American's life choices. He attempted to do this with resources more scarce, media more skeptical, and a Congress more paralyzed by interest groups than in JFK's time.

A program that tapped into the American people's best impulses was almost killed by Washington's worst.

Almost.

In the end, Clinton had—however awkwardly—called on Americans to do something grander than following their own self-interest. Congress had—through however precarious a process—passed the bill. Together, they provided some hope that in the long run, the idea will conquer the cynicism instead of the other way around.

Epilogue

On July 31, 1995—less than ten months after the first AmeriCorps members were sworn in—the U.S. House of Representatives voted to eliminate the program. Two months later, the Senate did the same.

The key intervening factor, of course, was the 1994 Republican takeover of Congress. Representative Dick Armey, who in 1993 had called national service a "welfare program for aspiring Yuppies," went from being a minor irritant for the Democrats to being the majority leader of the House. Senator Kassebaum went from critic to chairwoman of the Senate Labor Committee. National service foe Representative Bill Goodling replaced Bill Ford as chairman of the House Education and Labor Committee (renamed the Economic and Educational Opportunities Committee). The new Speaker of the House, Newt Gingrich, called AmeriCorps "coerced volunteerism" and said the participants were "not only useless but dangerous."

The more Clinton protested, the more insistent they became. "Since the President has chosen AmeriCorps as the battleground for his first counterattack against cutting big government, conservatives should oblige him," wrote John Walters, president of The New Citizenship Project, a group chaired by Republican strategist Bill Kristol. "Killing AmeriCorps should become a priority."

The Republican leadership decided to knock out the program through the appropriations process. They did not actually touch the

National and Community Service Trust Act of 1993. They simply voted to prohibit any money from being spent to implement that act. All those tortured negotiations in 1993 over whether the authorization should be two or three or five years became moot.

Gingrich understood that because Clinton loved the program so much, AmeriCorps could become a useful hostage during the end-of-the-year budget standoff. The GOP could eliminate national service in May and offer to restore it in October in exchange for some major Clinton concession. While many Republicans heard positive reports from their districts, they only amounted to squeaks drowned out by a chorus of other interest-group demands. The Corporation for National and Community Service had spread the money so thin—350 projects at 1,200 sites in the first year—that some congressional districts had only a handful of volunteers. In retrospect, the Republican success in 1993 in trimming the initial funding levels had made it harder for AmeriCorps to develop a critical mass of support for later budget fights.

Perhaps the most intriguing reason for the loss of the program in the House was the lack of enthusiasm among liberal Democrats. In early budget skirmishes, Clinton had White House negotiators tell Republicans that AmeriCorps, above all, had to be saved. Privately, that infuriated liberals who thought he should have fought for other programs like summer jobs for poor teens or low-income energy assistance. When it came time for the House Appropriations committee to consider the regular 1996 spending bill, Representative David Obey, the leading liberal on the committee, shocked AmeriCorps supporters by voting to eliminate the program. He said he couldn't justify funding AmeriCorps over traditional social programs like subsidized housing. In that sense, AmeriCorps was undermined by the same ancient tensions that had killed the Moskos-DLC service-for-loans plan of 1988 and that had fueled the attacks from the United Negro College Fund in 1993.

In the Senate, Republicans provided a textbook case of how to misuse statistics. The General Accounting Office had concluded that the Corporation was spending an average of $17,600 per recruit, including the $8,000 stipend, $4,725 scholarship and the cost of running the local program. Opponents added to that number the amount that local governments and private companies contributed to programs, arriving at a total of $27,000 in "resources per volunteer." Even though that included gifts from local companies—exactly what Republicans ought to be applauding—Sen. Charles Grassley of Iowa started referring to the $27,000 figure as the federal "cost per volunteer." Other lawmakers then distorted the distortion. During the Senate floor debate on September 26, 1995, Rick Santorum, who defeated Harris Wofford in Pennsylvania, complained that these young people serve only because they "get paid $30,000 a year." In addition to being misleading, these numbers were beside the point. Microsoft Inc., one of the most efficient companies in the nation, had a per employee cost (using these accounting methods) of $173,000. The logical flaw: the amount "per recruit" does not consider what, if any, services the employee delivers. That should have been the real question about AmeriCorps.

Most disheartening, opponents attacked AmeriCorps even when it was departing from typical government behavior. For government to operate efficiently it must be willing to reward success and punish failure, just as in the private sector. After the first year, AmeriCorps refused to renew funding for 48 programs. I think they should have pulled the plug on more, but this is a much better track record than any government program I've ever come across. And yet during the debate, these defundings were sighted not as proof of a government reinvented but as evidence that the whole AmeriCorps program was a failure. No wonder government officials so often refuse to admit mistakes.

Despite the pathetic quality of the debate, AmeriCorps proponents almost saved the program through an amendment on the Senate floor. They lost because, despite a last-minute appeal from Vice President Gore, two Democrats—Herb Kohl and Russell Feingold of Wisconsin—insisted that the money be spent on low-income housing instead. The vote provided one more devastating reminder that support for national service among many Democrats was tepid.

Here is my best assessment of whether AmeriCorps was working:

Doing Real Work. AmeriCorps members served at so many sites, it's impossible to say what percentage of programs were high quality —and that, in itself, is a problem. So it was easy to find examples of money that could have been better spent. For instance, AmeriCorps members in Dallas, Oregon, built a retaining wall at a local Community College—useful, to be sure, but not exactly the Lord's work.

But I did come across many AmeriCorps programs that seemed to not only be doing "real work" themselves but improving the efficiency of existing charities and government bureaucracies. At the Habitat for Humanity in Miami, 24 AmeriCorps members helped supervise 1,200 volunteers to build 90 low income houses for the poor to live in and own. "Our ability to engage this many people in the work of Habitat for Humanity is directly attributable to the success of the AmeriCorps program," said Habitat official Kevin McPeak. A YMCA official running a program in Brockton, Massaschusetts, reported that regular public school teachers became "reenergized" when the new AmeriCorps members arrived. At a Kentucky tutoring program called SLICE, AmeriCorps volunteers gave second-graders attention the regular teachers couldn't, and as a result, reading comprehension scores increased 116 percent in about six months. A housing authority official in Massachusetts told the General Accounting Office that AmeriCorps members who moved into the projects to help improve tenant self-sufficiency provided services "at approximately half the cost of an employed social worker."

A consulting firm, Aguirre International, compiled a list of AmeriCorps accomplishments from 52 sites. Consider that these represent only a fraction of those mentioned in the report—itself compiled from only 8 percent of the program sites over the course of only half the year—and one can begin to sense the dimensions of AmeriCorps' impact.

AmeriCorps members planted 212,500 trees; removed 2,000 pounds of trash from an urban river; fought two major forest fires and saved one national park road from washing out; built, restored, or maintained 311 campsites, 88 miles of parkland trails, 17 bridges, and one mile of forest service road; and completed 61 inner-city neighborhood cleanups—including a city-wide graffiti removal. They tutored 7,638 preschool, elementary, and junior high school students; established afterschool and educational vacation programs for 4,656 children; screened 1,100 low-income children for lead toxicity and other health risks; provided emergency medical services to over 1,500 people.

They escorted 8,500 children to school through safe corridors; started 258 neighborhood safety programs and patrolled 250 vacant buildings to prevent drug-dealing; provided each of 470 victims of sexual and domestic violence with 30 days of counseling and assistance. And they helped 123 elderly persons, 50 visually impaired adults, and 9 visually impaired children live independently; renovated 238 inner-city housing units and 99 rural homes; distributed food to more than 16,625 low-income people and packed 7,000 dinners and 32,000 breakfasts for the hungry.

Helping the Servers. The program clearly altered the personal aspirations of some of the roughly 20,000 people who joined AmeriCorps in its first year. "I wasn't doing anything but hanging out on corners, going out with my friends, and stealing cars," one volunteer told the *Galveston Daily News.* After working on a Seaborne Conservation Corps run by the Pentagon and National Guard, he now feels certain he'll become a firefighter.

In some cases, volunteers started off viewing AmeriCorps as just another job but eventually raised their aspirations. "In the beginning I just wanted some kind of training but as time went by I began to learn about water conservation, about recycling, and to be motivated to the point that I want to go to school and do my degree in geology and hydrology," says Alicia Cayce of the Los Angeles Southern California Urban Water Conservation Program.

Bringing People Together. Here, AmeriCorps did better than I thought they would. Ethnically, 47 percent of servers in the first year were white, 31 percent African-American and 14 percent Hispanic, a more balanced mix than the previously existing service corps had achieved. About a third were from very poor families, and 12 percent were from families with incomes over $50,000. The rest were from families with household incomes between $15,000 and $50,000. "The hardest part has been learning to trust everybody because we all come from such different backgrounds," Chris Avila of Sioux City, Iowa, told the Silada (Colorado) *Mountain Mail.* "It gets to be like a real family. We have some spats and arguments, especially on trips where you're spending 24 hours a day together, but for the most part, everybody likes it."

One red flag: National numbers don't mean much if the local corps are homogeneous. (After all, if half the programs were all-white and the other half all-black, the aggregate "result" would be a 50-50 mix.) Ominously, AmeriCorps officials could not or would not give a detailed breakdown of program demographics.

Educational Opportunity. In the first year, only 28 percent of the AmeriCorps participants had already completed college. So most were going to use the $4,725 to pay for future or current costs.

Developing a Civic Ethic. The Corporation tried to create a national identity for the disparate local programs, designing, among other things, an attractive orange-on-gray logo to be worn by all members. (Those colors were chosen because they were the only colors not associated with a street gang.) But too many programs simply didn't seem to have a selfless spirit of service. An official running one program in Texas told a TV interviewer that it was a "jobs program." And on average, only 12 percent of the program costs were picked up by private contributions, a sign that local corporations have not yet become sufficiently invested in making it work.

What about the structure of AmeriCorps? The state commissions, not surprisingly, were an eclectic group, some excellent, some lousy. North and South Dakota didn't bother setting one up. In South Carolina, the commission met only once in the first year. Other states, like Washington and Rhode Island, worked closely with groups and drew out the best in quality. Ironically, the decentralized structure that was supposed to make government leaner and more efficient created all sorts of bureaucratic hassles. One community non-profit group in Boston had servers provided by five different AmeriCorps programs, each unaware of what the others were doing. A study by Public Private Ventures concluded, "The overall funding mechanism proved unhelpful." What I've seen in the first year has not removed my concerns about the decentralized nature of the program. Given the paucity of resources, it seems crazy to give the money to states that don't care enough to spend it well.

As of October 1995, the fate of AmeriCorps was still undetermined. Eli Segal had announced plans to leave. The President nominated newly unemployed Harris Wofford to fill his place. The program had support in public opinion polls so the expectation was that through persistent veto threats, and promises of program reform, Clinton could possibly save the program for another year. But even if he did, national service would be on shaky political ground for years to come.

Direct lending and pay-as-you-can loans got off to a surprisingly good start. College financial aid officers raved that the program had simplified the process and saved money. The competition from the government seemed to spur banks into offering better loan payment terms. The Department of Education expanded the reach of the reform by putting together a "loan consolidation" program, in which students who already had loans through banks could combine them into one big direct loan. The idea proved popular. In the first year, the department consolidated 25,000 loans worth $200 million. Under pressure from lenders and Republican lawmakers, the Department agreed to stop aggressively advertising the option, lest they steal too much business from banks. That struck me as a bit odd; if we want government to act more like a business, shouldn't it be able to market its product?

The best news was about the pay-as-you-can option. Even though the feature had been virtually unpublicized, 37 percent of those consolidating chose to repay "as a percentage of income over time"; 22 percent selected the next most popular repayment option. In the second year, *almost half* chose pay-as-you-can.

Nevertheless, the new Congress quickly moved to kill direct lending. The banks and other financial entities that had almost blocked direct lending in 1993 had an easy time convincing Repubicans that this represented Big Government intrusion in the "private" sector.

They faced one major obstacle: those irksome budget rules decreed that direct lending saved money. The Republicans devised an amazingly brazen solution: change the budget rules! With a simple technical amendment, they ordered Deb Kalcevic and the Congressional Budget Office to count the money a different way—a way that made direct lending a money *loser*, instead of a money saver. *Without changing anything about the program.* One year Congress saved money by creating this program; two years later they saved money by eliminating it.

With the "scoring" no longer a problem, the Republicans were free to roll back the program. The House wiped it out entirely. As of late October, the Senate had voted to allow direct lending for 20 percent of loan volume. The odds of the program surviving at all looked slim. And, not surprisingly, there was virtually no discussion of the most important issue: if direct lending disappeared, so would pay-as-you-can loans.

During the 1995 legislative fight, as in 1993, there was a jarring inconsistency between that strange biosphere known as Capitol Hill and the rest of the country. In the field, the loan and service programs were deemed to be working imperfectly but well. That translated into a Washington debate about programs that were *disastrous* or *triumphant.* All activity seemed to get put into a high-speed information-smasher that ejected all bits of nuance, leaving only pure, toxic exaggeration. It pained me to see what was being said about the national service program by its adversaries because I had seen how much good it already had done. The debate was profoundly dishonest, even more so than in 1993. In the case of student-loan reform, policy was still being determined by warfare between the same batch of interest groups. The main change from 1993 was that this time the banks were winning.

Clearly, a political battle only begins with the passage of the bill. In a time of budget scarcity and electoral volatility, those who want to truly shape the final outcome must remain in the fight when regulations are written, grants awarded, programs chosen, and appropriations voted. In one sense, that's quite positive. Officials at the Department of Education and AmeriCorps know they'll be under constant scrutiny and have to make their programs work. The bad news is that their performance may not determine the fates of their programs. In the end, cynical politics may win after all.

Appendix

Service

To find out how to join AmeriCorps, call 1-800-94-ACORPS.

New College Loan Repayment Options

Through Individual Education Accounts, borrowers may repay their loans under any of the following four repayment plans:

1. *The Standard Repayment Plan:*
   - Allows borrowers to make fixed payments for ten years.

2. *The Extended Repayment Plan:*
   - Allows borrowers to make smaller payments for a longer period of time.
   - Borrowers will repay their loans in 12 to 30 years depending upon the amount of their debts.

3. *The Graduated Repayment Plan:*
   - Allows borrowers to repay their loans by making small payments at the beginning of their repayment periods when their incomes are likely to be modest and larger payments in later years.
   - Borrowers will repay their loans in 12 to 30 years depending upon the amount of their debts.

4. *The Income-Contingent (Pay-As-You-Can) Repayment Plan:*
   - Allows borrowers to repay their loans as a small percentage of their incomes.
   - Borrowers will pay between 4 and 15 percent of their incomes each year for up to 25 years.
   - If a borrower does not fully repay a loan within 25 years, any unpaid amount is forgiven.

> **To find out more about pay-as-you-can loans and other loan repayment options, talk to college financial officers or call 1-800-4FEDAID.**

ILLUSTRATIVE BORROWER TYPES: COMPARISONS OF INCOME-CONTINGENT, STANDARD, GRADUATED, AND EXTENDED REPAYMENT PLANS FOR A SINGLE BORROWER

Plan Type	First Year		Year 10		Term/Balance Remaining After 25 Years	Total Amount Repaid	Total in Inflation-Adjusted Dollars
	Monthly Amount	Percent of Income	Monthly Amount	Percent of Income			
Borrower Type 1: Low income & debt ($10,000 starting income and $3,500 debt)							
Income Contingent[1]	$ 36	4.3%	$ 36	3.0%	12	$ 5,183	$ 4,341
Standard	50	6.0%	—	—	8	4,800	4,282
Graduated	30	3.6%	57	4.8%	10	5,103	4,317
Extended	n/a	n/a	n/a	n/a	n/a	n/a	n/a
Borrower Type 2: Low income/high debt ($10,000 starting income and $20,000 debt)							
Income Contingent[1]	$ 65	7.8%	$ 93	7.8%	36,212	$ 32,484	$ 20,920
Standard	232	27.9%	232	19.6%	10	27,866	24,084
Graduated	119	14.3%	159	13.4%	20	40,447	28,816
Extended	155	18.6%	155	13.1%	20	37,214	27,553
Borrower Type 3: Typical income & debt ($30,000 starting income and $10,000 debt)							
Income Contingent[1]	$ 103	4.1%	$ 103	2.9%	12	$ 14,809	$ 12,403
Standard	116	4.6%	116	3.3%	10	13,933	12,042
Graduated	60	2.4%	104	2.9%	15	19,623	14,720
Extended	90	3.6%	90	2.5%	15	16,179	12,937

(cont'd)

Plan Type	First Year		Year 10		Term/Balance Remaining After 25 Years	Total Amount Repaid	Total in Inflation-Adjusted Dollars
	Monthly Amount	Percent of Income	Monthly Amount	Percent of Income			
Borrower Type 4: Typical income/high debt ($30,000 starting income and $50,000 debt)							
Income Contingent[1]	$ 345	13.8%	$ 491	13.8%	16	$ 87,090	$ 67,120
Standard	581	23.2%	581	16.3%	10	69,665	60,211
Graduated	297	11.9%	350	9.8%	25	119,784	78,344
Extended	353	14.1%	353	9.9%	25	106,017	73,060
Borrower Type 5: High Income & debt ($50,000 starting income and $50,000 debt)							
Income Contingent[1]	$ 514	12.3%	$ 514	8.7%	12	$ 74,043	$ 62,017
Standard	581	13.9%	581	9.8%	10	69,665	60,211
Graduated	297	7.1%	350	5.9%	25	119,784	78,344
Extended	353	8.5%	353	6.0%	25	106,017	73,060
Borrower Type 6: Very high income & debt ($100,000 starting income and $100,000 debt)							
Income Contingent[1]	$1,028	12.3%	$1,028	8.7%	12	$148,087	$124,034
Standard	1,161	13.9%	1,161	9.8%	10	139,330	120,421
Graduated	595	7.1%	657	5.5%	30	256,421	159,597
Extended	665	8.0%	665	5.6%	30	239,509	153,748

NOTE:
[1] Under the income-contingent plan, borrowers are assumed to pay the lesser of the formula calculation or 12-year fixed-payment amortization. The income-contingent payback rate is 4% plus 0.2% per $1,000 borrowed.

Source: U.S. Department of Education

Notes

Much of the reporting for this book was done as part of a special project for *Newsweek*. In the beginning of 1993, I approached people who I thought would be important in the coming legislative drama and offered them the following deal: If they let me sit in on private meetings, I would agree not to publish what I heard until after the bill passed. This idea was modeled after a highly acclaimed *Newsweek* project on the 1992 presidential campaigns. I gained varying levels of access. Some people—members of Congress, staff, lobbyists—allowed me to sit in on private meetings. I regularly attended the private lobbying meetings of the American Council on Education, the National and Community Service Coalition, and Youth Service America. I also was able to sit in on several pro–direct lending strategy sessions on Capitol Hill. Officials at the Career College Association and the American Student Assistance Corporation allowed me to attend private staff meetings as well.

Just as important, I spoke to about fifty people on an ongoing background basis, and to another fifty more sporadically. In some cases, individuals gave me private memoranda; in other cases I gained documents through the Freedom of Information Act. Some sources shared notes they took at meetings. I was not, however, allowed to sit in on meetings conducted by President Clinton in the White House. The accounts of the Clinton meetings are reconstructions. I have tried to base the narratives on multiple sources, backed, where possible, by a source's notes. Nevertheless, reconstructions are not as reliable as eyewitness accounts. They are based on the subjective memories of the participants. Sources sometimes gave differing versions of the same events. In a few cases, I simply chose the version that I thought was true based on secondary factors. But in those instances, I also have included the alternative view in the endnotes. If sources disagreed and I had no way of plausibly arbitrating, I left it out of the narrative.

I have tried in the endnotes to indicate which private scenes I actually witnessed (all the public scenes fit into that category); if a description of a private scene is not labeled as an eyewitness account, it can be assumed to be a reconstruction.

Chapter 1

4 *the DLC had adopted* . . . : The DLC stated its views in a 1988 pamphlet written by Moskos and Will Marshall. "A move toward national service is a step away from the prevailing ethos of entitlement—the notion that any segment of society has a permanent right to favors and privileges bestowed by government," the treatise stated. The Democratic Leadership Council, "Citizenship and National Service: A Blueprint for Civic Enterprise" (Washington, D.C.: May 1988), p. 54. Moskos wrote his own book, which laid out the plan and also provided an excellent history of service. Charles C. Moskos, *A Call to Civic Service: National Service for Country and Community* (New York: The Free Press, 1988).

5 *The plan, declared Representative Bill Ford* . . . : Phil Kuntz, "Nunn-McCurdy Plan Ignites National Service Debate," *Congressional Quarterly*, March 25, 1989, p. 647. At congressional hearings, one witness after another vehemently attacked the plan. "Any legislation that would substitute service for access to education would be a cruel hoax to play on black youngsters," testified Johnnetta Cole, president of Spelman College, before the House Education and Labor Committee. "The Nunn-McCurdy provisions would be disastrous for Texas A&I!" the school's president, Steven Altman, declared. A Yale University student active in volunteer work testified that the bill "creates a poverty draft. Community service becomes the privilege for the rich, but a punishment for the poor."

6 *an idea called "income-contingent loans"* . . . : The idea originated with Milton Friedman in the 1940s but over the years would have an impressively eclectic group of advocates including John Silber, Robert Reischauer, William Bennett, and Edward M. Kennedy. The most significant recent income-contingent loan proposal came from Representative Tom Petri, a Republican of Wisconsin. Others were later offered by Senators David Durenberger of Minnesota, Paul Simon of Illinois, and Bill Bradley of New Jersey.

6 *Is it a coincidence . . . :* George Bush served as U.S. Navy pilot from 1942 to 1945. Ronald Reagan enlisted in the reserves as a second lieutenant in 1942, made training films, and was discharged as a captain in 1945. Jimmy Carter graduated from the U.S. Naval Academy and served as an officer on battleships and submarines from 1946 to 1953. Gerald Ford enlisted as a reserve ensign in 1942 and was discharged in 1946 as a lieutenant commander. Same with Richard Nixon. Lyndon Johnson served as a special duty officer in the naval reserves in 1940 and won the Silver Star when flying a bomber attacked by the Japanese. John Kennedy served as a lieutenant (jg) from 1941 to 1945. Dwight Eisenhower served in the military from 1911 until 1948. Harry Truman enlisted in 1917 as a first lieutenant and was discharged as a major. Franklin Roosevelt did not serve in uniform but was from 1913 to 1920 the secretary of the navy. Herbert Hoover in 1900 helped in the defense of Tientsin during the Boxer Rebellion and from 1914 to 1918 chaired relief efforts in Belgium. So really one has to go back to Calvin Coolidge to find someone with as little experience with the military as Clinton. Joseph Nathan Kane, *Facts About the Presidents* (New York: H. W. Wilson Company, 1981.)

7 *The image of Clinton . . . :* Clinton's classmate Carolyn Staley remembers Mackey declaring that the flag "wasn't just a piece of fabric, it was lives, the symbol of what people died for," and when it passed by, students were expected to, and did, put their hands over their hearts.

8 *Clinton read and reread . . . :* C. S. Lewis, *Mere Christianity* (New York: Macmillan, 1943).

8 *At Yale Law School . . . :* Michael Kelley, "Hillary Rodham Clinton and the Politics of Virtue," *The New York Times Magazine,* May 23, 1993, pp. 22–25.

9 *He said "Probably," . . . :* From 1965 to 1970, roughly 80,000 men did perform alternative service as conscientious objectors. During that period, courts broadened the definition of conscientious objector status to include a secular opposition to war. But they never accepted the notion of "selective conscientious objection." The Peace Corps allowed volunteers to defer their military service for two years, but with a peak enrollment of 16,000, it was a relatively minor means of draft avoidance. John Whiteclay Chambers II, "Conscientious Objectors and the American State from Colonial Times to the Present," in Charles C. Moskos and John Whiteclay Chambers II, eds., *The New Conscientious Objection: From Sacred to Secular Resistance* (New York: Oxford University Press, 1993).

9 *Clinton's experiences . . . :* The GI Bill covered all tuition, fees, and books, and provided a monthly stipend of $75, about $500 in current dollars. The Korean War GI Bill provided similarly generous benefits.

12 *enormous in scope and import . . . :* Eli Segal and others would later try to claim that the president never actually promised that any student who wanted to serve away his or her debt could do so. But Reed's memo clearly shows that they always had in mind precisely that. Other comments during the campaign reinforced that point, the most significant being the language in the pamphlet "Putting People for First" put out during the primary campaign. "To give every

American the right to borrow money for college, we will scrap the existing student loan program and establish a National Service Trust Fund. Those who borrow from the fund will be able *to choose how to repay the balance*: either as a small percentage of their earnings over time, or by serving their communities for one or two years doing work their country needs [my emphasis]." "Putting People First: A National Economic Strategy for America," written by the Clinton campaign in June 1992. Indeed, an undated campaign "talking points" memo made it sound as if community service would be the primary way of paying for college. "He'll establish a National Service Trust Fund to make sure that Americans can borrow for college—and pay the money back through community service."

13 *Nevertheless, Reed did . . .* : Reed based his estimates for the flexible loan repayment on an income-contingent loan plan proposed by Senator Bill Bradley, in which students were allowed to borrow $10,000 a year. That essentially cost the government nothing over time, because students would pay back the money. As for the rest of the plan, Reed suggested giving servers a $10,000 scholarship for each year they worked. The average cost of four years at a public college was roughly $20,000, so $10,000 would be "better than any deal they can get now, except the military." He suggested limiting the size of the corps to 500,000 per year, "to keep costs down and to give it some prestige." That would mean about one of every three students could do the program.

The third page of Reed's memo outlined ways of paying for the program. Cutting federal bureaucratic overhead could provide some money, as could the "peace dividend." But the most important source would be from existing student-aid programs. "We're not proposing the elimination of Stafford loans (although if you don't mind taking a hit from the interest groups, we certainly could), but our plan is such a better deal that it will quickly become the preferred method for everybody. In 1990, we spent $11 billion on student aid programs— $5 billion on Pell Grants and $6 billion on loans. Once our program is under way, we'll no longer need the separate loan programs (savings = $6 billion). If you're willing to phase out Pell Grants, we'll save another $5 billion." In addition, by having the government give out the money directly from a "trust fund" instead of paying subsidies to banks, the government could save billions of dollars, Reed believed. The spending on service slots, minus the savings from student-loan programs, meant the net cost to the government would be $8 billion a year.

Reed concluded, "Our GI Bill is about a third the size of the original GI Bill, which cost 10% of GNP. The return on that investment was the most spectacular economic boom the world has ever seen."

13 *Not everyone . . .* : "The economy, stupid" has become so legendary that one might imagine a huge banner behind Carville's desk. Actually, the phrase was merely scrawled in Magic Marker on a bulletin board in the center of the War Room—along with two other mottoes: "Change vs. more of the same" and "Don't forget health care." These were answers to the question "What's the theme of this campaign?"

14 *Polls had him running . . .* : The Washington Post–ABC News poll released June 2, 1992, gave Perot 34 percent, Bush 31 percent, and Clinton 29 percent of the vote.

14 *As the Democratic convention . . . .* : Advisors launched the "Manhattan Project," an effort to probe voters' innermost thoughts about Clinton. Again, they found that the New Democrat themes of work and responsibility played well, with national service reinforcing, but not driving, the message. Clinton's comments on CBS were excerpted in *The New York Times*, June 16, 1992, p. 23.

14 *So far neither . . .* : Meanwhile, some in the Republican Party were urging Bush to try to co-opt the service theme. According to an account in *The New Republic* by former Bush aide James Pinkerton, Senate minority leader Bob Dole had suggested to the campaign that Bush advocate bringing back the Civilian Conservation Corps. Pinkerton made the same suggestion to first son George W. Bush after the Rodney King verdicts. George, Jr., liked the idea, but, according to Pinkerton, called back the next day. "The president was unenthusiastic: 'Isn't this the sort of thing that we're fighting against?' "

17 *In the sheer . . .* : Author's eyewitness account.

Chapter 2

21 *Many severe social problems . . .* : Alzheimer's example: William F. Buckley, Jr., *Gratitude: Reflections on What We Owe to Our Country* (New York: Random House, 1990), p. 103. Statistics on Germany: Jurgen Kuhlmann and Ekkehard Lippert, "The Federal Republic of Germany: Conscientious Objection as Social Welfare," in Charles C. Moskos and John Whiteclay Chambers II, eds., *The New Conscientious Objection: From Sacred to Secular Resistance* (New York: Oxford University Press, 1993). The Ford Foundation study: Richard Danzig and Peter Szanton, *National Service: What Would It Mean?* (Lexington, Mass.: Lexington Books, 1986). Donald Eberly, "Youth National Service Can Meet Many Needs," *USA Today*, April 11, 1985; reprinted in Donald J. Eberly, *National Service: A Promise to Keep* (Rochester, N.Y.: John Alden Books, 1988). Cost effectiveness numbers: Edward M. Kennedy, "Enacting the National and Community Service Trust Act of 1993," in John F. Jennings, ed., *National Issues in Education: Community Service and Student Loans* (Bloomington, Ind.: Phi Delta Kapp International, 1994), p. 24.

22 *waiting lists for publicly assisted day care . . .* : Children's Defense Fund, Washington, D.C.

22 *One in eleven kids . . .* : Author's cover story, "Lead and Your Kids," *Newsweek*, July 15, 1991.

22 *Nomination for most creative . . .* : This example comes from Nicholas Lemann, *The Promised Land* (New York: Alfred A. Knopf, 1991), p. 180, which has an excellent summary of the Community Action Program problems.

23 *"The volunteers could empower . . .":* Charles Peters, *Tilting at Windmills* (New York: Addison-Wesley Publishing Company, Inc., 1988), p. 123.

24 *cultural divides continue to grow . . . :* The top ten TV shows among blacks in 1992, according to Nielsen ratings, were: *Fresh Prince of Bel Air; Roc; Martin; In Living Color; Blossom; A Different World; In Living Color: First Season; Out All Night; Where I Live;* and *Hangin' with Mr. Cooper.* The top ten overall were: *60 Minutes; Roseanne; Home Improvement; Murphy Brown; Murder, She Wrote; Coach; NFL Monday Night Football; CBS Sunday Night Movie; Cheers;* and *Full House.*

Housing is only marginally less segregated than it was forty years ago. The percentage of blacks wanting an all-black political party doubled from 23 percent to 46 percent from 1988 to 1994. In the workplace, most whites believe affirmative action discriminates against them; most blacks say discrimination against minorities is a far more serious problem. At Oberlin College, the Lesbian, Gay and Bisexual Union broke into Gay Men of Color, Lesbians of Color, White Lesbians, and Gay White Men, according to Jacob Weisberg's *New Republic* article, "Thin Skins" (February 18, 1991). Students lived in ethnic heritage dormitories and then studied in ethnically specialized academic majors. "I have no black friends," one Jewish senior explained. "My entire social circle is Jewish and WASP. That was never true before."

24 *middle-class families . . . :* Paul A. Jargowsky, "Economic Segregation in U.S. Metropolitan Areas." Jargowsky, an assistant professor of political economy at the University of Texas at Dallas, presented his finding to the IRP-ASPE Poverty Research Seminar Series, Washington, D.C., May 13, 1994. Similar results were found in Paul Glastris, "A Tale of Two Suburbias: The Decline of Blue-Collar Suburbs and Growth of 'Edge Cities' Create a New Kind of Isolation," *U.S. News & World Report,* November 9, 1992, p. 32.

24 *A twenty-six-year-old John F. Kennedy . . . :* This description of Kennedy's PT boat comes from Mickey Kaus, *The End of Equality* (New York: Basic Books, 1992). During the 1950s, 64 percent of eighteen-to-twenty-four-year-olds served in the military. Even more impressive, 75 percent of male high school graduates and 70 percent of college graduates served, according to Charles Moskos, *A Call to Civic Service* (New York: Free Press, 1988). In Vietnam, however, high school dropouts were twice as likely to serve as college graduates; "more people evaded the draft through legal and semilegal means than were conscripted," Moskos wrote.

24 *The military is shrinking . . . :* Today's all-volunteer force still operates as one of the most successful means of mixing races and classes, but a tiny percent of young men and women will have the experience. And as the military shrinks, the subsidiary social impacts of military service will dwindle too.

25 *His model . . . :* The idea for Clinton to visit City Year came from Joel Berg, a former DLC staffer working in Little Rock. Berg had written a policy paper for the DLC's newsletter on City Year. He felt that a meeting with enthusiastic City Year youths could help the program and underscore Clinton's message emphasizing "rights and responsibilities." Berg also knew that Boston TV stations transmit across the southern part of New Hampshire.

25 *In December 1991 . . . :* Clinton arrived with a small entourage of TV cameras and print reporters, who figured this would be another photo op centered on a well-meaning liberal social program for the disadvantaged. The pictures of the Kennedys and Martin Luther King on the wall of the small conference room did not diminish that expectation. One of the City Year workers, Steve Spallos, welcomed Clinton, gave him a hat and mug, and began telling his story. He had been in trouble with the law and was told he could either go to jail or join City Year. "I considered City Year more like City Jail," Spallos said. Clinton began taking notes as Spallos explained the dramatic transformation. "In those nine months I grew more than in the previous twenty years," he said. "This is what I want to do for a career." An inspiring tale, but just about any self-respecting poverty program, no matter how pathetic, can trot out at least one drug-dealer-turned-productive-taxpaying-citizen.

The next story Clinton heard was intriguingly different. Laura Rivera described how she joined City Year after she had chickened out of going to college in Idaho. She joined City Year and hated it for the first few months. But while working as a teacher's aide at the Blackstone Community School in a low-income part of Boston, she began to notice one little girl beating up other kids. The troublemaker had been held over a second year in kindergarten, and Rivera heard the teacher say things like "That little girl's crazy, get away from her." Rivera was devastated. "How can a teacher be like that?" she asked herself. One day in class, the little girl grabbed Rivera and wouldn't let go.

"Let go of me, Ivalese," Rivera said.

But the girl refused. "I need your help!" she said.

"What's wrong?"

"I don't know how to write my name," the girl said, ashamed.

Rivera went on to describe how she taught Ivalese how to write her name, and how this seminal event led her to become a full-time paid team leader for City Year. Clinton listened to the story intently, maintaining eye contact with Rivera throughout.

Then Jim Kim, a burned-out prep-school student from Texas, told Clinton about planting a community garden in a low-income area and the thrill he felt when neighborhood kids came out to help volunteers build a playground.

Clinton was impressed that a former drug dealer was working side-by-side with a burned-out preppy to rebuild their city. "You make a statement every day that this really is an American community," he told the group.

City Year became Clinton's mental image of what national service should look like.

25 *Consider Earl* . . . : From Suzanne Goldsmith, *A City Year* (New York: New Press, 1993), epilogue.

28 *Service programs may "develop"* . . . . : "Youth Conservation and Service Corps," study by Public/Private Ventures of Philadelphia, December 1987. "The California Conservation Corps: An Analysis of Short-term Impacts on Participants," by Wendy C. Wolf, Sally Leiderman, Richard Voith of Public/Private Ventures, June 1987.

28 *national service could foster* . . . : William F. Buckley, Jr., *Gratitude: Reflections on What We Owe to Our Country* (New York: Random House, 1990), p. 153.

29 *like a Swiss Army knife . . . :* Why not mandatory service? Some, including my former boss Charlie Peters at the *Washington Monthly,* argue that national service should be compulsory. Indeed, some of the benefits I've described could be attained through compulsory service even more easily than through the Clinton system. But I've come to believe the basic Clinton approach is as good or better. Given the difficulty government has had in recent attempts to find meaningful work for young people (despite the many needs), I strongly doubt that the government could handle such a massive influx as a draft would create. Also, in a service program, one would want people who are enthusiastic, because they would perform better. A soldier under fire will fight for his life and the lives around him whether he volunteered or was drafted; but a social service worker, say, dealing with a senile or incontinent senior citizen, had better want to be there. A bitter or patronizing volunteer can be more demoralizing to those being helped than no volunteer at all.

The main advantage of a compulsory system over a voluntary system is the sense that everyone, no matter what economic or educational station, has the same obligations to serve. The most effective draft in terms of class-mixing was the World War II draft, because it dragged a broader net than did the drafts for Vietnam, the Civil War, or World War I. The Peace Corps and VISTA have recruited from a much narrower slice of America, mostly well educated in the first case, mostly low-income in the second.

Clinton's plan attempts to retain the advantages of a voluntary system while addressing some of its drawbacks. In order to draw people of different backgrounds into the system, he offers a lucrative college scholarship. To put it crassly: he is bribing the middle class to serve. But one could also look at it this way: Clinton figured out a way to make the middle class feel invested—literally, financially invested—in helping disadvantaged communities. I don't mind that some might be lured there by the prospect of a generous college scholarship, because college aid is a worthwhile goal anyway. The federal government already spends billions in college aid for middle-class kids; at least now some of them will be giving something back.

If national service succeeds and grows, it can gradually replace the existing student-aid system as the primary way of paying for college. The old argument against Nunn-McCurdy—that it discriminated against the poor—doesn't really hold true anymore under the Clinton plan. For one thing, it's simply not true that national service penalizes the poor because only the poor need financial aid. Right now, college costs have increased so much that about half of students get some form of financial aid. What's more, someone attending a low-cost community college would actually benefit proportionally more than an affluent kid going to Harvard. A $10,000 scholarship would pay for four years at a community college, but just one semester at Harvard.

29 *The cost of a college education . . . :* "Making College Affordable Again," report of National Commission on Responsibilities for Financing Postsecondary Education, February 1993. Statistics on the amount of aid coming from loans versus grants comes from the American Council on Education. Statistics on debt burden: Joseph D. Boyd and Carol Wennerdahl, "The Characteristics of Student Borrowers in Repayment and the Impact of Educational Debt," monograph published by the American Council on Education in 1993.

29 *The thirty-year trend . . .* : While overall college attendance rates have risen consistently over the past three decades, this is largely because of sharp rises in the percentage of women attending.

29 *A family's financial status . . .* : Thomas Toch, "The Great College Tumble: Education Is Becoming More Stratified by Class," *U.S. News & World Report*, June 3, 1991. Also helpful on this subject: Paul William Kingston and Lionel S. Lewis, "Undergraduates at Elite Institutions: The Best, the Brightest and the Richest," in *The High-Status Track: Studies of Elite Schools and Stratification*, Paul William Kingston, Lionel S. Lewis, eds. (Albany, N.Y.: State University of New York Press, 1990); and Charles T. Clotfelter, Ronald G. Ehrenberg, Malcolm Getz, and John J. Siegfried, *Economic Challenges in Higher Education* (Chicago: University of Chicago Press, 1991).

Why did tuition increase so rapidly? As college tuition rose in the inflationary 1970s, the middle class began to feel priced out. Congress reacted by opening up the Guaranteed Student Loan program to middle- and upper-middle-income students, while failing to increase Pell grants, the primary scholarship program for low-income students. Since students and families appeared to be dutifully paying the higher tuition—they had loans, after all—private colleges continued to raise tuition. As tuition at private schools went up, state legislators felt they could boost tuition at public colleges without losing students. (Where else could they go?) The end result: the poor and middle class became increasingly reliant on loans.

30 *Over the past fifteen . . .* : Beth Belton, "No Degree? Welcome to the Wage Gap," *USA Today*, February 15, 1994.

30 *The idea of easing . . .* : Milton Friedman and Rose Friedman, *Free to Choose: A Personal Statement* (New York: Harcourt, Brace, 1980). The original proposal was put forth in a 1955 essay called "The Role of Government in Education," which was reprinted in revised form in *Capitalism and Freedom* (Chicago: University of Chicago Press, 1962).

31 *That is most obvious . . .* : Some law schools have tried to make it possible for graduates to become public defenders or poverty lawyers by offering loan-forgiveness programs. But most law students attend schools without such an option. Medical school statistics come from "Making College Affordable Again." Statistics comparing debt's impact on life choices in 1985 and 1991 come from Boyd and Wennerdahl's "The Characteristics of Student Borrowers in Repayment and the Impact of Educational Dept." In addition, a 1991 University of Wisconsin study concluded that college students who take out loans are more likely to enter fields with higher starting salaries *and* choose academic majors more likely to lead to higher pay.

Chapter 3

34 *system was rigged . . .* : As a result of the commission's recommendations, the party created more primaries, reduced the power of political machines, kicked out the "old coalition . . . based in blue-collar constituencies," and installed a new coalition that "was white-collar from top to bottom," according to scholar Byron Shafer, in *Quiet Revolution: The Struggle for the Democratic Party* *and the Shaping of Post-Reform Politics* (New York: Russell Sage Foundation, 1983). By taking decisions out of the hands of traditional power brokers such as labor unions, and by creating opportunities for well-organized candidates to blitz primary states, Segal's changes made possible the nominations of George Mc-Govern in 1972 and Jimmy Carter in 1976.

37 *a classic bureaucratic parlor game . . . :* The agencies that contributed staffers to ONS included: the Domestic Policy Council, ACTION, and the Commission on National and Community Service.

38 *[massive grassroots movement]:* The best histories of this are Roger Landrum's 1992 unpublished paper, "National Service: Roots and Flowers," and Charles Moskos's *A Call to Civic Service.* Among those who pushed national service programs in the 1970s and 1980s were Ed Koch, Paul Tsongas, Pete McCloskey, Daniel P. Moynihan, Claiborne Pell, Robert Torricelli, Gary Hart, and Leon Panetta.

The best way to understand how broad-based the movement became is to scan the list of local corps compiled by the National Association of Service and Conservation Corps in their report, "Youth Corps Profiles 1993." Almost all were created since 1976, and most since 1983: Albany Service Corps; Arizona Conservation Corps; Berks County Conservation Corps; Berkshire Conservation Team; Bradford Area Conservation Corps; California Conservation Corps; Chatham-Savannah Youth Service Corps; Chattanooga Youth Corps; Cheektowaga Conservation Corps; Chesapeake Bay Youth Conservation Corps; City Volunteer Corps; City Year, Inc.; Civic Works; Colorado Youth Conservation and Service Corps; Colorado Youth Corps; Community Year; Confederated Tribes of Umatilla; Confederated Tribes of Warm Springs; Conservation Corps of Long Beach; Dallas Youth Services Corps; Denver Urban Conservation Corps; D.C. Service Corps; Durham Service Corps; East Baton Rouge Urban Corps; East Bay Conservation Corps; Erie Youth Conservation Corps; Fayette County Citizens' Conservation Corps; Flint Youth Service Corps; Florida Conservation and Service Corps; Florida Youth Conservation Corps; Fort Lauderdale Conservation Corps; Fresno Local Conservation Corps; Georgia Peach Corps; Greater Atlanta Conservation Corps; Greater Jackson Youth Service Corps; Greater Miami Service Corps; Hull Environment and Service Corps; Iowa Conservation Corps; Kansas City Urban Youth Corps; Kickapoo Youth Conservation Corps; Lake County Forest Preserves; Lane-Metro Youth Corps; Lehigh Valley Youth Service Corps; Los Angeles Conservation Corps; Maine Conservation Corps; Marin Conservation Corps; Maryland Conservation Corps; McDowell County Citizens' Conservation Corps; McKeesport Youth Service Corps; Michigan Civilian Conservation Corps; Milwaukee Community Service Corps; Minnesota Conservation Corps; Missouri Youth Service/Conservation Corps; Montana Conservation Corps, Inc.; Montgomery County Conservation Corps; Nevada Business Services Youth Corps; New Hampshire Conservation Corps; New Jersey Youth Corps; New Jersey Youth Corps of Newark; New Mexico Youth Conservation Corps; New Orleans Youth Action Corps; Northshore Employment Training; Northern Penobscot Tech Region III Conservation and Youth Service Corps; Northwest Youth Corps; Ohio Civilian Conservation Corps; Oneida Indian National Youth Corps; Opportunity Knocks; Orange County Conservation Corps; Oregon Youth Conservation Corps; Orlando Youth Service Corps; Oswego County Conservation Corps; Partners in School Innovation; Pennsylvania Conservation Corps; Pennsylvania Service Corps; Philadelphia Ranger Corps; Philadelphia Youth Service Corps; Portland Youth Service and Conservation Corps; Region C Service Corps; Rennsselaer County Youth Conservation Corps; Riverside Youth Service Corps; Sacramento Local Conservation Corps; San Francisco Conservation Corps; San Francisco Urban Service Project; San Jose Conservation Corps; Save A Generation; Schuyler, Chemung, Tioga BOCES Conservation Corps; Seattle Conservation Corps; Serve Houston; Service Corps of Rochester; Southeast Alaska Guidance Association; Saint Lawrence County Youth Conservation Corps; STEP Youth Corps; Student Conservation Association; Suffolk County Conservation Corps; Sullivan County BOCES Summer Conservation Corps; Tri-County PIC Youth Service Corps; Topeka Youth Corps; Tucker County Citizens' Conservation Corps; Tulare County Conservation Corps; Urban Conservation Corps; Urban Conservation Corps of the Palm Beaches; Urban Corps of San Diego; USDA Forest Service Youth Conservation Corps; Vermont Youth Conservation Corps; Washington Conservation Corps; Washington County Service Corps; Washington Service Corps; West Seneca Service Action Team; Winston-Salem/Forsyth County Service Corps; Wisconsin Conservation Corps; Wisconsin Service Corps; Year One, Inc.; Year-Round Conservation and Youth Corps; Year-Round Syracuse; Youth Conservation Corps; Youth Energy Corps; Youth Force: Salt Lake County Service and Conservation Corps; Youth in Natural Resources; Youth Opportunity Corps; Youth Resources Development Corporation; Youth Service Conservation Corps; Youth Volunteer Corps of America; YouthBuild USA.

40 *the "service movement"* . . . : Statistics on participation in new programs come from "What You Can Do for Your Country," the annual report of the Commission on National and Community Service, January 1993, p. 109. In addition to 15,000 in the Youth Corps, there were 6,300 in the Peace Corps; 3,300 in VISTA; 3,300 in religious service programs; 1,300 in Teach for America; 1,000 in the National Health Service Corps; 900 Bonner Scholars; and 2,200 in other miscellaneous programs.

41 *By the time of Clinton's inauguration* . . . : The various service interest groups were quite busy too. They spent December 1992 and January 1993 jockeying for influence in the new administration. Programs formed "coalitions," which created "working groups," which begat "task forces" and "steering committees." Youth Service America put together recommendations about promoting youth service under Clinton. But senior citizens' groups objected that service should include the elderly, so YSA changed the recommendations to take advantage of the seniors as a political asset. A small group of recent college graduates formed Young People for National Service, which proposed putting all new local programs under a loosely constructed national program they called AmeriCorps. The Points of Light Foundation hired a lobbyist to make sure they didn't get wiped out. The lobbyist: Bud Blakey, the same man who was helping John Dean fight against Clinton's student-aid reform.

42 *The only DLCer* . . . : The Kennedy camp was suspicious of Galston at first. The Communitarians, the group he had helped found, emphasized ideas like strong state action against crime and less emphasis on individual civil liberties. Galston had also written issue papers for the DLC. But he knew enough about the violent history of the Nunn-McCurdy fight to realize the sensitivity of his position. As soon as he got the assignment, he asked one of his assistants, Joel Berg, to write a paper for him on the politics of Nunn-McCurdy. "Groups and individuals that rarely agreed on anything joined together to condemn the DLC and Nunn-McCurdy national service proposals," Berg reported in his eleven-page history. Galston defined his role not as advocate for the DLC, but as honest broker between the different schools of thought. "I wanted to reassure them that I wasn't coming in to fight the battles of the past," Galston explained during the transition. "I came in as a broker, not as the heavy."

44 *Bill Galston's transition team recommended* . . . : The early drafts of the commission's report suggested that one million servers by the year 2000 was a "reasonable target" given Ford Foundation estimates that there is useful work for 3 million national service participants.

46 *"Obviously, if you read it carefully . . ."*: Segal's argument is worth savoring, since it is so typical of Clinton himself. Remember Clinton had craftily stated that he had never broken American drug laws, implying he hadn't smoked marijuana. Technically he told the truth: he smoked marijuana in England (but didn't inhale). Segal's spin on the national service campaign promise, later repeated by other White House officials, fit the same model of a legalistic quasi-truth with just enough literal veracity to let the speaker convince himself he was being honest. The YSA meeting described was witnessed by the author.

47 *Neither Panetta nor . . . Rivlin . . .* : Panetta and Rivlin advocated caution, but not vigorously. They obviously knew how much Clinton cared about national service; more importantly, they were closet service advocates themselves. As a congressman, Panetta had sponsored legislation to set up a massive national service plan. In fact, Michael Brown, the City Year founder, had worked for Panetta. And Rivlin was active on the board of directors of the DC Service Corps, a local service program. Indeed, a remarkable number of Clinton administration officials had such connections: Al Gore's sister was in the first class of the Peace Corps; Donna Shalala, the secretary of health and human services, had served in the Peace Corps; and Secretary of the Interior Bruce Babbitt worked in VISTA.

48 *On February 11 . . .* : There were somewhat contradictory memories of whether particular Clinton comments were made at the first meeting or the second. Everyone involved was sitting through meeting after meeting, and they tended to blur together. So it is possible that a particular comment I have attributed to Clinton at the February 11 meeting might have actually occurred at the meeting a few days earlier, or vice versa. But I feel confident that he said these words, or phrases very close to them, at one of these two meetings, and that I have accurately captured the spirit of his comments. I also have a feeling Clinton had several apples at the February 11 meeting, but I can't prove it.

49 *"The Washington Post was so unfair . . ."*: Clinton explained that Segal was describing the decision to allow pre-college kids as a pilot program. "And *The Washington Post* treated it like it was our whole proposal," Clinton said. To the president, this was a major distinction. He had always thought of the program as being for college graduates, and he had only recently agreed to add a new pre-college component. "We were going to add sixteen to twenty thousand, which was a *new* part of our program . . . and they thought it was our whole proposal and they went after us."

49 *On February 17 . . .* : Segal's office issued a press release touting the $5.8 billion "allocation" over three years to show that the president had *"fulfilled his promise* [their emphasis] to young Americans who were encouraged by his call to service by proposing significant resources for a strong and compelling national service initiative." To deal with those who felt that wasn't enough, Segal sent "Talking Points on National Service" explaining the administration's spin to key legislators. (In a reflection of the malleability of budget numbers, the talking points referred to $5.8 billion, the White House budget charts said $6.03 billion, the text summary accompanying the budget said $7.4 billion. And if you added up all the numbers in the budget chart, the total was $9.43 billion. Whatever. The important thing was that it seemed *big*.) "The President will 'ramp up' the national service initiative as the infrastructure for it develops," the cheat sheet said. "As a new kind of Democrat, Bill Clinton knows that good programs don't grow from the Washington bureaucracy, they grow from the genius of the American people." The statement fully qualified as a clutch rationalization.

Chapter 4

52 *gave special incentives . . .* : They also got a "special allowance," which works like this: The government guarantees the student an interest rate of 8 percent. If the market interest rate goes above that, the government pays the banks the difference. Specifically, they define the market rate as being 3.1 percent above the going rate on ninety-day Treasury bills. So if the Treasury bill rate is 9 percent, the market rate would be considered 12.1 percent, and the government would pay the bank an amount equivalent to 4.1 percent of whatever loans they give out.

58 *[what he didn't know . . .]*: Hultin's analysis prompted Reed to cut the national service program in half, which could only be good for Sallie Mae. The smaller the program, the less the student-loan industry would have to be trimmed to pay for it.

60 *Heather would end up paying nominally . . .* : I say "nominally" because of the economic concept known as the "time value of money." If Heather pays $100 over forty years, the value of that $100 is going to be much less in year thirty-nine than in year ten. Also, if Heather pays $100 insted of $300 she will have an extra $200 free for other activities that might generate more value. In other words, saying it's harmful because she would pay back $30,000 instead of $20,000 is misleading. It is also a bit paternalistic, since the implication is that the young people could not decide for themselves whether it made more economic sense to spread out the payments or not. No one would dare make that argument about a family taking a thirty-year mortgage, yet Nassirian regularly argued that students were not capable of deciding how much debt to incur.

61 *Pell grants . . . as the key . . .* : Part of the reason loans fared better than grants in the 1980s has to do with the politics of congressional budgeting. Student loans are an entitlement, grants are not. In 1990s budget chatter, the term *entitlement* had come to mean any program that profligately provides benefits to constituents, but it has a precise legislative meaning. An entitlement program increases in size automatically, according to the number of eligible recipients. Social Security is an entitlement, because anyone who meets certain terms must be given a payment. Guaranteed student loans are an entitlement, too; anyone who qualifies gets the federal subsidy. Congress does not have to approve an annual appropriation. Pell grants, however, fit into the category of "discretionary" spending, which includes everything from the FBI's budget to NASA's. For these, Congress must specifically appropriate the money each year for the program. In tough budgetary times, discretionary spending fares worse than entitlements. In 1992, Representative Bill Ford pushed to make Pell grants an entitlement, forever putting the grants on an equal footing with loans. The Bush administration opposed the effort as creating another new rapid-growth spending program. The Pell grant entitlement lost.

61 *USSA conference:* Author's eyewitness account.

62 *Simon decided he wanted . . . :* When Clinton called on Simon to ask for his support in the crucial 1992 Illinois presidential primary, the senator had just two issues he pushed on the Arkansas governor: the balanced budget amendment and income-contingent loans.

63 *a delicious opportunity:* Shireman asked Galston if Clinton would join the fray. Clinton was scheduled to announce his national service plan March 1 at Rutgers University in New Jersey. Couldn't he attack the banks while he was at it? Galston thought it wasn't a bad idea, and drafted a paragraph, which writer David Kusnet included in the speech draft that went to Clinton. At the last minute, however, Clinton himself scratched out the paragraph, for fear it would detract from the message of the day about service.

63 *a flustered John Dean . . . :* Author's eyewitness account.

66 *"Wouldn't be pretty" . . . :* One source claimed that Clinton specifically urged the aides to "find a role" for Sallie Mae, but others remembered no such comment. There was some difference of opinion about the wording of Clinton's comments on Sallie Mae, although there was widespread agreement that the subject had come up and a reference made to Hultin.

Chapter 5

69 *college students gawking . . . :* Earlier, I got the same charge following around the single most important person in New Jersey that day: MTV's redheaded reporter Tabitha Soren. MTV was producing an hour-long special on the national service plan, which would prove to be the most serious piece of TV journalism on national service over the course of the next six months. As the marching band warmed up playing "Jesus Christ Superstar," Soren walked up the bleachers and students broke into cheers. Several slipped her pieces of paper and ticket stubs and asked for her autograph.

Even my friend Jonathan Alter, a *Newsweek* correspondent who does occasional appearances as a pundit on TV, was approached for his autograph. "Hey, you're Jonathan Alter!" the college student said. "Boy, oh boy! Jonathan Alter!" He shook his head in amazement. "Boy, oh boy!"

70 *Over the course of the year . . . :* In fact, Christopher Georges wrote in *The Washington Monthly* that George Bush's tiny Points of Light program actually got more positive coverage than Clinton's national service initiative. Christopher Georges, "Bad News Bearers: The media really were mugging Bill Clinton. Here's the proof," *Washington Monthly*, July/August 1993, pp. 28–34.

72 *preferably using sports metaphors:* When I first came to Washington, I had lunch with a respected veteran political reporter who gave me one piece of advice: "Covering politics is just like covering sports—just a different group of players."

73 *Clinton's own advisors reinforced . . . :* I sympathize with these reporters because I've had firsthand experience with how deeply paranoid the White House's media operation was, particularly in the first six months of Clinton's administration.

In December 1992, I began pushing to get good enough access to produce a vivid fly-on-the-wall article. I met with scores of different men and women on Capitol Hill and among interest groups. By March, I had made access arrangements with about fifty key players on all sides of the issues, but I was having little luck with the White House—and without material from inside the White House, my editors would likely lose interest. Penetrating Paul Simon's office was not their idea of pathbreaking journalism.

At this point, I had to confront a personal dilemma. I have a brother, Michael, who is two years older than I. I was delighted when Mike moved to Washington to work for Ralph Nader. I was proud of his commitment to the public interest and satisfied that I could steer clear of articles on tort reform and pesticides.

In the summer of 1992, the Clinton campaign asked Mike to come to Little Rock to help with issues development, particularly on campaign finance and political ethics reform, two of his specialties. I began working on my national service idea in October, but figured that even if Clinton won it would be pretty easy for Michael and me to avoid each other. Unfortunately, Michael is extremely talented. During the transition, his star rose; he helped write the inaugural speech, and his star rose some more. When Clinton announced his appointments, he made my big brother a special assistant to the president for policy coordination in the communications office.

I wondered, would I be able to write objectively about Clinton with Michael working in the White House? Would I shade my writing toward the positive to protect him? Or, just as likely, would I shade my writing toward the negative to prove my independence? I considered whether Mike's presence in the White House made it impossible to write about national service. My bureau chief, Evan Thomas, thought it would not be a problem as long as Michael didn't work on that issue. So over dinner at a nearby Thai restaurant, the two Waldman brothers negotiated a deal, divvying up issues as we once had negotiated over strawberry Jell-O portions. I would avoid writing about campaign finance and lobbying, and he would ask to recuse himself from working on national service. We made a solemn pledge—which we kept—not to talk about my project or about whatever he might have heard about national service. The deal was done.

Throughout this time, I tried negotiating access agreements with the White House. Bruce Reed, who was policy director during the campaign, had sounded positive, so I thought my chances were decent. Since the Clinton campaign always complained that the press focused on politics or personal trivialities, I thought they'd jump at the chance to help a newsmagazine devote resources to one of the president's favorite policy proposals. Shortly after the election, George Stephanopoulos faxed me a note saying, "I think we might be able to work something out." He told me to talk to press secretary Dee Dee Myers. I was ecstatic.

But, oddly, over the course of the next month I couldn't get anyone to return my calls. Dee Dee said she would talk to Eli Segal and get back to me. She never did. I wrote and called Segal. No response. I wrote a letter over the signature of Evan Thomas and cornered Segal at a community service meeting to stuff it into his hand. The letter modified our basic request: we no longer asked to sit in on meetings as our campaign reporter had, but rather simply to have regular background briefings. Still no response.

Eventually I talked to Bob Boorstin, a special assistant to the president in the communications office. Boorstin, to his credit, immediately took my call—a first—and told me bluntly that he had killed the idea because he thought that to have me sitting in on meetings would prevent honest discussion. I said, "Yes, but as I've explained to half a dozen people over the past month, we're just asking for regular interviews, not to roam the halls of the White House or camp out in the president's bedroom. In fact, at this point I'd settle for having my phone calls returned at all." "Well, anyway," he said, "I think you have a conflict of interest." He meant, of course, the Big Brother problem. "I know you have an arrangement," he said, "but I just can't see it working. I just think it's unfair to him."

I, and *Newsweek*, had invested about three months of time—a lifetime in reporter years—operating on the assumption that we would get "inside" the White House. Not only were we not getting cooperation, but they were treating us like we were investigative reporters for the *Draft-Dodger Gazette*. Now, in mid-February, just a few days before the president would make the key decisions on national service, Boorstin was telling me the White House wouldn't cooperate with the country's second-largest newsmagazine—with 3.4 million in circulation, and 10 million readers—on an in-depth piece about Clinton's favorite policy initiative . . . because it would be unfair to my big brother, Mike?

Eventually, the misunderstanding was cleared up and ONS began to be more cooperative. From about April on, the Office of National Service was fairly generous with its time and always friendly.

I mention all this for two reasons. The first, of course, is vengeance. They made me suffer for months. More importantly, though, I was struck at how antagonistic their attitude was even toward a substantive project by a sympathetic reporter on a subject they believed to be win-win for the president. *Never again could I listen sympathetically to their complaints about the press's unwillingness to cover issues instead of "the horse race."*

It is interesting to note that the tone at the White House did, in fact, change when David Gergen came in as a communications czar. His brilliant insight was pretty straightforward: If you deny reporters information, they become mean, like sharks who've been denied food and then smell a drop of blood. If you keep them steadily fed, even if it's on junk food, reporters will be happy. The Reagan administration manipulated the media not by denying them information but by controlling it. Many of the Clinton administration's problems with the press during the first six months stemmed from this basic misunderstanding.

Chapter 6

74 *the modern budget process* . . . : When Congress votes on the budget resolution it is implicitly making hundreds of other decisions—how much will go to agriculture versus housing, guns versus butter, etc. Presidents love budget resolutions because they can get a single up or down vote on an abstraction. If a president proposes cutting, say, the mohair subsidy, some congressman will stand on the floor to attack the reduction as an affront to all hardworking mohair-makers around the country. But if the president proposes simply spending $100 million less on agriculture, that same congressman can feel free to cheer the president's good sense.

75 *How on earth* . . . : Congress prefers *guarantee* programs, in which the government encourages private banks to make loans, because those programs accomplish important social goals—aid to farmers, to small businesses, to students—without costing a penny, at least until the farmers, businesses, or students start defaulting and Uncle Sam has to make good on the guarantee.

78 *Cyberspace then buzzed* . . . : Nassirian sent a Q & A about direct lending over the Internet:

> Why is direct lending a better alternative for borrowers than guaranteed student loans?
>
> By reducing the number of intermediaries and, most important, by eliminating the existing profit-driven incentive structure, direct lending will permit alternative terms and conditions that will be to the taxpayers' and borrowers' benefit. The savings from direct lending, estimated by the Congressional Budget Office to be at least $6.052 billion over the next five years, can either be reinvested in new programs of federal support for higher education, or they can provide better terms for borrowers.
>
> In other words, under the current system the folks at Paiselley College dealing with Heather Doe's loan would have to deal with Heather, and her local bank, and her local guaranty agency. But for Heather's roommate, they would have to work with a different bank and guaranty agency, perhaps on the other side of the country. Under direct lending, they would work directly with the federal government for all their students.
>
> Can the Education Department handle direct lending?
>
> Yes. This catch-all objection fails to note the functional complexity of the present arrangement. The General Accounting Office recently rated the program one of the six riskiest federal credit programs.
>
> Can [schools] handle direct lending?

Yes. . . . Direct lending will free [college] resources by reducing the number of steps involved.

81 *March 15 meeting . . .* : Author's eyewitness account.

82 *One man in the higher-education . . .* : ACE meetings with Gray and, the next day, with Blakey are author's eyewitness accounts.

Chapter 7

88 *Commission on National and Community Service . . . staff meeting . . .* : Author's eyewitness account.

89 *Just two weeks earlier . . .* : YSA meeting is author's eyewitness account. At the meeting, Frank Slobig, one of the leaders of YSA, interjected an interesting historical note: Seven years earlier, City Year's approach had been viewed as "against the grain" because it advocated "reaching out to the middle class." Now, thanks to Clinton, the pendulum had begun swinging the other way. Programs targeting the disadvantaged had begun to feel defensive.

90 *"There is this romantic notion . . ."*: Peel away the outer layers of the argument and one eventually hits deeply rooted assumptions about the role of government, the distribution of power, and even the roots of poverty. In fact, burrow all the way to the core, and you eventually get to different views of human nature.

Implicit in the integrationist model are several important assumptions. Integrationist programs accept the notion that there is a self-reinforcing "culture of poverty." People who grow up poor too often learn behaviors that will ensure they remain poor: a tendency to discount the value of education; failure to act responsibly at work; alcohol or drug abuse; becoming parents when they're unequipped to raise kids; etc. Socioeconomically diverse programs enable people to witness other behaviors, successful and unsuccessful. A major reason for poverty is the inability of the poor to imagine a better life or to understand how to obtain the tools of advancement. One young man I met at City Year, Tyrone McFadden, wasn't planning to go to college—not because of lack of money, but because the thought had never occurred to him. Some young people from disadvantaged backgrounds are stunned to realize that they are, in fact, just as smart as their well-to-do colleagues, and have just as much right to achieve.

Advocates of targeted programs accept the notion that poor kids need role models but argue that the most plausible and effective role models are those who are, or who started out, in similar circumstances. Dorothy Stoneman also argued that nothing can be a stronger motivator than the sense of rebuilding one's own community. If the community happens to be all white or all black, then the service program should be the same. Some advocates for targeted programs dispute the "culture of poverty" idea entirely; they say that people remain poor because society denies them opportunities.

The race- and class-mixing approach also assumes that segregation inevitably suppresses advancement for minorities and the poor by depriving them of access to informal career networks. You get a job from the father of the guy you went to prep school with; if you have no access to prep school, you won't get that job. Adherents of targeted programs are more likely to accept the basic premise of Afrocentric curricula and black colleges—that the key tool a disadvantaged person lacks is self-confidence, and he or she is more likely to gain emotional strength among supportive people who won't begin the relationship with negative assumptions.

The integrationist model further assumes that segregation and racism hurt everyone, not just minorities. By fearing or remaining aloof from minorities, whites lose out on an entire pool of potential friends, lovers, and advisors who could teach them and change their lives, the integrationist model assumes. The same goes for middle-class or affluent young people who avoid the poor, and vice versa. Those for whom success comes easily can learn from those who had to struggle. If they don't know any minority people, even the most liberal, well-meaning person cannot possibly understand the situation minorities face. At the very least, racial integration can reduce fear by helping a white kid discern what type of black youth might cause him harm and what type would not (just as blacks already have to make those distinctions).

Targeted-program advocates don't necessarily dispute that whites could benefit from working with blacks, but they argue that priorities must be set. In a time of scarce resources, they believe, society should funnel money toward the bigger problem: the material poverty of the poor, not the spiritual poverty of the burned-out preppy.

97–98 *Sagawa and Susan Stroud . . .* : Author's eyewitness account.

100 *Inside the* VA *. . .* : The Department of Veterans Affairs, the Senate Armed Services Committee, and the Office of National Service all did comparisons, each of which came up with different numbers. In each case, though, the scholarship level for the veterans was, in fact, lower. According to the Veterans Administration, someone who served for three years would get $14,400, or an average of $4,800 per year served, compared to $6,500 for the civilians. The veterans concentrated on this number in making their case. The White House, on the other hand, looked at total compensation, pay and scholarship. By that count, the annualized benefit was $21,250 in the army and $15,000 in national service.

Chapter 8

102 *He was watching a politically mixed group . . .* : Reconstruction.

104 *On the morning of March 15, 1933 . . .* : Press conference, executive offices of the White House, March 15, 1933, 10:25 a.m., excerpted in Edgar B. Nixon, ed., *Franklin D. Roosevelt & Conservation 1911–1945*, vol. 1 (Hyde Park, New York: Franklin D. Roosevelt Library, 1957), pp. 139–40. When Roosevelt tried to convince the public of the CCC's success, he focused less on employment or personal development than on conservation. In a speech at Glacier National Park, August 5, 1934, Roosevelt began by saying the CCC was "helping these men to help themselves and their families." But the rest of the speech was about what they had done: "Hundreds of miles of firebreaks have been built, fire hazards have been reduced on great tracts of timberland, thousands of miles of roadside have been cleared, 2,500 miles of trails have been constructed, 10,000 acres have been reforested. Other tens of thousands of acres have been treated for tree disease and soil erosion. This is but another example of our efforts to build, not for today alone but for tomorrow as well."

109 *Jonathan Rowe's hilarious account . . . :* Jonathan Rowe, "I Was a Spearcarrier in the War on Poverty," *Washington Monthly*, November 1984.

110 *Clearly, having a program . . . :* There were other issues as well. What should service programs pay the more highly trained "professional corps" like teaching or police? Would they be paid at minimum wage? If you paid minimum wage to someone teaching alongside someone earning $30,000 a year, that would inevitably drive down the wages of the permanent teacher. In early drafts of the White House proposal, planners had provided a substantial subsidy for national service teachers and other professionals to raise their salaries up to the salary levels of the people with whom they would work. But the police and teachers' unions objected, arguing that the feds would then be subsidizing municipal payrolls. And if a city could get a national service teacher for nearly free, why hire a regular teacher for $30,000? So the ONS staff changed the provision so that any program paying more than a $10,000 salary would get *no* federal help. Advocates for professional-type service programs, such as Teach for America, argued that the White House had now gone too far in the other direction. Finally, Segal's team hit upon what seemed like an ingenious compromise. The feds would provide an amount equivalent to 75 percent of the minimum wage, or less. Professional corps could feel free to pay $30,000, but they would have to come up with the rest of the money on their own. Given Clinton's desire for a strong professional corps, however, Lew and Sagawa were not certain he would agree. That went on the options memo too. Clinton loved the idea.

114 *The state commissions would have to get "concurrence" . . . :* As AFSCME put it in their private written recommendations to the White House, "As a condition of receiving funds, applicants for federal funds must provide written certification from a labor organization representing employees in the area who are engaged in the same or similar work as that proposed to be carried out, that it concurs with the proposed projects."

115–117 *the April 12 meeting . . . :* Reconstruction.

118 *the Peace Corps and the space program . . . :* The other successful government programs have been the ones in which Washington gave money directly to the individual beneficiary, bypassing the local governments or contractors: Social Security, food stamps, the GI Bill, and Pell grants.

Chapter 9

119 *conference . . . on national service . . . :* The conference was run by the National Strategy Forum, funded by the Robert R. McCormick Tribune Foundation.

120 *Why wasn't the military . . . :* The White House did have Major Rob Gordon (not to be confused with Robert Gordon the college student), a White House fellow working at ONS. But most people in the service movement seemed to distrust the military deeply, to fear that it didn't understand the problems of at-risk youth. I had seen no evidence up to that point that the administration really believed the military had much to offer this program.

125 *flipping a coin:* Pat Rissler, staff director of the Education and Labor Committee, disputes this account. She says that Ford meant no ill will toward McCurdy. He merely decided he had already sponsored enough legislation that session and could afford to let some of the more junior members on the committee get some glory.

126 *the peculiar rules governing budget bills:* Direct lending could go on the budget reconciliation bill because it saved money. Under Senate rules, however, costly new programs like national service could not be initiated on the budget reconciliation bill. The White House couldn't take direct lending *out* of the budget bill, because it needed the savings; it couldn't put national service *on* the budget bill because of the rules. So they ended up in two separate bills.

129 *"For most Americans . . .":* This is according to Greenberg's own recollection in January 1994. When I asked Greenberg whether they had considered the realities of the policy when deciding to emphasize college aid, he laughed. "Don't bother me with the details." Quickly, he added, "That's a joke. That's a joke. I deal with message, not policy. I give advice on how to present this. Of course they ought to make policy on its own terms."

130 *Friday morning, April 30 . . . :* The one bit of bad news of the morning was the *USA Today* headline, across the top of the front page, referring to $6,500 per year in loan benefits, for a total of $13,000. The paper had gone to press with the story before the veterans' uproar had forced the cut to $5,000. But at least the White House got real coverage.

Chapter 10

132 *lobbyists milking their clients . . . :* Some figure out creative billing techniques. A Hyundai executive recalled thinking little of it when the company's new lobbyist, Daniel Murphy, said he was going to be in South Korea and wanted to make a courtesy call on the chairman. The executive was disturbed, however, when he discovered that Murphy charged Hyundai not only for his time but for his travel expenses as well. Murphy worked at the time for Gray and Company, whose founder, Bob Gray, was notorious for racking up $1,000 lunches by including in the bill to clients his own $450-an-hour fee as well as the hourly pay of the staffer who briefed him, the secretary who made the reservations, and the chauffeur who drove him to the restaurant. In other cases, lobbyists will trick clients into thinking a crisis is imminent—to justify a bigger lobbying budget—or will take credit for things that would have happened anyway. In other words: Just because a company hires a high-priced lobbyist, they are not necessarily buying real influence.

133 *massive issue-oriented political campaigns:* In the mid-1980s, for instance, a group of clothing retailers hired Reese Communications Companies to block a protectionist textile bill that would have increased the price of imported clothes. Reese began with a pool of 3 million names drawn from its own database and from rented mailing lists. He went through an elaborate process of weeding out those unlikely to respond. "The most *sympathetic* individual was the yuppie buying Armani ties," said Michael Graham, Reese's president. But sympathy and proclivity toward action are not the same. Yuppies are notoriously bad letter writers. Retirees, on the other hand, are usually good letter writers, but in this case the Reese Companies' evaluators feared the seniors might hold lingering anti-Japanese feelings from World War II. Using polls and "psychographic" studies of life-styles and values, they whittled the list down to 600,000 middle-aged, well-educated voters living in districts of key representatives. Reese sent those voters lobbying packages and of those, about 50,000 wrote letters or phoned legislators.

133 *Teams of technical experts . . .* : Included in the lengthy briefing notebook given to Sallie Mae staff was an intimidating series of charts showing fifty-seven separate steps for giving out direct loans, including some scary ones, such as "Borrower authorization will be needed to credit loan proceeds to student's account," and some that on close inspection didn't sound terribly onerous, such as "School obtains borrower signature on note."

Sallie Mae's packets were misleading because they relied on the administration's very earliest plans from back in December. The Department of Education had since promised that any school that didn't want the hassle could have a private contractor process the loans. Nevertheless, the conclusions from this "objective" analysis were gloomy indeed: "Existing staffing levels are inadequate to support new direct lending activity. . . . Existing aid administration office space will not support staff expansion and equipment. . . . Schools will need to invest in new computer hardware and peripherals, as well as software development and integration. . . . Schools will not have sufficient time to prepare for direct lending." A Sallie Mae spokeswoman defended the packets as being based on the most solid information they had at the time. In a monthly newsletter Sallie Mae sent just to financial aid administrators, CEO Lawrence Hough bluntly declared that direct lending would "eliminate your service choices." It "could risk students' access to loan funds," he stated, and "result in poorer service for your graduates." All this would likely happen because under direct lending "the timely delivery of loan funds would hinge not on the competitiveness of the private marketplace but on the responsiveness of a federal bureaucracy."

133 *"Ninety-five Questions . . ."*: Among them were such loaded questions as "Are the Department of Education and the Internal Revenue Service capable of carrying out all of their new responsibilities in a much more timely and accurate manner than they have carried out current responsibilities to date?" Some merely hinted at vaguely ominous possibilities—"What forms of liability insurance will be required?"—while others evoked a new world where the beleaguered financial aid administrator would become a combination loan officer/tax collector/banker: "What if an individual borrower never works but files a joint tax return with a spouse?"

135 *flown to Washington by Sallie Mae . . .* : Sallie Mae had actually offered to fly someone out to Wisconsin to brief Kraig, but the student had said no. So Sallie Mae agreed to fly the students to Washington.

136–138 *"Let's go through the Senate Democrats . . ."*: Author's eyewitness account.

138 *the Career College Association . . . :* CCA did allow me to sit in on several strategy and lobbying meetings, including visits to senators and officials of the Department of Education. CCA lobbyists were not, however, invited to attend the weekly Monday-morning sessions hosted by ACE at One DuPont circle. Other education lobbyists sneered at CCA's trade schools for not being institutions of higher learning. Cultural bias explains some of the contempt. The higher-education lobbyists had gone to prestigious colleges and universities, often for advanced degrees; they hadn't studied to be mechanics or refrigerator repairmen. But there was another, more substantive reason for this coldness: trade schools had been the major reason for the startling increase in student-loan defaults that had given the entire program a black eye.

The worst of the proprietaries are simply cynical financial scams that prey on disadvantaged young people trying to better themselves. Some sent employees to set up camp outside welfare offices or housing projects; they recruited students with promises of a high-paying job, then gave them a lousy education in a field with few job openings. Students often left worse off than when they'd entered: without skills but now with $1,000 in new debt. They soon defaulted on the loan, making it impossible for them to get a loan should they ever want to try a reputable school.

In 1992, the four-year colleges and universities supported government efforts to crack down on sleazy trade schools—but the CCA fought hard to block the most stringent of these efforts, which they felt hurt good schools along with bad. Many in the higher-education community questioned whether the CCA had a built-in conflict of interest, since the trade association also ran the accreditation service for schools. The association, therefore, derived some of its revenue from fees paid by the schools it was supposedly trying to police. Moreover, some of the schools with high default rates were very influential within the CCA.

Feeling besieged, the CCA in 1992 decided to shift its lobbying emphasis away from Washington toward the grass roots. The trade association had a bad reputation, but the hardworking local businessmen who ran their schools still had credibility. The CCA hired Bob Beckel, Walter Mondale's former campaign manager (and substitute host on *Crossfire*), to set up a grassroots network throughout the country called "Skills 2000." They trained local trade-school operators to form state organizations, and hired a Washington staff of former congressional aides to serve as regional coordinators.

139–140 *national conference . . . on May 12 . . . :* Author's eyeswitness account.

139 *Lesson number one . . . :* The discussion of campaign fund-raising was instructive. "Clearly if you're supportive of a member it doesn't hurt to *support him*," Pave said. "You can volunteer to be a member of his finance committee. You can hold fund-raisers. And you can give money to the CCA PAC. All of these are ways of supporting people who support us—all are good ways of making a connection with members of Congress."

Although she didn't speak more of the political action committee at this session, visitors were asked to give to CCA PAC. A list of talking points given to the CCA staff to help drum up enthusiasm for the PAC laid out the basic pitch: "It is really important for you make a PAC contribution now rather than waiting until later. . . . We must work with Members of Congress from committees that we have never worked with before, such as the Energy and Commerce

Committee. Our PAC can help us to begin relationships with some of the key players on these committees." In addition, the talking-points memo stated, "The PAC must file a report with the FEC in June that details our fund-raising for this year to date. In the current political climate for CCA, it is very important that our PAC looks strong and has a good balance."

139 *anything to make themselves known* . . . : Deborah Dunn, who ran the Restaurant School in Philadelphia, recounted her success with this technique. One member of Congress had asked her for help getting some unemployed people for a photo opportunity on the economy. She rounded them up immediately. "You have to do things where you never even raise an issue of concern to the school," she explains. "It's very important that you look for those opportunities. Believe me, it turns them around faster than anything else. I have a district manager from a congressman who calls me all the time now. I know when he has staff problems or he's having a really bad day." Author's eyewitness account.

140 *Senator Specter* . . . : Author's eyewitness account.

140 *local banks refused to give loans* . . . : Trade schools charge relatively small tuition compared to four-year colleges, and programs sometimes last for only a year. Lenders prefer working with larger amounts, for longer periods of time.

The CCA really had two agendas with their direct lending lobbying: The first was to influence the outcome; the second was to be *seen* helping the Clinton administration pass its proposal. The CCA and the Department of Education had been at war under President Bush; the CCA viewed direct lending as an opportunity to prove its usefulness to the new regime. Apropos of that, the CCA officials held perhaps their most important lobbying meeting with top Department of Education officials. The goal of this was obviously not to persuade the Clinton administration to support direct lending, but to make them aware of what good friends they had at the CCA.

Madeleine Kunin chaired the meeting at a conference table in her office; her colorful, dangly bird earrings helping to set a relaxed tone. "Grassroots support would be very important for us," she said. "The other side is using it and they have a lot of money. We are prohibited from lobbying ourselves so we're relying on other groups."

That was a perfect setup for Stephen Blair, the executive director of CCA. "We have deemphasized the role of Washington lobbying and are pooling our efforts into building constituent support. We represent 1.5 million students, 1,600 schools."

"The scare tactics [from the industry] are what's worrying me," Kunin said, referring to several local campaigns by guaranty agencies to convince students they would lose their loans under the White House plan.

Sensing an opportunity, Blair chimed in by talking about *his* big guns—the corporations who hire the trade-school students. "We have major corporations —Carrier, Humana, General Electric. We can deliver major corporations," he pledged.

"That's something no one else can bring," CCA lobbyist Nancy Broff added.

140 *postcards to Specter* . . . : Most kept it short and simple. "Dear Senator Specter, please vote for the direct lending program." Others added their own special touches. "I feel that the direct student loan program needs a yes vote from you," one wrote. "Most students I know who attend the Restaurant School need these loans to finish or attend the school of their choice. I plan to go into the hotel business after graduation."

Chapter 11

142 *Ford. . . . would be Clinton's footsoldier . . . :* There was some important recent history simmering in Bill Ford's political subconscious. Ford had an axe to grind with Sallie Mae. After taking over as chairman of the committee in 1991, Ford had slowly, carefully guided the Higher Education Reauthorization Act of 1992 through Congress. This bill included many important provisions, hammered out through months of compromise, to expand eligibility for middle-class student loans. It also included a pilot program to try direct lending in five hundred schools, or about 5 percent of the total. When the Bush administration learned about the pilot program, Secretary of Education Lamar Alexander issued a terse statement, pledging that the president would veto the entire reauthorization because of the direct lending program. In the end, the dispute was resolved when a delegation of Republican congressmen appealed to Bush personally. But Ford blamed Sallie Mae, which was influential in the Bush White House, for virtually ruining his maiden voyage as chairman of the committee. He had felt personally betrayed. "It's one thing to vote against Ford," Representative Rob Andrews said. "But to spend *his* political capital and then trample all over him, that's another thing. Bill Ford holds grudges."

142 *a solid piece of legislation . . . :* The key had been constant hectoring from Gene Sperling and Bill Galston, and the work of Maureen McLaughlin, a talented career employee at the department who was appointed to the political job overseeing the loan reform.

149 *hearing on student-loan reform:* So many questions had been raised about the Department of Education's ability to run the direct lending program that Kunin had to restore some confidence in the department. In fact, Shireman scribbled a note to Simon at the hearing saying, "I think it's best to let *Kunin* handle the detailed points on savings, etc." It had to be Kunin herself impressing the senators. She departed from her original text and launched into a detailed exposition on all the ways the department was trying to reform itself. "Kunin was superb," said Senator Pell's staff aide David Evans, who was skeptical about direct lending.

149 *Pell mumbles so meekly . . . :* Riley's and Kunin's efforts to build personal rapport with the senators was crucial in raising confidence in the Education Department. Kunin's only gaffe during the hearing came when she said the budget for Pell grant funding "will put Pell on solid footing." The fragile-looking Senator Pell blushed with embarrassment, as the room cracked up.

150 *loyal old man . . . :* Even Pell's own staff was surprised at the senator's increasing steadfastness on this issue. Fearful that Pell might compromise too soon, Evans cautioned the senator not to agree to anything when he talked to Kunin by phone over the Memorial Day weekend.

"You mean don't give away the store?" Pell asked.

"Well, yes," said Evans, embarrassed that he had been caught lacking confidence in the man he respected more than anyone in the Senate. It was a reminder to Evans of something he had learned in the past: Pell was a team player, but every once in a while, on issues he deemed matters of principle, he became stubborn and immovable.

151   *"A presidential phone call . . .":* Back at Pell's office, David Evans couldn't believe the president hadn't called his boss. He wanted Pell to oppose direct lending and feared that a presidential call would immediately stop him. "The best way to handle us would have been a presidential call," Evans said later. "I think you would have had the senator very, very willing to help [Clinton] out." But the call never came.

151   *Pell's plan included . . . savings for students . . . :* Galston had been quite blunt with Senate staffers: the purpose of direct lending was to reduce the deficit and pay for national service, not to give students a fee cut.

153   *"When he gets his mind set . . . :* Had the White House looked far enough back in Pell's past they would have found clues to his latent toughness. In the 1940s, Pell was arrested several times by the Nazis for trying to help concentration camp inmates, according to his Senate office.

153   *The night before markup . . . :* Sallie Mae lobbyists, meanwhile, were desperately trying to divine what the negotiations were producing. That Friday night, June 4, Winkie Crigler called Kennedy aide Suzanne Ramos in a panic because they heard the legislation might cap the salary of Sallie Mae's CEO. (Evans had indeed included such a provision at the behest of Republican Senator Judd Gregg.)

156   *The next morning . . . :* Even though the compromise had been struck, the staff was dashing back and forth across the room as if something horrible had happened. The problem: The old language was still in the bills sitting on the senators' desks. No big deal, a novice might say, just cross it out. But the politics of that simple stroke of a pen were significant. If the senators started off the markup with the phrase in, they would have to vote publicly to cut it out. That would give satisfaction to the Republicans, but could be perceived as a slap at the administration. After several tense moments of consultation, Suzanne Ramos of Kennedy's staff went around to each senator's desk and crossed out the language.

That crisis passed.

Chapter 12

161   *commission had to be "bipartisan" . . . :* No more than 50 percent—plus one—of the voting members could be from the same political party.

161   *NASCC was pushing . . . :* NASCC suggested eliminating the requirement that eight of the new directors of the corporation come from the Commission on National and Community Service. How does that help the poor? Again, the real intent was apparent only if one looked between the lines. The White House had required the corporation to transfer some of the commission board members in order to preserve some of the commission's clout. But several of the corps represented by NASCC disliked the commission, and believed it had discrimi-

nated against them because they weren't sufficiently mixed racially. (The commission did show a preference for diverse programs, but also came to believe that many of the corps were of poor quality.) They wanted the commission's influence *decreased.* Sofer agreed to the change.

NASCC also suggested requiring that the state commissions include individuals "who have experience in developing and administering effective national service programs" instead of just "experts regarding national service." This would knock out someone like Charles Moskos, an academic expert, and emphasize—surprise!—the directors of the existing youth corps.

Earlier, NASCC, along with Representative Xavier Becerra, had gotten in the requirement that half the money going through the states be targeted toward programs that work in *and recruit from* distressed communities. Sofer rejected three NASCC amendments that targeted the program even more toward the poor: NASCC wanted penalties against those states that didn't meet the poor-participant quota; it wanted to eliminate the requirement that every participant have a high school diploma or work toward a GED; and it wanted the law to set aside 30 percent of all funds explicitly for youth corps. NASCC also suggested including in the law's preamble the "finding" that "residents of low-income communities, especially youth and young adults, can be empowered through their service to help provide future community leadership." Sofer added it to the bill.

163 *"Most people [in the House] . . .":* While the Commission on National and Community Service had built up a strong following in the Senate, ACTION had far more allies in the House. "The only constituency here is the ACTION employees," one aide said. "Nobody gives a shit about the commission." Commission staff began to hear rumors that ACTION employees were bad-mouthing them behind their backs. "The ACTION people have been spreading things around attacking the commission as being too young, having a staff in over their heads," one observer said.

164 *The White House gave in:* The White House negotiators privately consoled themselves that the civil service committee had done such a bad job of drafting the provision that the president could probably sneak in some extra flexibility when they wrote regulations.

They further strengthened the clout of VISTA and ACTION by requiring that the corporation establish an office in each state. This is a classic case of how legislation can include protection for a particular interest group without explicitly identifying the group. The committee couldn't actually say "the corporation will be required to use ACTION employees" as the federal representatives on the state commissions. But follow the crafty logic and you see how they end up with the same result: They could require that the corporation establish "an office" in each state. They knew that, since ACTION already had setups in each state, the new corporation would be virtually forced to use those as their state offices. And it only made sense that the head of the corporation's state office should also be the federal "spy." Therefore, the federal spy would be the state's ACTION official.

Chapter 13

171 *President Clinton had announced Summer of Service . . .* : The White House originally wanted the Summer of Service to be a *year* of service. John Kennedy, after all, had gotten the Peace Corps going almost immediately, by executive order, before the legislation had been approved. But Catherine Milton told the White House it obviously didn't have any conception of how hard it would be to whip up a yearlong domestic service program on a few months' notice. Furious negotiations ensued over the details, but the White House soon agreed to a summer program.

In his March 1 Rutgers speech, Clinton asked for interested young people to mail in postcards. Significantly, about 40 percent of the people who sent in cards emphasized the financial aid benefits more than service, the ONS staff estimated. The public seemed to be absorbing the bumper-sticker concept that national service was a means of creating educational opportunity. One young man wanted to participate in Summer of Service because "in order to get financial aid I would much prefer to help people."

Another girl wrote from Gardena, California: "I heard about your National Service Plan, on MTV a few weeks ago. I feel that your plan is what I need. Oh, by the way, I would like to thank you for giving a youngster like me a chance to make money for college. I am a eighteen year old teen on my way to graduate and looking for some type of financial to help me to get to college. But my family and I are having real financial problems."

Others viewed it as a job. "Dear president Clinten [*sic*]: Or do you prefer Bill? Whatever the case may be, I'm writing you because I saw Al Gore on TV last night pitching national service. He also said there would be 1,000 jobs available this summer so here's my application." The man was forty-one years old, had an aviator's license, and hadn't been able to find work. "One thing's for sure, I'll never be able to pay rent, buy food and make my student loan payments on minimum wage. I need some alternative Mr. Clinten."

171 *The Summer of Service staff was ecstatic . . .* : The atmosphere at the commission on deadline day was a cross between Christmas and April 15. Anticipation rose each time the Federal Express courier wheeled in a cart of applications. Staffers were thrilled by the efforts programs made to participate. One person carried his application by plane to get it to Washington on time. Another called from an airport and held the phone out so the commission staff could hear his flight being canceled.

The commission received more than 430 applications and sent them to several groups of evaluators—service professionals from the field—which winnowed, ranked, and finally, selected. On May 6, the commission announced the winners, sixteen programs in eleven areas. In the tradition of all great federal programs, this one gave advance notice to congressional representatives from those districts so they could take credit for it—and help generate more local press. "Congressman Flake Announces New York National Service Recipients," read the release from Representative Floyd Flake of Brooklyn, whose district would be helped by some of the programs. "Sarbanes Hails Award to Maryland Summer of Service Program," declared another. "Foglietta Announces Philadelphia Wins Summer of Service program." "Bradley Commends Selection of Newark Summer of Service Program."

171 *Everything seemed to be going according to plan:* They had just one small problem. They technically had no money to pay for the Summer of Service. The funds for SOS had been provided in the president's economic stimulus package—which had been defeated by the Republican filibuster. The Office of National Service kept waiting for a chance to attach a funding amendment to some other bill, but as June 19 approached they still had no appropriation. In a $1 trillion budget, wasn't there some way of getting a measly $15 million? They scoured the existing service programs and decided that some of the money that was appropriated for the new Civilian Community Corps in the defense budget could be spent on Summer of Service. But this was not the first priority of the Pentagon, which hadn't gotten around yet to sending the money over to the Commission on National and Community Service. So commission staffers tracked down someone at the Defense Department and asked him to transfer the money. They received a strange response: Okay, come pick up the check. The check? Somehow, in this day and age, with tens of billions spent each day, it hadn't occurred to anyone that they would actually get a check, which they would then deposit into a bank account. Surely this must be done via some high-speed electronic computer transfer. Nope. Chris Gallagher from the ONS staff went out to Andrews Air Force Base to pick up an envelope. Inside was a check from the U.S. Department of Defense authorizing their bank to "Pay to the Order of Commission on National and Community Service, $40,000,000.00."

172 *The irritation was compounded . . . :* The commission was running the event, but Phil Caplan, a former advance man for the Clinton campaign, and Major Robert Gordon, a former West Point teacher, were keeping tabs on it for the White House. Caplan had begun to grow worried that for all their knowledge of service programs, the commission staff didn't know how to organize a large retreat like this. He kept asking about the communications system, to which the commission staff replied, somewhat annoyed, that they would all be on the same base—why would they need communications gear? On Sunday, however, a participant got sick and the staff found it impossible to communicate about what to do. So Caplan and Gordon, as the training was beginning, went into the streets of San Francisco and rented sixty walkie-talkies, which then became essential tools during the week. "They figured this was Robert Gordon playing army and the White House political guy being a jerk," Caplan said later. "But it was symptomatic of the service community's inability to manage this event."

175 *Segal began talking:* The meeting was tape recorded. Segal did not realize that at the time.

178 *not one highlighted the difficulties . . . :* The only publication in America to report anything even close to an accurate version of what happened that summer was the *Chronicle of Philanthropy*, a specialty publication that covers the nonprofit world. Kristen Gross did the best reporting.

Chapter 14

181 *It did nothing to consolidate* . . . : Barnes O'Connor pointed out that the corporation does not actually consolidate any of the existing seventeen service-related federal programs, but just puts them together under one extra new roof, the Corporation for National Service. In addition to the roughly one dozen different programs under ACTION and the commission, there were: the Civilian Community Corps and National Guard Civilian Youth Opportunities programs, funded by the Pentagon; the National Health Service Corps and the Indian Health Service, at the Department of Health and Human Services; the YouthBuild and Urban Revitalization Demonstration programs, at Housing and Urban Development; the Student Literacy Corps and Innovative Projects for Community Service, at the Department of Education; Summer Youth Conservation Corps, at the departments of the Interior and Agriculture; and the Senior Community Service Employment Program, at the Department of Labor.

181 *"True service is that which is freely given* . . . : from Kassebaum's chapter in *National Issues in Education*.

182–183 *At a July 1 strategy meeting* . . . : Author's eyewitness account.

183 *when service groups gathered* . . . : Author's eyewitness account. The National and Community Service Coalition was housed in the offices of Youth Service America. But because YSA's tax status prevented it from direct lobbying, the service groups established the coalition as a separate entity and hired a former congressional aide, Sara Hartman, to run it.

185–186 *On July 14, Segal worked the phones* . . . : Author's eyewitness account.

186 *With this group, Segal stressed* . . . : Author's eyewitness account.

196 *they began singing a little ditty* . . . : Author's eyewitness account.

196 *"Have you seen this* . . . *?"*: Author's eyewitness account. The letter was signed by ACE, the American Association of Community Colleges, the American Association of State Colleges and Universities, the Association of American Universities, the Association of Community College Trustees, the Association of Catholic Colleges and Universities, the National Association of College and University Business Officers, the National Association of Independent Colleges and Universities, the National Association of Student Financial Aid Administrators, and the United States Student Association.

197 *Ford demanded a letter from ACE* . . . : The national service supporters viewed the ACE letter as a sneak attack—a stab in the back. What had actually happened was more pedestrian. At the Monday-morning lobbying meeting on July 19, the colleges' Washington representatives had discussed their position. On the one hand, they didn't want to publicly oppose their Democratic allies in Congress or pick a fight with a generally pro-education Democratic president. But they had to think carefully about how the college presidents—their bosses —would react if the ACE didn't back an amendment ostensibly geared toward improving funding for Pell grants or campus-based aid. "If we get asked, we have

to support it," Terry Hartle concluded. "But I don't think we should look for trouble."

At 4:30 on July 20, Rose DiNapoli from Goodling's office called Becky Timmons of ACE and asked if they would support either means testing or trigger amendments. Timmons said no on means testing, but that she would check with the schools about the trigger. She surveyed the other college lobbyists and found near-unanimity in supporting it. ACE tried calling Ford, but couldn't get through. So they faxed the letter to him and Molinari simultaneously. As one higher-education lobbyist put it later, "The Molinari amendment was totally consistent with our public positions. If we hadn't supported it, we would be very vulnerable to accusations of being partisan, supporting Clinton just because he's a Democrat." Acknowledging that it looked a little bit spineless to come out for a trigger amendment at the last minute, she said, "We may not have courage, but we have convictions. We're wimps but we're principled wimps."

197–198 *"This is going to be . . ."*: Author's eyewitness account.

199 *The votes happened so quickly . . .* : Another amendment, offered by T. Cass Ballenger, would have removed the provision requiring programs to consult unions if jobs would be displacing unionized positions. It lost 276–153.

And a second Molinari amendment, cutting the stipends for volunteers, was also defeated by voice vote.

200 *a $10.8 billion program . . .* : The House Republican opponents had referred to it as a $7.4 billion program by adding up the projections in Clinton's original budget request, before the authorizations had been cut back. The Senate Republicans simply added on a fifth-year estimate, raising the sum to $10.8 billion.

201 *"You know the Republicans . . ."*: Author's eyewitness account.

201 *the Republican senators gathered . . .* : After the meeting, the rumor spread that it was Dole who had said, "No cheap victories for the president." Based on conversations with people in the room, I think it was D'Amato, but it is a subject of some disagreement.

205 *"Tempers are high . . ."*: Cheever now realized that the industry had made a major blunder by not focusing more on the problems with income-contingent loans and IRS collection. The administration had focused on direct lending, and so the industry had too—and got tarred as the evil "special interest" as a result.

Cheever had developed an intense bitterness toward Sallie Mae; he blamed its behavior for many of the industry's problems. "They had a kind of imperial arrogance about all this." Now, he said, their fates were in the hands of those four or five senators who were skeptical about direct lending.

208 *chess masters battling . . .* : Another analogy: In Woody Allen's movie *Sleeper*, adults in the future get stoned by merely rubbing a special orb. Instead of actually conducting a filibuster, Dole now just rubs the filibuster orb.

209 *Don Nickles . . . argued . . .* : Nickles said the "$10 billion program" warped the spirit of volunteerism by offering stipends. "I doubt that Mother Teresa is on the Indian government's dole!"

221 *Metzenbaum offered a proposal* . . . : Actually, Metzenbaum's proposal was devised by Kennedy but he wanted someone else to offer it. Kassebaum quickly blew his cover by stating, "This is really Senator Kennedy's suggestion but I do think it has merit."

225 *nerve-racking problem* . . . : After a careful reading of the Solomon proposal, Ford decided he would offer to accept the amendment, but only if he got something in return. "Let us make a deal right here and make everyone feel good," Ford said to Solomon. "I say to the gentleman, I'll take your amendment and you vote for the bill." Solomon declined the offer, so Ford said he couldn't accept the amendment. Cliff Stearns of Florida again appealed to Ford to accept the amendment. Ford asked him: If Ford accepted the Solomon amendment, would he get Stearns's vote on the whole national service bill? Stearns said no.

"I am offering to say yes, but the gentlemen are not giving me much respect," Ford concluded. "Mr. Chairman, I will have to oppose the amendment."

226 *The Solomon amendment passed* . . . : After it was clear the administration had lost, Ford gave the signal that it was okay for Democrats to switch their votes so they wouldn't be on record opposing veterans. This is standard practice on controversial votes. After much vote-switching, the amendment carried 259–171.

226 *"We cannot stand by* . . .": The American Legion sent out bulletins to all fifty-eight departments of their organization around the country: "The morale of the armed forces is in a nose dive. First came defense cuts and involuntary discharges. Then came the plan to lift the ban on homosexuals and place women in combat. Now comes an education package for 'national service' that's superior to the GI bill and, the veterans don't even have an opportunity to participate in it."

Unfortunately, the House leadership and the White House had focused their energies on T. Cass Ballenger's amendment intended to curtail the rights of unions. The White House won on that, but in the process the Democrats neglected to "whip" the Stump amendment—that is, the Democratic whip's organization had not done a formal vote count, so they didn't know how many votes they had.

228 *for all intents and purposes, a two-year authorization* . . . : To get the third year, Congress would still have had to vote to reauthorize.

231 *Pryor had to go to Arkansas* . . . : Senators cannot vote absentee on bills on the floor.

231 *The tiny, ornate Senate meeting room was packed:* There weren't even enough seats for staff, let alone lobbyists (although, to the deep envy of the other lobbyists, Sallie Mae's David Starr managed to get in on the arm of his former boss Howard Metzenbaum).

233 *turning into delirium:* Shireman was also growing frustrated at Kennedy's bipartisan strategy. It was already clear that they could have proposed going up to 60 percent if Kennedy were willing to blow off Jeffords and Kassebaum. At one point, Shireman saw Littlefield and Waddles talking and decided to send a signal to the House side. He whisper-screamed at Littlefield, "Let's go to sixty.

We have the votes for sixty!" He knew Littlefield would not accept the suggestion, but wanted Waddles to understand that the House could push harder.

234 *meeting among Riley, Kunin, and Ford.:* Author's eavesdropping plus reconstruction.

238 *The Republicans were done:* Well, no, not exactly: nothing's ever quite done in the Senate. Dole's motion required *unanimous* consent from all the senators, and one senator was refusing to give that consent. Dole spent the next hour trying to get the bill unstuck. They were not able to finish that night.

239 *Despite the frantic rush . . . :* I had my interview with Clinton on August 2, 1993, right after the agreement was reached in the Senate. I had never interviewed a president before, so I brought two tape recorders in case one broke, continuously reviewed my questions, and went to the bathroom four times before leaving my office. I walked through the White House security gate, down the long, curved driveway, and into the press briefing room. There, a young aide gathered me up and took me through the narrow hallways of the west wing to the president's office.

The best description of the private sections of the White House came from Diana Aldridge, who likened it to a "badly designed bed and breakfast," with its blue carpet, Federal-style architecture, and rows of framed pictures of the president in various poses and scenes. I had imagined long, somber hallways with a lone marine guard standing at attention. In fact, it's cozy and compressed. The Cabinet Room was next door to the Oval Office. The vice president's office was close enough that he and the president could (in theory) shoot rubber bands at each other. Stephanopoulos's office was connected to a dining room that adjoins Clinton's office. There was a small outer chamber where two aides sat.

The door opened and Clinton's personal assistant, twenty-five-year-old Andrew Friendly, motioned for me to come in. I walked through the door and, panning left to right, saw a still photographer, a three-person video camera crew, Segal, Aldridge, and, finally, Bill Clinton. I shook his hand. The cameramen recorded the moment.

Only then did I realize something bizarre about the Oval Office: it is *oval*. Somehow I had not contemplated what an oval-shaped office would look like. More startling, still, was Clinton's face. His features were large, and there was one jarring characteristic I had never before noticed.

The president is very pink.

Not red. Pink—something between cotton candy and raspberry sorbet. It was disconcerting to be surprised by a physical attribute of the most recognizable man in America.

I was guided around toward the sitting area of the office, where two couches faced each other. We sat down in the two gold chairs in which Clinton is forever conversing with newly elected Third World presidents.

When I asked questions, Clinton looked directly into my eyes, making me feel—as those who meet with him in private always seem to feel—that each one of my words was extremely important. We marched through the evolution of his ideas about service, the means-testing debate, why the program was so much smaller than the campaign promise. As others have reported, he has an incredible command of detail. When I asked about the loss of IRS collection, something that had received no public attention, he discussed the Ways and Means politics and his hope for a technical compromise in which the IRS would share information with the Department of Education.

He still insisted national service would be among his most important legacies. "You know, I could have the best economic policies in the world and [if] we keep losing kids, we're not going to have a healthy economy. And there will never be enough tax money to solve some of the problems that we've made for ourselves as a society. That's why I feel so passionately about this. This will enable us to bring people into contact with one another in ways that many government programs don't." He expressed the belief that the program would work so well, the public would demand more.

Clinton seemed forever tempering his idealism with his pragmatism, or vice versa. He continues to talk about national service as a society-changing force, even though his team had compromised much along the legislative path. Often Clinton pretends this tension doesn't exist. But sometimes he strikes a good balance, painting in sweeping strokes without losing his sense of realism. That's when he's most impressive. "We had *twenty four* people killed in this town in *one week* a couple of weeks ago. Now, is national service going to change all that? No. But will it make a difference? Will it rescue some kids? Will it give kids a chance to lead a different life? It certainly will."

239 *the new program would . . . be called AmeriCorps:* This name was pushed by Young People for National Service, a small group of college students and recent graduates led by Diane Jackson and Malkia Lydia, as well as Senator Wofford's office. The only argument against calling it AmeriCorps apparently came from Native American representatives, who argued that America meant all the lands of the Western Hemisphere.

Chapter 15

242 *Oddly enough, they did . . . :* Milton cited three reasons for the stronger emphasis on this mission. First, the Summer of Service had demonstrated that diversity would not just happen on its own; a stronger federal role would be required. Second, in the relative calm of the rule-making process the corporation staff had been able to focus on key principles that had been lost in the din of the legislative fight. Finally, questions from the press (i.e., from me), had forced her to examine the issue more closely. "We just got totally wrapped up in the details, so many forces going in different directions," Milton said. "Being asked questions by a reporter in fact influenced the course of what we did. The questions reminded us, 'Oh yes, this is really important. If we have the local programs define their own approach, this key value will get lost.' "

243 *engaging in political advocacy . . . :* The regulations not only prohibited "influencing legislation and union organizing"—a standard provision in most social legislation—but also forbade programs to organize "protests, petitions, boycotts, or strikes."

Index